Nussbaum's Politics of Wonder

Also available from Bloomsbury:

Advances in Experimental Philosophy of Free Will and Responsibility,
edited by Thomas Nadelhoffer and Andrew Monroe
A Philosophy of Comparisons, by Hartmut von Sass
A Philosophy for Future Generations, by Tiziana Andina
Exploring the Philosophy of R. G. Collingwood, by Peter Skagestad

Nussbaum's Politics of Wonder

*How the Mind's Original Joy
Is Revolutionary*

Jeremy David Bendik-Keymer

With images by Misty Morrison

BLOOMSBURY ACADEMIC
LONDON • NEW YORK • OXFORD • NEW DELHI • SYDNEY

BLOOMSBURY ACADEMIC
Bloomsbury Publishing Plc
50 Bedford Square, London, WC1B 3DP, UK
1385 Broadway, New York, NY 10018, USA
29 Earlsfort Terrace, Dublin 2, Ireland

BLOOMSBURY, BLOOMSBURY ACADEMIC and the Diana logo are trademarks of
Bloomsbury Publishing Plc

First published in Great Britain 2023
This paperback edition published 2024

A catalogue record for this book is available from the British Library.

A catalog record for this book is available from the Library of Congress.

ISBN: HB: 978-1-3500-7607-5
       PB: 978-1-3502-9361-8
       ePDF: 978-1-3500-7608-2
       eBook: 978-1-3500-7609-9

Typeset by RefineCatch Limited, Bungay, Suffolk
To find out more about our authors and books visit www.bloomsbury.com
and sign up for our newsletters.

From real people, real good is born.
(My handwritten note in a children's book, Chicago, Thursday,
August 20th, 1998)

FOR EMET

Contents

Contents

Prologue

After listening to Mahalia Jackson on my parents' vinyl from the '60s, then a selection of Christmas records that Misty had found damp in her parents' barn inherited from Grandma Em – one in German, another in Ukrainian, some Polish, others Russian. After Art Blakey & the Giants of Jazz, with scratches, and following a mis-spin of Bob Dylan's "Boots of Spanish Leather," I found an old cassette from time in France, 1988–89: Maurice Duruflé's "Quatre motets sur des thèmes grégoriens" (1960). Around '83, I'd sung those motets in Utica, New York.

My first cousin once removed on my mom's side, "Aunt" Ruth, was visiting from New York City, and my father, Dave, was with Misty, ten-week-old Emet and me. Emet's first Christmas.

A few days later, I thought: With some work, a book written as a series of polyphonic choruses, them the idiosyncrasy and durability of family – that'd make a counterpoint by which to disagree with Martha C. Nussbaum and open up the politics of wonder. Family is an education in relationships – how to disagree; be angry, true, and loved.

Grateful for the polyphony, I was grateful for the bizarre thought, too.

Motets came to be used in jazz and funk.

Then why not also punk.

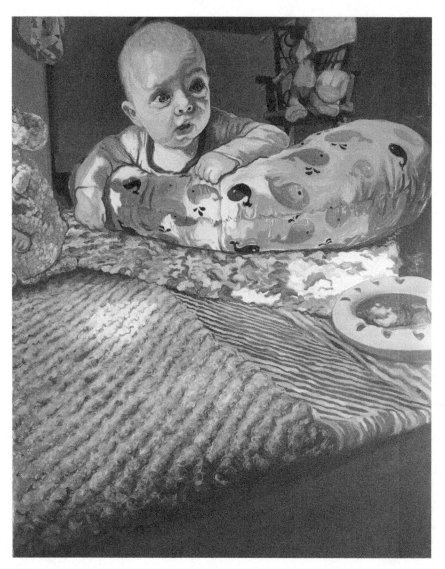

"Seeing what Emet sees," 2020

SETTING – *WHEN PEOPLE NO LONGER WONDER, DOMINATION'S HOLDING DOWN THE SYSTEM*

For Ruth in New York City,
a get-away for philosophy

The most political thing about wonder is right there at the beginning. When
wonder[ing] gets hammered out of folks, drained out by a thousand cuts, or
deadened by endless suffocating days, this is the result of domination
[somewhere in the system]. The presence of the absence of wonder[ing] shows
us the afterlife of domination, the world that must be changed.[1]

Deerhunter's "Punk," live at Le Trianon, Paris, France
22 Mai 2013

Let me get some things out of the way. This is a not a secondary source on Martha C. Nussbaum's philosophy. It's an original, philosophical essay that develops something implicit in her work. Disagreeing with her on several assumptions, I reorganize her political vision. The result is an interpretation of what Nussbaum has to offer quite different than what she's avowed. Still, I believe that it is true to her intentions. "Nussbaum's politics of wonder" is the topic in the sense of the place – *topos* – wherein realizations I've had about politics have fallen into view down to the ground of my world, like leaves from overwintering trees. The topic has been the occasion for awakening into a hibernal world, fraught with domination and narcissism.[2] I see that clearly now.

I won't give you an overview of Nussbaum's philosophy. But I will work on an insight. Thinkers shouldn't be spared coming to a great scholar's work on their own. Kierkegaard taught me that. If you took up this book looking for an easy way into Nussbaum, forget it. Close the book now. I'm assuming that you have spent some time with Nussbaum's work, enough to form an opinion and to wonder. She deserves that as any life-long, prolific scholar does. Instead, I'm giving you a place to sit with your opinions and to see what falls out when you consider them in light of what I will elaborate. I trust in the difficulty that comes from having to mull things over. I aim to slow things down and to give room for a polyphonic, multisided existence.

The moral intention behind my approach is coherent with the place where I live. The way I see things now, it's a time to shake up our cognitive agency in the coldness of the present. The United States of America in 2022 is especially

---

[1]   Author's reply to Anders Schinkel, personal email correspondence, April 11th, 2021.
[2]   "Topic," "occasion," *Oxford American Dictionary* (Apple Inc., 2005–20). "Occasion" comes from Latin *occasio,* a juncture or reason, itself developed out of *occidere,* to fall or set, from *ob* – towards – and *cadere* – to fall.

troubled and conflicted. It's a settler colonial state recycling histories of violence, and we are reeling from a pandemic that has laid bare a vastly unjust, morally unaccountable system driven by selfishness and "organized irresponsibility"[3] at scales that are planetary. Goddamn, it makes me so mad.

In times when it is possible for there to be abundance enough for folks to meet their vital needs, if people no longer wonder, this fact in and of itself reveals that there's domination somewhere in their system. Now their system may be their family, their school, or their society. But since humans are born to wonder, if people no longer wonder, it must be because it is no longer safe to do so. Since the precarity isn't the result of absolute deprivation in their world, the blame falls on the system.[4] People then close their minds to avoid threat. They live dominated.[5]

The literature on domination is extensive of late.[6] I view domination after Philip Pettit's original version of neo-republicanism.[7] Unlike Petit recently, I don't have qualms saying that arbitrary power over others is the essence of domination.[8] What Pettit calls, "the eyeball test"[9] tells us when things get arbitrary between us: Is it *imprudent* to look others squarely in the eyes and ask "Why?", to object, or to demand a justification of their behavior or views from them? Are you reasonably afraid of what will be done if you demand that things make sense? Is there a threat involved in demanding to be reasoned with in good faith? Are you subject to the arbitrary sway of another's will or of some institution? Do you have to shut up and look away, lest you get hurt? These are some things that are dominating. Disagreement isn't arbitrary when we're trying to make sense together.

When Pettit writes in *On the People's Terms* that "Someone, A, will be dominated in a certain choice by another agent or agency, B, to the extent that B has the power of interfering in the choice that is not itself controlled by A,"[10] the

[3] Robert Jackall, *Moral Mazes: The World of Corporate Managers*, 2nd ed. (New York: Oxford University Press, 2009), "*Moral Mazes* and the Great Recession," 221–40.
[4] I am bracketing the case of people who suffer from chemical depression and related mental illness. Those of us who are not born to wonder so easily due to physical causes obviously do not cleanly fit inside my syllogism. Nonetheless, it is worth noting that one cause of the persistence of mental illness is the social cause of domination: feeling unsafe to get help for one's condition and to demand that society accommodate basic human needs.
[5] In "Who Gets to Feel Secure?" *Aeon* (October 30th, 2020), Olúfẹ́mi Táíwò holds that domination cannot account for deprivation, that there is a form of existential insecurity coming from how societies distribute opportunities. But domination holds the system down somewhere. Otherwise, people would demand what they need. They wouldn't accept an arbitrary "no" for an answer.
[6] Cf. Christopher McCammon, "Domination," *Stanford Encyclopedia of Philosophy* (2018).
[7] Philip Pettit, *Republicanism: A Theory of Freedom and Government* (New York: Oxford University Press, 1997).
[8] In his *On the People's Terms: A Republican Theory and Model of Democracy* (Cambridge: Cambridge University Press, 2012), 28, Pettit focuses instead on "another's power of uncontrolled interference" in one's choices.
[9] Ibid., 47.
[10] Ibid., 50.

issue is not whether A can control something that B claims authority to do, but whether A should, and when possible can, find legitimate what B has the power to do to A's choices. The issue isn't *control*; it's the intention to seek *justification*. I may not have delegated to B the power to stop me from hurting C; but that doesn't mean B dominates me in stopping me from hurting C. If B has good reason to protect C by stopping me and B is willing to justify it to me, then B does not behave arbitrarily. B's attention to justification makes B open to reasoning, i.e., to being looked in the eye should I protest. Heck, B will accept that they should hear the protest when it comes from me honestly.

I open with these remarks on domination because we need to remind ourselves both what is up against wonder *and* what wonder can unsettle when we refuse to shut our minds up. Presuming that wondering is not a lost cause, that domination only goes so far for you as a reader (how could you be reading this?), I've written this book to stir us to wonder. I want its form to be subversive in the way that tuning out the arbitrary world to hear music can attune us to how another world becomes imaginable – even in glimpses and fragments.

I've written the four essays in this book around recurring themes, each essay with a central word hovering in their background. The essays slowly circle (the first chapter), unfold (the second), spiral out (the third), and drive toward (the last chapter) important *notes* for a politics beyond domination. I had music in the background while writing them. That music is noted in an epigraph at some point before, within, or just after each motet, including where and when the music first entered my life. Please find the music when you can and hear it sometime. It originated in the spirit of Duruflé's *Quatre motets*, mainly the *Ubi Caritas*. But when it was done, the second essay felt like it belonged to a different circumstance. I updated the epigraph accordingly.[11] The four works of contemporary music behind the book overlay Duruflé's four motets as memories that make me wonder.

The word "motet" inspired me to write around a single word. That musical tradition hearkens back to the French diminutive form of "mot," word.[12] A "motet" is *a little word that is a polyphonic song*. The motet is one of the most enduring and evolving musical forms of classical music. Beginning in medieval

---

[11] The Deerhunter song mentioned at the start of this setting, the live version, is available only on the internet for as long as it will remain posted. If it ever gets deleted, note that most of the nineteen minutes is gorgeous, harmonic feedback as the very end of the concert. I heard something like it live at the Beachland Ballroom in Cleveland in September 2013. During the final stretch of revising this book, rediscovering Deerhunter's magnificent, subtle, and fun *Monomania* carried things along.

[12] "Motet," *Oxford American Dictionary*.

plain chant as it emerged into polyphony, the motet was central to the Renaissance, and evolved over the next centuries into areas outside the classical canon. The motet began in religion but came to find secular themes. Polyphonic, punctuating silence in their surprising brevity, changing in form, motets suit the topic of wonder and its positive, restless anxiety.

What I will call "lostness" is the "little word" of the first motet, while "devotion" is that of the second. The word is held silently there. "Honesty" is the word of the central and third motet, and so the central word of the book. "Vulnerability" is my last word on wonder. These words suggest a collection of qualities well-fitting to the character of political judgment that Nussbaum explores in her reading of Henry James's character Hyacinth Robinson from *The Princess Casamassima*: a "consciousness of a certain sort" on whom "nothing is lost," being among the "more deeply wondering."[13] Nussbaum thinks that he's an exemplar of humane judgment. I'll add another layer of maturity to this sensitive one, too, so that he can be angry in an accountable way. Let him protest.

The first motet circles around what wonder is and how it works, parsing it as the mind's excitement. That motet is sprawling, contemplative, and incremental – thinking in slow motion. The second motet explores the premise that humans are born to wonder, emphasizing how wonder emerges in environments with wonder in them. It moves quickly, born around a real story in my life. The third motet works out where freedom involves wondering in our relations. It's here that my opening claim about domination and wonder starts to grip the nature of politics. This central motet is the longest in the book and takes up two extended experiences around wonder from the last decades of my life. The final motet exhorts readers to view anger as a protest for others to wonder about how to make sense of the world together. It ends with an imaginary address. Reader, I wrote this book as a protest.

The book is excitable, and each of its four parts aren't entirely filled in. The notations (for that is what the motets are) have space within and between them. The space gives us leeway to come to things, room to think. I follow Misty Morrison who uses incompleteness in her visual work to provoke the viewer's subjectivity.[14]

Misty's series "With Wonder" creates a parallel exploration alongside the essays in this book. We created this book in tandem, two lines of a drawing in

[13] Martha C. Nussbaum, *Love's Knowledge: Essays in Philosophy and Literature* (New York: Oxford University Press, 1990), 198–9.
[14] See Misty Morrison, "An Interview about *Oblivion*," https://soundcloud.com/mistymorrison/an-interview-about-my-upcoming-show-oblivion-and-the-process-behind-it, 2021.

sound. I wrote words taking shape by seeing Misty paint her exploration of wonder. She discusses her series after the last motet (but please look at the images first). From Misty, I learned that the qualities of being open to possibilities and of seeking unseen connections are part of wondering. Translating her visual sense into my auditory one, I felt that the essays' forms should oscillate, building up an experience of searching for sense and meaning.

So, the motets try something out (*essay* it), and only in this way prove themselves. To "prove" comes from a root meaning to try or test something for its durability or the like.[15]

But as I suggested, the essays are "little words," not big ones. The polyphony of the essays – like the many voices of motets – demands subtlety. The relationships in which people can fulfill their mind's excitement aren't made of monologues but of "subtle interplay."[16] The exploratory tentativeness of wondering absorbs such subtlety, considering many possibilities together, supported best by a social form of power where people can search for sense together and see each other as wonders.

There's a close connection between wondering and creativity,[17] and it's good to have make-believe with us. It helps make us human.[18] Little else than control takes root in the shadow of imperious sayings. I want you to comment, for us to think together creatively.

For that, I'm going to be vulnerable. Because wondering is a basic human need and because people are mysterious to each other always to some degree, relationships without domination have wonder in them.[19] To relate well to each other requires a capacity to consider each other's worlds as we seek to find how we make sense together, starting with considering what really does make sense and what we truly and deeply need by our own lights. Anything we can confidently call "our" world becomes an achievement in potentially confusing, sometimes contentious, relating. Anything we can trust as relating involves wondering about each other.

15 "Prove," *Oxford American Dictionary*.
16 Martha C. Nussbaum, *Upheavals of Thought: The Intelligence of the Emotions* (New York: Cambridge University Press, 2001), 213ff.
17 Vlad P. Glaveanu, *Wonder: The Extraordinary Power of an Ordinary Experience* (London: Bloomsbury, 2020).
18 William Pène du Bois, *Bear Party* (New York: Viking Press, 1951).
19 The claim about the mysteriousness of each other is developed convincingly by Theodore Zeldin in his *An Intimate History of Humanity* (New York: HarperCollins, 1994). A related view of the complexity of people appears in João Biehl and Torben Eskerod, *Vita: Life in a Zone of Social Abandonment* (Berkeley: University of California Press, 2013). I'll be citing some readings like these that aren't exactly scholarship on my topic so that you can get a sense of the ethos around this book.

A book that conveys some of the subtlety of interpersonal wonder is a good medium for wondering.[20]

Looking back at the sometime tortuous process of writing this book, I'd say that I had to risk something and let things get lost. Wondering involves considering the different ways things can make sense. We wonder around, about, and over an area where we're lost– maybe, the sense of our society and its arrangements (does it really make sense?), or the strange history and experience of another (what was it like to be them?). Genevieve Lloyd speaks of wonder in the context of "the movement between knowing and not-knowing which is crucial to the ongoing activity of the mind."[21] By contrast, the largely anglophone and post-Humean understanding of wonder views wonder as a "delightful" and sudden emotion, a kind of winged flight into fancy. This doesn't lend itself to the largely post-Kantian and to some extent ancient Greek tradition of wonder as a fundamental cast of mind, a virtue of understanding.[22] But wondering often proceeds slowly right on the inside of our drive to understand.

In my philosophy, the capacity to form good relationships and wondering are bound up as family. Our potential to wonder about each other's lives and inner worlds is the antipode of our potential to relate to each other badly. Good and bad relationships are a microcosm of the larger problem. Take a society suffused with violence and undismantled domination.[23] There, the wills of others threaten to be out of our control. And then, given the ghosts of histories of violence, relationships can be interrupted by "narcissism" – especially around issues that are profoundly important to one's world. This narcissism is the opposite of wonder, the bad relationship (hardly a *relating* at all) the opposite of a good relationship.

---

[20] Sometimes an imaginative mood is helpful for locating an intuition behind a concept so that it does not remain empty. Take the portraits of relationships in Krzysztof Kieślowski's *Trois couleurs: bleu, blanc, rouge* (1993–4). Especially *Bleu* (blue), developing camera work used to great effect in his 1991 film *La double vie de Véronique*, involves many silent close-ups of eyes or point-of-view shots in peri-phenomenological moments, each evoking simultaneously the intimacy possible within each of our lives when we let ourselves be vulnerable and the mystery involved in reaching out to (or into) another's world where connection is an event of meaning. Kieślowski's films show the subtlety of interpersonal wonder. Krzysztof Kieślowski, *Trois couleurs: bleu, blanc, rouge* (Paris: MK2 Productions, 1994); *La double vie de Véronique* (Paris: Sidéral Films, 1991).

[21] Genevieve Lloyd, *Reclaiming Wonder: After the Sublime* (Edinburgh: University of Edinburgh Press, 2018), chapter 8, "Thinking with Arendt about Refugees."

[22] See Sophia Vasalou, *Wonder: A Grammar* (Albany, NY: SUNY Press, 2016) and my "Wonder & Sense: A Commentary," *Studia Wratislaviensia* 15:2 (2020): 65–70. Vlad Glaveanu holds as I do that wonder's many expressions appear on a continuum from quietly meditative to suddenly ecstatic. See his *Wonder*.

[23] Kyle Powys Whyte, "Settler Colonialism, Ecology, & Environmental Injustice," *Environment & Society* 9 (2018): 129–44.

By "narcissism," I mean the tendency to either ignore or to want to control the wills of others as a way of protecting that one's perceived needs are met.[24] This understanding of narcissism is developed from Nussbaum's work in *Upheavals of Thought*, chapter 4, itself indebted to D. H. Winnicott and others. The *Oxford American Dictionary* defines "narcissism" as "selfishness, involving a sense of entitlement, [and] lack of empathy" among other qualities. Here, the emphasis is on disregard of others, not on the tendency to want to control them. But both Nussbaum and much psychotherapeutic practice proceed on the more robust understanding of narcissism as seeking to neutralize, in some form, the "objects" in one's social world (an oddly narcissistic way of putting things).

Popular psychotherapy, in turn, is consistent with such an analytical understanding of narcissism, adding many of the other traits that are grouped in the DSM.[25] The tendency in this literature is to point to attention-seeking, low empathy, being self-serving in social interactions, wanting others to shore up one's self-esteem, and either grandiosity or entitlement. The DSM only lets narcissism reach the bar of a personality disorder when such traits interfere with personality functioning and interpersonal relationships.

Some of the popular books on narcissism self-published by therapists focus on gaslighting and other forms of epistemic control over the perceptions of others.[26]

In these diagnostic and current therapeutic discussions, the analytic premise of narcissism being an orientation toward controlling the wills of others is largely implicit. For instance, attention-seeking is premised off of the need to neutralize others' wills by having them approve or align with one's own. Low empathy is a way to block out the distinct reality and separateness of others. *The simple point is that the problem of others being out of one's control is the core premise of all of the traits.* Moreover, the various trait adaptions can be read as seeking to neutralize, co-opt or otherwise control the independent reality of others who are out of one's control.

Understood in an ordinary way, "narcissism" is as deep as infancy.[27] Especially when we are born into volatile worlds, narcissistic tendencies can have pernicious

---

[24] E.g., Martha C. Nussbaum, *Citadels of Pride: Sexual Assault, Accountability, and Reconciliation* (New York: W.W. Norton & Co., 2021).

[25] American Psychiatric Association, *DSM-5: Diagnostic and Statistical Manual of Mental Disorders, 5th Edition* (Philadelphia: American Psychiatric Association, 2013).

[26] See, e.g., Christine Louis de Canonville, *When Shame Begets Shame: How the Narcissist Hurts and Shames their Victims*, https://narcissisticbehavior.net/, 2018.

[27] Nussbaum, *Upheavals of Thought*, chapter 4, section II–III & VI; *Hiding from Humanity: Disgust and Shame in the Law* (Princeton: Princeton University Press, 2004), chapter 4, section II; and *Political Emotions: Why Love Matters for Justice* (Cambridge, MA: Harvard University Press, 2013), chapter 7.

and perverting effects – often subtle – in life between people, leading to various ways that people deny the independent worlds of others and seek to disregard or control them.[28] Narcissism then tends toward reproducing domination, control over others, and manipulation (it can become commonplace to some degree). Nussbaum writes of narcissism as internalizing an experience of the social world not having involved a "facilitating environment" – an environment that was caring enough that one learned to trust in it.[29] But when an environment appears trustworthy, the negatively anxious impulse to control it ought to begin to disappear. Anything more persistent is pathology. The environments that matter here can include our political systems, reaching us *before* we are born!

Working on wonder in our relationships contributes to working toward something beyond narcissism and domination in our society. Within good relationships, wonder between us helps us imagine how "another world is possible" (a phrase that comes from Saidiya Hartman's *Wayward Lives, Beautiful Experiments*); I tend to hear "possible" as *imaginable*, if only in glimpses and fragments. This personal domain supports what Nussbaum believes, namely that being civic-minded and politically engaged is an outgrowth of cultivating our humanity. Good relationships pursue justice and realize compassion to the point of being deeply critical of the political order in which they are formed, even seeking to transform that order. The search for justice ought to be grounded in an emotionally capacious and relationally mature form of love, informed by a compassion that is imaginatively open only through wondering (this is even the thesis of Nussbaum's *Political Emotions: Why Love Matters for Justice*). To work on wonder in our relationships bears the seed of something revolutionary.

Accordingly, this book's style is intended to project an imaginative space as intimate as some aspects of personal relationships. I have oriented it toward the soulfulness I find in good relationships so that you, reader, can think about your own relations in your own, idiosyncratic ways. One way to sustain wonder against background domination in a society is to form good relationships with wonder inside them. Not the wanton but the wonderers are subversive.

Of course, relationships aren't perfect unions, but they form, like this book, a little place to oppose insecurity in the world.[30] They can help us head out into the

---

[28] Racism is an ideology, but it is also a medium for narcissism – and for breaking free of it. Cf. Saidiya Hartman's *Wayward Lives, Beautiful Experiments: Intimate Histories of Riotous Black Girls, Troublesome Women, and Queer Radicals* (New York: W.W. Norton & Co., 2019).

[29] Nussbaum, *Upheavals of Thought*, 186ff. The term comes from her work around Winnicott.

[30] See Sidra Shahid and Jeremy Bendik-Keymer, "A Little Place to Oppose Insecurity in the World," *Blog of the APA*, June 25th, 2021.

world keeping life-sized and soulful. The lines of this book, personable, fragmentary, and musical, are meant to call out real relations.

*

Let me now say more about wonder before exploring, in the first two motets, what wonder is and how it originates. (1) Wonder is a mode of anxiety, and (2) anxiety is at bottom positive, meaning that it gives us something significant that we need to flourish. *We have inherited histories of violence that lead us to identify anxiety with its narcissistic expressions, depriving us of important areas of our flourishing such as good relationships and self-realization.* Thinking of anxiety negatively makes sense within conflicted and precarious social environments where our needs are unlikely to be met. Within a history of violence, being excited is often reactive. Reactivity haunts your society and your soul. But not all anxiety is negative, threatening to imperil our flourishing, and we shouldn't lose track of anxiety's fundamentally positive nature.

Anxiety includes creativity – the excitement of making things – leadership – opening up possibilities for action – and sociability – the fluidity of relating with others.[31] According to technical philosophical taxonomy, *creativity* is positive anxiety in the domain of practical reason concerned with producing, i.e., *poiein* (Greek "to do, to make", the root of "poetry"). In the sense of going ahead (or apart) from inherited norms and finding new possibilities for action, *leading* is the positive anxiety of the domain of practical reason concerned with deeds. *Sociability*, in turn, is positive anxiety in the domain of relational – i.e., interpersonal, or second-personal – reasoning, e.g., in loving, being a friend, or even simply being moral with others.[32] Since sociability is a broad category, it includes the positive anxiety of sex – erotic innovation – just as well as the positive anxiety of hospitality, e.g., warmth and affection so that others can feel at home during the mutual adjustment to differences involved in the shuffling possibilities for interaction of welcoming strangers.

Now within this taxonomy, *wonder is the positive anxiety of considering things* – the mind's excitement in seeking understanding. Technically, wondering is

---

[31] In his inaugural Freiburg lecture on anxiety, Martin Heidegger noted love and its excited joy alongside dread and boredom. See Martin Heidegger, "What Is Metaphysics?" in David Farrell Krell, ed., *Heidegger: Basic Writings* (1929; New York: Routledge, 2015), chapter 2.

[32] On relational reason, see my "The Moral and the Ethical: What Conscience Teaches Us about Morality," in Vasil Gluchmann, ed., *Morality: Reasoning on Different Approaches* (Amsterdam: Rodopi, 2013), 11–23; "'Do you have a conscience?'" *International Journal of Ethical Leadership* 1:1 (2012): 52–80; *Solar Calendar, and Other Ways of Marking Time* (Brooklyn, NY: Punctum Books, 2017), study 4; *The Wind ~ An Unruly Living* (Brooklyn, NY: Punctum Books, 2018); and *Involving Anthroponomy in the Anthropocene: On Decoloniality* (London: Routledge, 2020), chapters 3–4.

positive anxiety in the domain of theoretical reason, i.e., when thinking. Insofar as we continue to consider things as we make them or act on them (through practical reason) or consider each other as we relate (with relational reason), wondering can be intertwined in an ongoing way with creativity, leadership, or sociability. Theory, practice, and relating cooperate in real life. They make us dynamically and multidimensionally human.[33]

It's probably new to think of anxiety as good. But consider the phenomenology of anxiety. Excitement over the unknown possibilities before us anticipates things that matter to us. We live elevated in attention, occasionally even elated, and open to the significant possibilities before us. This seems different than being angsty. There, we become agitated by something that feels like it could be fear but, in the analysis of one of Kierkegaard's pseudonyms, is without object.[34] We roam around ourselves seeking answers, or at least some calm. We find here excitement that has gone wrong or turned bad. Coming from a deontological culture, Kierkegaard's pseudonym speaks of impending guilt, but one can also dread under the aspect of the bad, dreading some undefined bad thing that might happen, not simply some sense of being in the wrong. The question is, though, *How could we dread things if they didn't first matter?* We have to be excited about the world's possibilities to turn around and dread them. The world cannot be simply dreadful to us unless it were once *promising.* Angsty dread is a negative form of the mind's excitement, anticipatory apprehension of unknown bad things or of somehow being in the wrong.

There's also this conceptual point. Dread depends on a proliferation of possibilities around a given nest of concerns. Søren Kierkegaard's pseudonym, "Vigilius Haufniensis," writes of anxiety that it is the "dizziness of freedom."[35] In such "dizziness," what's possible outpaces what is actual so that one's world swims in possibilities to the point of undermining one's ability to respond to them. So, one understandably becomes reactive, seeking to control the situation. But possibilities proliferate in wondering and in imagination, too. Those needn't be negative. Can't they be pregnant?[36] The relationship between anxiety and possibility suggests that why anxiety *must* be negative is mysterious.

---

[33] See my "'Do you have a conscience?'" and the premise of *The Wind*'s structure in three stretches.

[34] Søren Kierkegaard, *The Concept of Anxiety: A Simple Psychologically Orienting Deliberation on the Dogmatic Issue of Hereditary Sin*, trans. Reidar Thomte (1844; Princeton: Princeton University Press, 1980).

[35] Kierkegaard, *The Concept of Anxiety*, p. 61 ("Subjective Anxiety").

[36] Compare Immanuel Kant's understanding of the beautiful in his *Critique of Judgment*, trans. J. H. Bernard (1790; New York: Hafner Press, 1951), First Book, especially section 11. This will be an important connection.

Even the possibilities in dread are possibilities of sense and meaning. Dread opens up *within* sense and meaning! Sense and meaning come first. Dread unsettles them and makes things seems senseless or potentially meaningless in the process. But none of that could occur if we weren't first attuned to the presence of sense and meaning, if our consciousness were not at first open to the world as a meaningful place where the sense of things is at stake, at least incipiently and inchoately.[37] As Nussbaum notes, one even sees such an original, mental joy in children.[38] The world matters to children in its givenness. Here the logical "first" of dread depending on the givenness of sense and meaning overlaps with the developmental "first" of kids meeting the world for the first time. Negative anxiety depends on the givenness of the world having some meaning and making some sense within the openness of our minds.[39]

Reflection shows that even sense and meaning depend on the proliferation of possibilities to be able to mean something or to make sense. Things don't make sense or mean anything outside a space of possibilities of sense and meaning. We have to be able to consider whether X could be Y or at least ~ X or, in the context of action, whether there could be another justification or angle on something that we think makes sense to do. *We have to swim in possibilities to live with sense and meaning.* Anxiety reflects that condition. Following Haufniensis, we should take anxiety as the appearance of that condition revealed by degrees to our souls. But against Haufniensis, we should hold that *the dread of the world being seemingly unable to make sense or to be meaningful depends on a deeper proliferation and free play of possibilities of sense and meaning.* Dread depends on a deeper, positive anxiety where things that matter come to light or are at stake. This is a strong, conceptual conclusion.

Take the experiences of meditation, long-distance running or swimming, or even spending long periods out in nature's waves of wind or water – all ordinary examples. These things help calm dread by easing us into living with the possibility of meaning, although the world does not make sense right now or things have become meaningless to us, fraught with senselessness and meaning. All of these experiences reveal the excitement at the base of consciousness.

---

[37] John McDowell, *Mind and World* (Cambridge, MA: Harvard University Press, 1994); Jean-Luc Marion, *Being Given: Toward a Phenomenology of Givenness*, trans. Jeffery Kosky (Palo Alto: Stanford University Press, 2002).

[38] Nussbaum, *Upheavals of Thought*, 189–90.

[39] Think even of what Immanuel Kant articulates in his *Critique of Pure Reason*, that we come into the world seeking to make sense of it through the demands of reason, always already taking the world as a place where sense and meaning get worked out. Susan Neiman, *The Unity of Reason: Rereading Kant* (New York: Oxford University Press, 1994).

When we have the space and time to let our minds search for how things can make sense or be meaningful, often by seeing how another world is possible, dread can slowly dissipate, revealing – as the narcissistic dimensions of the ego recede – that consciousness is fundamentally fecund and free, in the sense of playing freely. The problem is out there, not in us. The problem is the world that shuts down wondering. My claim in this book is that wonder is the manifestation of positive anxiety in the realm of thinking where we consider sense and meaning amid the free play of possibilities around any given thing. Wonder is the mind's excitement seeking understanding.

*

I'm going to reorient Nussbaum's work in a way that may be counterintuitive if you've read much of it. Her work uses ideal theory,[40] pursues the project of political liberalism,[41] and disvalues anxiety and anger.[42] But by developing Nussbaum's strongly suggestive, pervasive, and mostly implicit understanding of wonder in ways that I have suggested, I extend her thought in the direction of critical theory, a form of socialism dependent not on liberty but on relational autonomy, and the validation of anxiety and of anger as crucial moral and political possibilities.

When I first realized that Nussbaum was using wonder to work out a politics, it was in the context of justice for other-than-human animals, specifically, when she assumed that all of life is wonderful.[43] Nussbaum avowed biocentrism not long ago.[44] Biocentrism is a common sort of environmental morality by which life as such, not just sentience or human dignity, calls directly for moral thoughtfulness, consideration, and responsibility.[45] For Nussbaum, wondering is central to appreciating the moral and ethical meaning of all other forms of life, not just animals.

---

[40] Martha C. Nussbaum, *Creating Capabilities: The Human Development Approach* (Cambridge, MA: The Belknap Press, 2011).

[41] Nussbaum, *Political Emotions*.

[42] Martha C. Nussbaum, *Anger and Forgiveness: Resentment, Generosity, Justice* (New York: Oxford University Press, 2016). See also Martha C. Nussbaum, *The Monarchy of Fear: A Philosopher Looks at Our Political Crisis* (New York: Simon & Shuster, 2018).

[43] See my "From Humans to All of Life: Nussbaum's Transformation of Dignity," in Flavio Comim and Martha C. Nussbaum, eds., *Capability, Gender, Equality: Toward Fundamental Entitlements* (New York: Cambridge University Press, 2014), 175–200.

[44] Martha C. Nussbaum, "Human Capabilities and Animal Lives: Conflict, Wonder, Law," *Journal of Human Development and Capabilities* 18:3 (2017): 317–21.

[45] As a "perfectionist," Nussbaum is not subject to John Basl's deflation of welfarist biocentrism in his *The Death of the Ethic of Life* (New York: Oxford University Press, 2019). See my "The Other Species Capability & the Power of Wonder," *Journal of Human Development and Capabilities* 22: 1 (2021): 154–79.

All animals are objects of wonder for the person who is interested in understanding ... [I]f we feel wonder looking at a complex organism, that wonder at least suggests the idea that it is good for that being to persist and flourish as the kind of thing it is. This idea is at least closely related to an ethical judgment that it is wrong when the flourishing of a creature is blocked by the harmful agency of another. That more complex idea lies at the heart of the capabilities approach.[46]

At first, I thought that Nussbaum brought up wonder mainly in the context of these discussions.[47] Once I looked, however, I began to read suggestions of wonder across Nussbaum's work. Wonder is much more central to her philosophical project than I had realized. I found Nussbaum invoking wonder in *Upheavals of Thought* at the heart of emotional development.[48] Something akin to wonder appeared in *Love's Knowledge*. She called it "searching." It develops our "sense of life."[49] Looking back from *Frontiers of Justice*'s animal politics, I read wonder into her 1970s commentary on Aristotle's *De Motu Animalium* (*On the Motion of Animals*), her first written attention to animal – and, in one explanatory essay, human – striving.[50] Wonder was also apparent in her appreciation of development's unfolding in *The Fragility of Goodness*.[51] Given, too, that wonder was implicit in reading literature in *Love's Knowledge*, I projected wonder into her work on literature and the law.[52] Most importantly, I realized that wonder was invoked as the ground of moral argument in one of her most important works:

We react to the spectacle of humanity so assailed in a way very different from the way we react to a storm blowing grains of sand in the wind. For we see a human being as having worth as an end, a kind of *awe*-inspiring something that makes it horrible to see this person beaten down by the currents of chance – and *wonderful*, at the same time, to witness the way in which chance has not completely eclipsed the humanity of the person.[53] [Emphases mine]

---

[46] Martha C. Nussbaum, *Frontiers of Justice: Disability, Nationality, Species Membership* (Cambridge, MA: The Belknap Press, 2006), 348–9.
[47] Ibid., chapter 6, "Beyond 'Compassion and Humanity': Justice for Nonhuman Animals," especially 6.iv: "Types of Dignity, Types of Flourishing: Extending the Capabilities Approach."
[48] Nussbaum, *Upheavals of Thought*, Index, "Wonder," p. 751.
[49] Nussbaum, *Love's Knowledge*, "Introduction: Form and Content, Philosophy and Literature," especially "C. The Starting Point: 'How Should One Live?'," 23–9.
[50] Martha C. Nussbaum, *Aristotle's* De Motu Animalium (Princeton: Princeton University Press, 1985), Essay 1, Appendix, "The Function of Man."
[51] Martha C. Nussbaum, *The Fragility of Goodness: Luck and Ethics in Greek Tragedy and Philosophy*, 2nd ed. (1986; New York: Cambridge University Press, 2001).
[52] Martha C. Nussbaum, *Poetic Justice: The Literary Imagination and Public Life* (Boston, MA: Beacon Press, 1995).
[53] Martha C. Nussbaum, *Women and Human Development: The Capabilities Approach* (New York: Cambridge University Press, 2000), 72–3.

Wonder had a role in grasping *human dignity* as such! By the time that I reread *Political Emotions,* my incredulity broke loose. There, Nussbaum's interweaving of childhood development, psychoanalysis, and politics recognized wonder's prominent role in any just and inclusive politics, especially when confronting various forms of intolerance and negative emotions, such as disgust.[54] There was a whole politics of wonder in Nussbaum's work as a whole.

But it was mysterious what she thinks that wonder is. As of 2022, she hasn't published an extended analysis of wonder.[55] This realization led me to look more closely at the texts where Nussbaum located wonder in human development and to think more carefully about them. Over time, I realized that there is a clear thought running through them:

> Nussbaum wants to think through and to then publicly cultivate a *non-narcissistic* relationship to the world involving others, including animals. The condition of this relationship is emotional maturity in which we cease seeking to control others or to overcontrol ourselves and are capable of *wondering* about others.[56] A consequence of this relationship is to support the capability of all animals, including humans, to be free, which is to say, dynamically alive in their own ways of being, something that is only possible through a fundamentally wondering relationship to them.

I think that this is Nussbaum's main philosophical idea. Its core assumption is that *a non-narcissistic relationship demands wonder.* Wonder and narcissism are antipodes. Wondering is central to our relationships with others. In wondering, we come to appreciate the other as another and not as a narcissistic extension of, or obstacle to, ourselves. Wonder allows the other to be who they are as they are and to consider their possibilities within and against our sense of life. Wonder is so important that loving others depends on it. Without some wonder in it, love

---

[54] Martha C. Nussbaum, *Political Emotions,* Index, "Wonder," p. 457. On intolerance, compare her *The Clash Within: Democracy, Religious Violence, and India's Future* (Cambridge, MA: The Belknap Press, 2007); *Liberty of Conscience: In Defense of America's Tradition of Religious Equality* (New York: Basic Books, 2008); *The New Religious Intolerance: Overcoming the Politics of Fear in an Anxious Age* (Cambridge, MA: The Belknap Press, 2012), and *The Monarchy of Fear.* On disgust, compare her *Hiding from Humanity,* and *From Disgust to Humanity: Sexual Orientation and Constitutional Law* (New York: Oxford University Press, 2010).

[55] Even her recent *Justice for Animals: Our Collective Responsibility* (New York: Simon & Schuster, 2022) has but a section of the first chapter on wonder, albeit reflection on wonder that is among the most condensed in her work as a whole. In what follows, I will not draw on *Justice for Animals,* as it did not come out until this book was in the final stages of production.

[56] On the notion of "overcontrol" of oneself, consider her early work on *sophrosyne* (the Greek cardinal virtue of self-control or temperance) in *The Therapy of Desire: Theory and Practice in Hellenistic Ethics* (Princeton: Princeton University Press, 1994).

becomes pathological.[57] As Nussbaum writes, wonder is entangled with true love
and play and is at the heart of justice. It is crucial to the equal respect that
Nussbaum, as a political liberal, wants to cultivate philosophically in the public
sphere:

> If even respect is to be sustained stably, there has to be a moment of generosity,
> in which one is willing to be at the mercy of another who is mysterious, and
> approachable *only in a spirit of play and wonder*. That generosity, that "yes," is
> made possible only by the spirit of love; or, more accurately, it is that spirit.[58]
> [Emphasis mine]

In other words, the spirit allowing respect to be qualitatively different than
narcissism depends on the generous spirit of love in turn involving wonder. In
the above passage, Nussbaum isn't explicit about the logical relationship between
wonder and love. But as I noted, in *Upheavals of Thought*, it is clear that wonder
is necessary for non-pathological love. Wonder is needed for love and lasting
respect.

By the end of the section just quoted from *Political Emotions*, Nussbaum links
the spirit of love to "decent [political and social] institutions [being] stably
sustained against the ongoing pressure exerted by egoism, greed, and anxious
aggression."[59] This coheres with her linking of "facilitating environments" to
political environments at the last sections of chapter 4 of *Upheavals of Thought*.
What Nussbaum does not directly consider, though, is how wonder can also
disclose dominating political and social institutions.

Note, too, how Nussbaum uses the adjective "anxious" as something negative.
For prominent examples, consider her use of Iris Murdoch's blanket
condemnation of anxiety as the lead epigraph of *The New Religious Intolerance*.
Note the subtitle of the book, too ("in an anxious age"), and then chapter 1,
which leads off discussing "a time of anxiety." Interestingly, however, there is no
entry for "anxiety" in the index. The concept has not been focused on. Also
consider *The Monarchy of Fear*, where anxiety trades with fear throughout the
book. Based on reading many of Nussbaum's works, I realized that, for Nussbaum,
anxiety has wholly *negative* connotations and makes one prone to narcissistic
impulses. Nussbaum implies that anxiety is an emotional disposition interfering
with such un-self-involved things as wondering. Worry crowds out wonder.

---

[57] See Nussbaum, *Upheavals of Thought*, chapter 4.
[58] Nussbaum, *Political Emotions*, II.7. "'Radical Evil': Helplessness, Narcissism, Contamination,"
especially section IV, "The Growth of Concern out of the Spirit of Love," 177.
[59] Ibid., 277.

But we should disagree with Nussbaum when it comes to her way of handling anxiety in her texts. Positive anxiety is a far cry from fear and is crucial to politics – ironic though that may be in light of Nussbaum's accounts. The same issues that Nussbaum discusses around problems of anxiety attest to the loss of a society's capacity to *live with* anxiety. Underneath that is a deeper misunderstanding of what anxiety is. By attending to wondering's phenomenological features and considering the conceptual structure of anxiety, we should realize that wonder is *aligned* with anxiety. They are both *good* for our flourishing. This unsettles Nussbaum's account and opens up unseen possibilities. Nussbaum's sense of anxiety doesn't exhaust how anxiety appears.

When we wonder, the head-swimming experience of considering possibilities is good, no worry at all. The experience portends the articulation of how things make sense, even if wonder itself is not fixated on our own good.[60] Wondering isn't self-involved but involves a moment of profound and simple opening onto the world – a consideration of all the possibilities we can soak up, so to speak, using the "free play of the imagination."[61]

When Kant introduces the notion of the free play of the imagination, he even goes so far as to claim that it must be "universally communicable" because everyone who thinks shares the experience of coming to try to conceptualize and make sense of things. In other words, although we may not understand what someone else is wondering about, it should be clear that they are wondering. Kant, in my view, suggests that an imaginative activity such as wondering is basic to being human and should make sense across humankind. Drawing on other sources, Nussbaum agrees. But she misses the connection to anxiety. The experience of wonder counteracts negative anxiety by keeping us in touch intuitively with another (organization of the) world we can glimpse. Nussbaum doesn't see that what counteracts negative anxiety is the mind's excitement, keeping possibilities of sense and meaning open as we seek to understand things. And that oversight matters because Nussbaum's philosophical work aims to cultivate a social and political world wherein we support each other in being creative, protect independent judgment, and love openly.[62] She wants us to be capable of being thoughtful, free to consider things with an imaginative cast of mind. She works for equal respect for all. *But this much implies that Nussbaum's*

---

[60] See Nussbaum, *Upheavals of Thought*, p. 191, on wonder being "non-eudaimonistic" in its focus, i.e., capable of being "disinterested" in Kant's sense from the Third Critique.

[61] Kant, *Critique of Judgment*, section 9, p. 52.

[62] This is one reason for her work to protect gay relationships. See especially *Hiding from Humanity* and *From Disgust to Humanity*, also *Love's Knowledge*'s dedication and donation of profit.

work aims for a society that engages in wondering and is at home in positive anxiety! Against a society with domination in it, another social world becomes imaginable where relational autonomy and emotional freedom prevail in the free play of their possibilities.

*

I find such utopianism powerful, on the side of the resistant and the oppressed. It helps to shatter worlds patterned by narcissism and abuse. Getting out of their headspace is an opening, and Nussbaum's philosophical striving seeks some such thing. But where?

While Nussbaum is negative about anxiety, her comfort with the mind's excitement appears when she reads literature. Nussbaum's sympathetic imagination is closest to the excited sense of life involving positive anxiety. So, I want to pause and take up some literature.

Consider some lines from an early poem by Arthur Rimbaud called "Roman" which I loved dearly in 1989 when I was an 18-year-old exchange student studying at the Lycée Corneille in Rouen, France:[63]

> *On n'est pas sérieux, quand on a dix-sept ans*
> *Et quand on a des tilleuls verts sur la promenade.*
>
> *You're not for real when you're seventeen*
> *& green lindens line the walkway!*[64]

These lines end the poem. The lyrical voice of the poem relates trees along the walk to the claim: "You're not for real when you're seventeen." The enigmatic claim is the poem's refrain.

There's wonder in it. The 17-year-old lyrical subject of the poem is flying down the walk outside cafés, bubbly as champagne and filled with incipient *eros*. What could it mean that one isn't "for real" when one is 17 and "green lindens line the walkway"?

Perhaps the green lindens are a power. But what kind, what power? We might put things this way: *Life stretching out is that power.* Then the lyrical subject is taken by the flourishing of the world. Rimbaud's poem is of summer: "Les tilleuls sentent bon dans les bons soirs de juin." "The lindens smell good in June's good eves."

---

[63] Arthur Rimbaud, "Roman" (1870; widely reprinted). Rimbaud was 16 when he wrote it. One thing I loved about this poem was its slightness, its honesty. "Roman" in French means "novel."

[64] To keep the feel of Rimbaud's lines, I was liberal with the word-for-word translation.

Rimbaud was struck by summer nights around this time. In the same year, he wrote "Sensation," which begins with the melodic line that rises into song: "Par les soirs bleus d'été, j'irai dans les sentiers / Picoté par les blés, fouler l'herbe menue." "In summer's blue eves, I go to the trails / shin-scraped by wheat, milling the slightest grass."[65] For Rimbaud's teenage voice, summer's life – foliage in sensation – is a power. Reading Rimbaud's poems, we might feel that the power of life outstretched is *excessive*. It calls for words that are songs. Air fills with purpose, although one doesn't know what that purpose is. Desire and imagination stir both fleshly and other than flesh. Out there is meaning, precisely ungraspable, for we would be too "serious" to stop and grasp it. The moment would already pass by. Yet life is *ongoing* down the walk swaying in the leaves and scents.

"Roman" is comic and ambitious, disobedient, and sly. Although lyric poetry, it calls itself a "novel," that vaunted literary form of the nineteenth century where social criticism lived. Is such genre-slippage a jest? Could jests be "for real"? What should we make of blurry life – the blur of genres, too, like the stretch along café walks; the importance of the moment that one cannot absorb as a "serious" person? In understated ways – for teenage excitement's ordinary – Rimbaud's poem flaps norms, introducing a trembling inside the importance of novels and of serious men. "Roman" gives us possibilities to consider.

At the root of the trembling where possibilities array is something that I hope we sense throughout this book: the background state of wonder. Wonder as a *background state* can be developed into *acts* of wondering.[66] We can exercise wonder's soulful excitement about the world to consider it, becoming lost in searching for what something means. Wondering, in turn, is the positive anxiety of consideration. When we wonder, we take in the world and turn over the sense of things in our lives. Here, I side clearly with what Ronald Hepburn identified as the "post-Kantian" tradition of wondering, rather than what I consider to be the Humean one that is largely prevalent in contemporary work on wonder as a sudden emotional upsurge of delight.[67] The emotional experience of delightful wonder is but one form of the much broader phenomenon of wondering. The process of wondering opens our minds and can even open our lives and who we are in this world.

The openness of wonder proceeds on the basis of letting the things of our lives, the things of the world, or the ones with whom we are related be separate

[65] Arthur Rimbaud, "Sensation" (1870; widely reprinted). The translation is mine.
[66] Cf. Glaveanu's *Wonder* for its intricate typology of wonder expressed in qualitatively different forms and intensities.
[67] R. W. Hepburn, "The Inaugural Address: Wonder," *Proceedings of the Aristotelian Society, Supplementary Volumes* 54 (1980), 1–23, and my "Wonder & Sense."

from our control, free to appear in their own way, even if it surprises us. In such freeness, wondering disrupts narcissism:

"There, right there, is everything free and alive around us."

"And who are we in this world?"

"Have we gotten outside ourselves to experience the world yet?"

"Is this life that we are living something that makes sense?"[68]

As the form that positive anxiety takes when we absorb things even unconsciously as Rimbaud's teenager appears to do, *wonder trembles orders of common sense, sending a vibration through everything around what we're considering*. Roland Barthes spoke of an "oscillation" around the meaning of things.[69] In its most profound form, wondering may make everything in the world tremble, alive with the proliferation of possibilities.[70] As we wonder, things open to different senses and take on unexpected shades and associations of meaning. They may stop making sense as they did. The oscillation within wonder is fecund – what Kant called "purposeful" but lacking a clear purpose.[71] We might say, *There is meaning there, but I do not know what it is yet*. Wondering becomes pregnant with sense and meaning.

In Rimbaud's poem, wonder follows summer entering into the porous consciousness of adolescence. This is consonant with the way Nussbaum uses wonder in the Aristotelian tradition where all of life has something wonderful

---

[68] Cf. Charles Larmore, *What Is Political Philosophy?* (Princeton: Princeton University Press, 2020), 1–2:

> [W]onder . . . the feeling that a whole dimension of our dealing with things, if not indeed the world itself, has ceased to make sense as it once seemed to do[,] . . . to stand back from ordinary concerns and seek the larger picture[,] . . . to arrive at a broad understanding of how everything fits together in one way or another.

He then adds:

> One need not suppose that everything [fits together] without tensions, conflicts, or even discontinuities.

[69] Roland Barthes, *The Neutral: Lecture Course at the Collège de France (1977-1978)*, trans. Rosalind Krauss and Denis Hollier (1978; New York: Columbia University Press, 2007).

[70] In personal correspondence, Rick Anthony Furtak pointed out that this passage hearkens back to Kierkegaard's *Upbuilding Discourses* from 1843 to 1844: "The discourses speak of an awakening concern for what one's life means 'for the world.'" Søren Kierkegaard, *Eighteen Upbuilding Discourses*, trans. Howard V. Hong and Edna H. Hong (1844; Princeton: Princeton University Press, 1990). There, the meaning of the world trembles around one's life's meaning as one seeks to relate oneself to the world.

[71] Kant, *Critique of Judgment*, section 11: "A Judgment of Taste Is Based on Nothing but the Form of Purposiveness in the Object (or of the Way of Presenting It)."

about it.[72] Caught up on the background state of wonder, we become open to the range of ways that things could make sense and to surprises in sense and meaning that come from letting the meaning of things unfold freely around us. This primes us to develop a more capacious understanding of where we are in this world and what it might mean to be human should we actually commit ourselves to wondering. In Rimbaud's poem, the power of the world's background generosity helps us see the way wonder can be excitement, even while it leaves out the commitment to wonder. But we will consider such commitment in this book.

*

What are the implications for politics when it is guided by wondering? Nussbaum's work calls for a more thoughtful, even soulful, politics. With Nussbaum's attention to both wondering and to free play in its background, Nussbaum seems to have seen how we ought to conceptualize thoughtful, not just "rational," people. To "make sense of humanity" – as one of her mentors urged – is not to find merely the "rational being," but to acknowledge an emotionally fuller and more imaginative human being.[73] Wondering helps to open up what makes sense in life, filling out the amplitude of what it takes to be thoughtful and revealing the *arbitrary constriction* of our social worlds in the process. This is really where Nussbaum's sympathetic imagining helps.

"Rational" people are capable of examining beliefs for their truth and also justifying them up to a point, depending on how much emotional intelligence is part of reasoning.[74] On an ordinary English way of hearing "rationality," though, not much is said of an imaginative and emotional orientation to our considerations in favor of or against things. But not so with "thoughtfulness."

In ordinary American English, "thoughtfulness" has soul in it. It adds humanity to rationality. It's more capacious than rationality while including reason.[75] "To be thoughtful" is more than simply thinking. It is also to be morally considerate of others.[76] Others have lives of their own, rich in sense and meaning,

---

[72] Nussbaum, *Frontiers of Justice*, 348.

[73] Bernard Williams, *Making Sense of Humanity, and Other Philosophical Papers, 1982–1993* (New York: Cambridge University Press, 1995).

[74] The subtitle of *Upheavals of Thought* is "the intelligence of emotions."

[75] Cf. my "The Reasonableness of Wonder" that discusses a parallel distinction between the "reasonable" and the "rational" by way of Rawls.

[76] Here, the comparison with Rawls is best made. See his *A Theory of Justice*, 2nd ed. (1971; Cambridge, MA: The Belknap Press, 1999). Rawls assumes equal respect as a condition on the rational becoming reasonable. The morality of thoughtfulness is explored by philosophers such as Cora Diamond, e.g., in her essays on animals in *The Realistic Spirit: Wittgenstein, Philosophy, and the Mind* (Cambridge, MA: MIT Press, 1995) and her "The Importance of Being Human," *Royal Institute of Philosophy Supplement* 28 (1991): 35–62.

and to relate to the meaning of them on their own terms, they mustn't simply be objects for our use of cognition. Instead, we must cultivate an openness within ourselves to someone outside us. This openness already disposes us to wondering about them.

What's more, thoughtful people aren't easily mentally dominated. The basically accountable and considerate nature of thoughtfulness isn't rule-bound or even heavily moralized. Many free thinkers focus on opening up people's relationship to the norms that guide their lives so that the norms aren't unquestionable. They also focus on learning to live without a ruler. Both of these things can be consequences of living in wonder.[77] Thoughtful people seek what makes sense in a capacious way, and respect that others do so, too. Moreover, without coming to share the world about which we are bound to disagree,[78] we cannot live a life wherein we find what makes sense consistently justified or refined by others. Thoughtful people thus mind their interpersonal relationships, yet not out of a moralistic demand to connect or to correct. Rather, they do so because it is the nature of living a life that makes sense that we consider each other and each other's worlds, and that we share *our* world together, each having our own perspective on it.[79] What makes sense in life just as how relationships can make sense are deepened and clarified during thoughtful people's lives. Once again, this takes wondering – a steadying out of positive anxiety into a virtuous disposition.[80]

I read Nussbaum's interest in imaginative people as an interest in thoughtful ones, especially in politics. A main preoccupation of this book is to suggest an intuitively imaginable starting point from which to begin answering the question,

[77] Compare Lynne Huffer's "ethics of wonder" as discussed in Sidra Shahid, "Genealogies of Philosophy: Lynne Huffer (part I)," *Blog of the APA*, March 5th, 2021; Michel Foucault, "What is critique?" in *What Is Enlightenment? Eighteenth-Century Answers and Twentieth-Century Questions*, ed. James C. Schmidt (1979; Berkeley: University of California Press, 1996), 382–98; and Immanuel Kant, "An Answer to the Question: What Is Enlightenment?" in Schmidt, *What Is Enlightenment?* (1794), 58–64.

[78] Cf. Charles Larmore, *The Morals of Modernity* (New York: Cambridge University Press, 1996), chapter 7.

[79] Rick Anthony Furtak, *Knowing Emotions: Truthfulness and Recognition in Affective Experience* (New York: Oxford University Press, 2018), chapter 7.

[80] For more on thoughtfulness, see my *The Ecological Life: Discovering Citizenship and a Sense of Humanity* (Lanham, MD: Rowman & Littlefield, 2006); "Species Extinction and the Vice of Thoughtlessness: The Importance of Spiritual Exercises for Learning Virtue," in Ron Sandler and Philip Cafaro, eds., *Virtue Ethics and the Environment* (New York: Springer, 2010), 61–83; "The Sixth Mass Extinction Is Caused by Us," in Allen Thompson and Jeremy Bendik-Keymer, eds., *Ethical Adaptation to Climate Change: Human Virtues of the Future* (Cambridge, MA: MIT Press, 2012), 263–80; *Solar Calendar, and Other Ways of Marking Time*, study 6, and *The Wind*, stretches 2 and 3. Compare Hanna Arendt's *Eichmann in Jerusalem: A Report on the Banality of Evil* (1963; New York: Penguin Classics, 2006) and in Susan Neiman's *Evil in Modern Thought: An Alternative History of Philosophy*, rev. ed. (Princeton: Princeton University Press, 2015).

"What is political thoughtfulness?" This book aims to clarify the wondering in thoughtfulness, relocating politics in a form of thoughtful relationship to each other, even in a society struggling with reproduced, historically deep domination and resultant insecurity.

Given the pervasiveness of domination, politics often gets pitched as antagonistic, interest-based, or cynical, with conflicting interests colliding in struggles over control. Here, politics seems fundamentally narcissistic, with recent politicians only bringing that truth to light.[81] People who are politically savvy – from French *savoir*, "to know how to do something" – should be manipulative, right? Why should we wonder except in moments of calculation? Politics involves *stratagem*, waging slow warfare against opponents in pursuit of your goals. It's born of the need to control the order of the "city," i.e., the *polis* (Greek for "city state" and the root of the word "politics"). Nothing political is born from getting lost together in wondering how to make sense together! That's for the gentle sheep to the political wolves.

But focusing on thoughtfulness subverts such an understanding of politics. It exposes so-called "politics" as pathological and self-contradictory. Assume that the autonomy of people is something to which we must be morally accountable. This is an axiom of egalitarian morality.[82] Next grant that politics is the process by which we come to govern our lives together. In such a light, politics proper depends on the sharing of norms between people to whom each of those norms must make sense. Anything else would contravene the autonomy of those involved. Governance would not be done together then. Politics thus appears to demand a form of what we might call "relational autonomy" – autonomy worked out only in and through relationships with each other in which moral accountability to each other is conserved.

As such, the thing, politics, is in direct contradiction with the common-sense word, "politics," at least in many common cynical usages in the media and in everyday complaint. In technical terms, politics *de res* (the thing itself) has come unstuck from politics *de dicto* (as a word). People controlling others irrespective of their autonomy isn't politics. It's domination. People manipulating others isn't politics. It's objectifying them. Presuming the cynical construction of the world isn't politics either. It denies people their freedom to imagine a better world. As

---

[81] Cf. Nussbaum, *The Monarchy of Fear*.

[82] R. Jay Wallace, *The Moral Nexus* (Princeton: Princeton University Press, 2019); Glenn Coulthard, *Red Skins, White Masks: Rethinking the Colonial Politics of Recognition* (Minneapolis: University of Minnesota Press, 2014). Coulthard understands autonomy through the figure of self-determination and its practices.

the sharing of norms by people who must be treated as autonomous, politics cannot be domination, objectification, or the denial of people's freedom to connect intuitively with a social world that could make sense to them and be meaningful rather than being apparently meaningless. Politics cannot be a stratagem when politics is supposed to be a shared endeavor.[83]

The fundamental contradiction between the thing, politics, and the everyday expression, "politics," is that a domain that must be free is often taken to be a domain of unfreedom. A good theory of politics will be able to explain how that contradiction comes to be. Redeploying Nussbaum's concerns with negative anxiety, this book provides an answer. The contradiction (of "politics" with politics) arises through people being overwhelmed by the anxiety of sharing norms with each other, often with good reason, given histories of violence, domination, privilege, and inequality. The causes of this anxiety can be explained to a great extent sociologically by antagonistic social systems, such as capitalism, industrialism (e.g., how it is selfish regarding the future onto which it offloads waste), or imperialism and extant colonialism with its structural racism, hierarchies, and intra- and inter-national exclusions and divisions.[84] The point is, the thing, politics, isn't narcissistic. Narcissism born out of a reaction to abuses of sharing norms as moral equals is the reason for the fundamental contradiction between politics and the everyday word, "politics."

Moreover, narcissistic politics is the consequence of an understandable, but still negative relationship to the fundamental social anxiety of sharing the world with others, shaped by "the monarchy of fear." Despite the history of one's society, making narcissistic reaction the basis of politics hands politics over to domination. If we can forge the minds through wonder to hold onto what politics should be between people, we can reveal domination as it has seeped into the political and thus into our everyday lives, tasks, and hopes. Then we might be better able to keep track of the domain of coming to share norms that govern our lives together as moral equals even in and through the persistence of bad facilitating environments.

Just as wonder works against narcissism in relationships, the wondering in thoughtfulness breaks through the narcissism of the political and its ingrown domination. To speak of the "politics of wonder" is most precise, then, for politics

---

[83] See my criticism of the role of stratagem in "The Neoliberal Radicals," *e-Flux Conversations* (February 1st, 2017).

[84] See my *Involving Anthroponomy in the Anthropocene*, chapters 1, 2, 4, and 5 and "Facing Mass Extinction, It Is Prudent to Decolonise Lands & Law: A Philosophical Essay on Respecting Jurisdiction," *Griffith Law Review* 29:4 (2020): 561–84.

when it advances through relational autonomy between people evolves from what sharing the world together must involve, and thus it must be born in part from wonder. Can we then say, at the least, that the corrupt chaos commonly called "politics" is in part the detritus of not forefronting wonder in sharing the world together?[85] Are those who own the word "politics" and debase it cynically shutting out the space for people to be thoughtful together, recycling systems of domination? Histories of repression and silencing only deepen the question.[86] The subversion of the narcissistic meaning of "politics" by focusing on political thoughtfulness (and the wonder in it) leads the way to showing how the politics of wonder can be revolutionary.[87]

*

Wonder isn't nearly enough for all that we need in politics, but it is sorely needed. Any politics in a society that is supposed to be shared freely depends on learning how to wonder. A common criticism of wonder in politics is that wondering is not sufficient for good politics.[88] But of course it's not. Moral monsters are perfectly capable of wondering in a limited way about or during monstrous things, although their wonder is narrowly ranged by pervasive, background narcissism. Narcissists can wonder about how to control others. The claim in this book is only that involving wonder is a necessary condition on a politics that we can trust. But that in and of itself is revolutionary (quietly so perhaps).

People do need to be free with each other. Otherwise, they won't work out what they need. What does it take to trust politics in a society with domination cycling through it?

*

I approach trustworthy politics through the egalitarian figure of relational autonomy, something that I find in Nussbaum's work under other names and somewhat in the margins. I want to know how we can relate freely when we have

[85] "Sharing the world" is an expression I found in Luce Irigaray's *Sharing the World* (New York: Continuum, 2008).
[86] Cf. Kristie Dotson, "Tracking Epistemic Violence, Tracking Practices of Silencing," *Hypatia* 6:2 (2011): 236–57, and the tacit role for wonder in "Making Sense: The Multistability of Oppression and the Importance of Intersectionality," in Namita Goswami, Maeve M. O'Donovan, and Lisa Yount, eds., *Why Race and Gender Still Matter: An Intersectional Approach* (London: Pickering & Chatto, 2014), 43–58. I discuss the connection in "Wonder, Capability Determination, and Epistemic Inclusion," MS, Human Development and Capability Association Annual Meeting, Buenos Aires, Argentina, 2018.
[87] "Revolution," *Oxford American Dictionary*; from late Latin *revolutio(n-)*, from *revolvere* "roll back."
[88] W. P. Malecki, "Against Wonder," *Studia Wratislaviensia* 15:2 (2020): 45–58.

a world with domination in it (what, for instance, is *free protest* in such a world?). The relational autonomy is there in Nussbaum, but not the full power of its potential to protest domination.

In an important passage from *Political Emotions,* Nussbaum draws on an aria from Mozart's *La Nozze de Figaro* ("The Marriage of Figaro"), "Duettino-Sull'aria."[89] Her discussion of Mozart's aria explores how the democratic ethos of an egalitarian society involves a process of reciprocal give and take that is, most precisely, "isonomic," a sharing of norms between autonomous equals, or as I will say, *a sharing of norms between us.* Within Nussbaum's work, there is a fragmentary view of autonomy within relationships wherein people come to an isonomic way of life together, and this governs their lives together as free.[90] Nussbaum's attention to the duet is significant in that it presents a memorable and stirring example of the possibility of the momentary isonomy between people when they relate together well.

Still, the aria Nussbaum interprets is a friendly affair, despite the intrusion of class distinctions that limits its power for glimpsing a more egalitarian world. The aria isn't a disagreement, let alone angry. This is a drawback for showing us autonomy in relationships. Egalitarian politics must grapple with histories of violence, domination, privilege, and inequality. When it does, it often involves sharp opposition, even revolt. But I want to know how the democratic ethos of isonomy should involve sharp disagreement in a way that is relationally autonomous – not arbitrary and disconnected from those whose views one might very well oppose or even despise.

This book approaches politics by diving down into isonomy as a process in relationships between people seeking to govern their lives together when attunement as harmony is *missing* and civic relationships need to be formed. Who is ready to be harmonious when there's so much domination?

From the standpoint of political thoughtfulness, one thing to focus on is the moral necessity of accountability in relationships. Within that moral landscape,

---

[89] Nussbaum is a lover of music, someone who is both trained in singing and known for memorizing the librettos of operas on her daily runs and walks. Alongside the literary, music is central to Nussbaum's imaginative work surrounding wonder. It should come as no surprise, then, that some of her most important intuitions emerge during her discussion of music. Her writing on music follows her mature work from *Upheavals of Thought* (2001) through *Political Emotions* (2013) to recent work on Benjamin Britten. See, for instance, Martha C. Nussbaum, "Crucified by the War Machine: Britten's *War Requiem* and the Hope of Postwar Resurrection," in Alison L. LaCroix, Jonathan S. Masur, and Martha C. Nussbaum, eds., *Cannons and Codes: Law, Literature, and America's Wars* (New York: Oxford University Press, 2021), chapter 7.

[90] In viewing isonomy as a process between people, I expand its conception from the modern meaning of isonomy in purely juridical terms as equality under the law. I also depart from the economic interpretation developed in Kōjin Karatani's *Isonomia and the Origins of Philosophy,* trans. Joseph A. Murphy (Durham, NC: Duke University Press, 2017).

I see anger as an attempt to *relate* – a morally accountable, embodied communication of one's perspective on the world and the wrong that is in it. This pushes pretty hard against Nussbaum's view of anger as at best a "signal" but as almost always morally problematic.[91] For her, there is so much residual narcissism in anger. How can anger be part of relationships involving wonder? But not only can it be. In conditions of historical violence, domination, privilege, and inequality, anger that is part of sharing the world together is wonderful. There have been wrongs done, and things have got to change otherwise. We have to consider some new possibilities that trouble this world. The key is expressing anger in a moral relationship, not out of fear and narcissism, and for that wonder is essential.

The lack of a space for outrage in Nussbaum's work and for properly appreciating the humanizing role of anger within moral life is a shortcoming. My question is how things might go in sharp disagreements when people hold onto what R. Jay Wallace has called "the nexus" of moral equality between them.[92] Nussbaum's vision of egalitarian reciprocity – the back and forth of being free and equal together – pulls against the arbitrary ignoring of others that is possible within some visions of liberalism where individual liberty licenses people to individualistically disregard what others think in a laissez-faire attitude. So does the place she gives to wonder in living successfully with others. One question, of course, is about how anger should figure in reciprocity. Beyond protecting and validating outrage, I will argue that the persistence of disagreement in all its soulful emotion is *good* for autonomy between people. Held within moral accountability, even outrage is positive, not negative. It opens up the sense and meaning of the world and is thus wonderful.

Not what anger is about, but the fact of someone expressing anger – insisting on dignity and good relationships in the bare assertion of the anger, summoning the power to speak – is wonderful. The sense revealed by the cry of outrage over moral wrong is real and extremely significant. It is much more than a "signal."[93] It is the beginning of a real relationship. My emphasis on anger opening up relationships is different than Myisha Cherry's "Lordean Rage," where the point is largely practical, to empower and focus people to continue until a dominating

[91] Nussbaum, *Anger and Forgiveness,* chapter 2; on it being a "signal," at best "instrumental," p. 37. Cf. her *The Therapy of Desire,* chapter 7. In *Justice for Animals,* she backs off on the rhetoric condemning anger, intuitively sensing – I think – that anger is important for social justice now. But she is still quite clear that, logically speaking, most anger is problematic, since what she calls "transition anger" takes such discipline.
[92] Wallace, *The Moral Nexus,* especially chapters 3 and 4.
[93] Nussbaum, *Anger and Forgiveness,* 37.

system is transformed.[94] I am on board with Cherry's practical focus, and Cherry agrees that rage at injustice can humanize those who have been dominated. But my emphasis remains more relational than practical, concerned with the surfacing of moral relationships through the interpersonal expression of anger. *The rage belongs to the restoration of the relationship.* When we come to wonder about what makes sense to each of us in a society of ingrown domination, it becomes true that outrage over moral wrong becomes needed for sharing the world together in a deep and lasting way. Restoring our moral relations is a prerequisite for being able to transform society and to heal.[95]

In this way, I see protest as a communicative act, often involving anger, situated within moral relations. "Protest" means witnessing shared between people concerning what ought to be considered when something important is lost from view, ignored, disregarded, misunderstood, unseen, and so on. "Protest" comes from Middle English (as a verb in the sense "make a solemn declaration"), from Old French *protester*, itself from Latin *protestari*, from *pro-* "forth, publicly" and *testari*, "assert" (from *testis*, "witness").[96] Since such witnessing involves shaking up the common sense of the world and asking that people see things in a new light, protest involves the positive anxiety of considering things, i.e., wondering. Something comes between us, and yet the egalitarian relationship between us is morally obligatory to develop and preserve. In protest, we can both develop and preserve our relationship only by considering the world together, and, as I understand it, that means only by wondering. But how can we view protest as wonderful?

I think that to do so is crucial for thoughtful politics. I have concluded that wonder is a necessary part of protest in a politics that doesn't recycle domination. In other words, anti-domination protest *must* be wonderful.[97]

Of course, "protest" can become narcissistic and degrade into mere "strategy" wherein subtle forms of pressure and even coercion come to play in the intention to manipulate or control others.[98] It is very hard to be consistently thoughtful when sharing our lives together, let alone when seeking to govern them in ways

---

[94] Myisha Cherry, "Anger Can Build a Better World," *The Atlantic* (August 25th, 2020). See her *The Case for Rage: Why Anger Is Essential to Anti-Racist Struggle* (New York: Oxford University Press, 2021).

[95] Cf. Colleen Murphy, *The Conceptual Foundations of Transitional Justice* (New York: Cambridge University Press, 2017).

[96] "Protest," *Oxford American Dictionary.*

[97] See my "Reconsidering the Aesthetics of Protest," *Hyperallergic* (December 7th, 2016), and "The Art of Protesting During Donald Trump's Presidency," *The Conversation* (January 20th, 2017).

[98] John Hulsey's "Reconsidering the Aesthetics of Liberalism," *e-Flux Conversations* (January 18th, 2017) and my "The Neoliberal Radicals" in reply.

that make sense to all of us as moral equals in a society that is troubled by domination. This is why it is crucial to consider protests that help us to wonder. When wondering, we consider the many possibilities of the sense of the world, especially when we are lost in the midst of the fragments of that sense. Such consideration is something we learn how to do better or worse, and as such it cannot be something merely psychological. Rather, wondering can be dispersed across many processes, including practices – educational, artistic, political, you name it.[99] Later in this book, I will consider two of them, one in education and another in social practice art.[100] The second is a protest. As a practice and as a moral relationshjp, protest helps us co-discover the sense of the world together, including reimagining it and understanding different ways that the world could make better sense.[101]

When we engage in protesting, we soak in how something could make sense. Even the rage underlines existence. What bringing out wondering in protest does it to help us, when we find ourselves coming up short in our understanding or sense-making of something, to imaginatively consider alternatives, trying to project the world in different ways. Bringing out the potential of protests to be wonderful underlines how, in isonomy, we must not control the sense of the world or the meaning of others but we try to find the world and to be open to others as they are fully themselves: to co-discover. In practices of isonomic protest, we must always seek sense and consider how people could make sense, even if strangely, even if it would mean we might have to change our understanding of the world, alter our relationships, or even, at the most profound point of wonder, change aspects of our lives. Doing this kind of thing is not something one merely automatically does as if by psychological talent. It's hard work that has to be learned. It's hard-won, thoughtful politics that involves learning how to wonder in the midst of disagreement and anger. (I put the point even more strongly, too. It helps to see how anger can be wonderful.)

---

[99] This is the most important single idea to take from Sophia Vasalou's important overview of the conceptual landscape around wonder – that learning to wonder depends on practices of wondering: see Vasalou, *Wonder*. The point is also implicit within Lorraine Daston and Katharine Park, *Wonder and the Order of Nature, 1150–1750* (Cambridge, MA: MIT Press, 1998).

[100] Nicholas Wolterstorff, *Art Rethought: The Social Practices of Art* (New York: Oxford University Press, 2015) and Gregory Sholette, Chloë Bass, and Social Practice Queens, eds., *Art as Social Action: An Introduction to the Principles and Practices of Teaching Social Practice Art* (New York: Allworth, 2018).

[101] On "co-discovery," compare "co-construction" (a seemingly *practical* term) in Daniel R. Scheinfeld, Karen M. Haigh, and Sandra J. P. Scheinfeld, *We Are All Explorers: Learning and Teaching with Reggio Principles in Urban Settings* (New York: Teachers College Press, 2008), on the Chicago Commons Head Start Family Centers circa 2000.

The picture of trustworthy politics here is this. With wonder being central to the process of trying to share norms, a good part of the active life of politics then comes to life within modes of consideration between us where we co-discover the sense of the world that we can share – and this includes within protests. Such a politics of wonder is thus iterative, coming to consider norms together as moral equals in our autonomy over and over again, even much more so when protest and legitimate outrage are involved. Along these lines, wondering gives politics a strongly phenomenological moment that responds in kind (as the positive anxiety of consideration) to the equally phenomenological moment of protest and legitimate outrage when these cry out that another social world be possible. The coming-to-share norms that is politics comes to depend on being open to what appears between us as we consider what makes sense to each of us and why, even in protest and outrage.[102] If this process of appearing halts – if practices of wonder fade from being dynamically present in our lives (if they ever were) – the projection of some common understanding between us deteriorates with each missed disagreement. Just as we must push, and shake, and be outraged when the world must become other than it is,[103] so it appears that we must cultivate, fortify, and protect practices of wondering for the sake of the shared governance of collectively autonomous politics. That's where political thoughtfulness leads, and it is subversive, even counterintuitive, to any group that organizes its politics narcissistically, whether on the "Right" or the "Left."

Given the reality of domination between folks who are supposed to be moral equals, learning effective practices of wondering within isonomic politics contributes to true politics – politics in which it could make sense to trust. For a moment, hear the word "true" with its connotations. "True" comes from the Old English *trȳwe*, in some relationship with the German *treu*. It is related to "truce." The sense of these is related to the idea of trust.[104] "True" politics, in this etymological and poetic array of connotations, would be politics that engages in trust and in which one can trust. Is it "true" politics even where there is anger, and we can hold it; where there is protest, and it unsettles sometimes everything, that being wonderful; where what is wonderful is positively anxious – not simply pleasant and surprising – an awesome, ground-level upswell of change in the world toward more sense and more meaning for everyone involved in society?

---

[102] Steve McQueen, *Small Axe* (London: BBC, 2020), "Alex Wheatle." See the documentary interlude accompanied by a protest poem accompanying footage of the Black People's Day of Action, March 2nd, 1981.

[103] A point and phrasing I owe to David Keymer.

[104] "True," "Truce," *Oxford American Dictionary*.

Wonder's capacity allows a high degree of pluralism in political life, structured by a minimal morality. Add wondering to relationally autonomous, moral accountability – to "the moral nexus"[105] – and processes of protest, outrage, and disagreement become potentially, profoundly transformative for our relations. They become a slow-moving revolution of their own sort, shorn free from reactive violence that locks up in narcissism and is all too easily used for perpetuating domination under the guise of policing dissent. Politics, as it appears through ongoing relating, should be just that: trustworthy, at least increasingly so. Why would we want any other kind of politics than one in which we can trust?

*

At one point in *Upheavals of Thought*, Nussbaum writes:

> [W]e need to posit an original need for cognitive distinction-making, and an original joy in sorting out the world, in order to explain why infants get going and pursue projects of their own in the uncertain world.[106]

She develops this claim after a close reading of Lucretius' *De Rerum Natura*. For her as for Lucretius, the mind's original joy motivates our powerful, cognitive agency. Wonder is part of our drive to flourish.

But some mornings, we might wonder what has happened to the world, starting with what has happened to our minds. How much more weariness can a person take – can their family take – their neighborhood, settlement, country? How can we break open the fantasy world that would rationalize that we live precariously, tugging at the edges of its contradictions that contain powerful, negative anxieties about whether we – and our families – can succeed in this life or not?[107] Where can we go to get the resources to continue to insist, "This is not enough. This life is not right. Things could be otherwise. There could be a society better than this"? When "meaning" comes down to resignation and common "sense" settles in either as avoidance of what makes us fearful or as imposing what is fearful on us, how can the world become meaningful to us, and how can what makes sense to us, not despite us, persist as an intuitive possibility? How can we keep mental and soulful space to negate this world while anticipating more meaningful and sensible ways to coexist?[108]

---

[105] Wallace, *The Moral Nexus*.

[106] Nussbaum, *Upheavals of Thought*, 189–90.

[107] Say that things are competitive and selfish, and we have "cruel optimism" to attract us back to our place. Lauren Berlant, *Cruel Optimism* (Durham, NC: Duke University Press, 2011).

[108] "Coexist," *Oxford American Dictionary*, from a Latin root implying that we "stand out together."

I hope that this book will lead you to reconsider ways that you can wonder regularly in your own life and especially in politics. Wonder, after all, surfaces the cognitive agency of those who practice it, helps us to imagine a world that could be otherwise, and preserves the possibility of a shared and conflicted world that is considerable to people in their disagreement, even if only through sticking with the trouble in our differences and working to have real relationships.

"Duckies," 2020

IN THE READER'S VOICE

I was lucky to have a good reader. In the voice of Sidra Shahid, here is a paragraph overview of the book's central claims:

> Wonder is a promising starting point for progressive [or] radical politics. To fully appreciate wonder, we have to understand that wonder is a form of anxiety, yet anxiety in a positive or productive sense . . . In light of long-standing negative associations, [this] book attempts to recover a positive meaning of anxiety . . . [O]ur prevalent strategic understanding of politics is narcissistic, governed by domination. That is the reason why you think much that passes for politics in our common vocabulary is only politics so-called and merits scare quotes . . . [P]olitics is non-domination at bottom and only subsequently, through histories of violence, becomes dominating and narcissistic . . . [F]actually speaking . . . in your view, social or political relations today (or in Western, capitalist, competitive societies) foster emotional immaturity . . . [T]o achieve emotionally mature social relations, we have to give wonder its due place.[1]

What will you find by reading these motets?

---

[1] Sidra Shahid, personal correspondence, October 2021.

"Wallpaper," 2020

Human flourishing depends on our capacity to be lost in wonder when the world does not make sense or could make more sense.

MOTET 1 – *WONDER IS THE MIND'S EXCITEMENT AND PROCEEDS BY GETTING LOST*

TEXTS: *Aristotle's* De Motu Animalium, *Frontiers of Justice*

WORD: "Lostness"

*In our most trivial walks, we are constantly, though unconsciously, steering like pilots
by certain well-known beacons and headlands, and if we go beyond our usual course
we still carry in our minds the bearing of some neighboring cape; and not till we are
completely lost, or turned round, – for a man needs only to be turned round once
with his eyes shut in this world to be lost, – do we appreciate the vastness and
strangeness of Nature. Every man has to learn the points of compass again as often
as he awakes, whether from sleep or any abstraction. Not till we are lost, in other
words not till we have lost the world, do we begin to find ourselves, and realize where
we are and the infinite extent of our relations.*

~ Henry David Thoreau, "The Village," Walden; or, Life in the Woods, *1854*

A lunar eclipse occurs when the Earth passes between the moon and the sun.
The Earth casts its shadow over the moon against the sun's light. A world bathed
in moonlight goes dark. Only the traces of stars remain. Now the path is no
longer where we walk but becomes the realm of sounds – rustle, cooing, chirp,
scratch, an almost oozing.

The night of the lunar eclipse was an emotional point in their lives. N., let us
call one, and O. – the other – had come to the point where they wanted to grow.

As the lunar eclipse began, O. was outside staring at the path at the end of
their road. The night thickened except for specks of stars, windows orange-
yellow, florescent white behind them far off into the interiors. The edge of the
brush where the road ended had disappeared.

Lately, N. had been closed-in, polite but not forthcoming. When N. was like
this, there was something on their mind. N. needed space to consider it.

O. didn't know where they wanted to go with their life either. Perhaps N.
sensed this or perhaps O. and N. worked in tandem, slow-moving questions
silently sent like waves.

"NO." O. didn't know why that night, but the lunar eclipse made them feel
unhinged. Standing at the end of the road and looking to where the brush should
be, O. felt electric, sparking aimlessly. Their mind pulsed with the momentary
silence coming from the dark. Turning abruptly, they shuddered and walked
directly back to the apartment, moving more quickly as they went.

Inside the living room, N. was lost in their cell phone reading. As O. came in,
the door swung back, latched. N. startled. *What was going on?*

"On that thing again." "What?" "*That* thing!" "I . . . I don't know what you're
asking for."

O. rushed past.

"*ON.*" O. didn't know why that night, but the lunar eclipse made them feel unhinged. Standing at the end of the road and looking to where the brush should be, O. felt electric, sparking aimlessly. Their mind pulsed with the momentary silence coming from the dark. The mind is funny. Things built up, sought relief. Maybe the environment expressed this.

This didn't feel good, but it was meaningful. O. breathed in, exhaled forcefully. No one saw them as they walked into the blackness.

With one foot before the other, stopping frequently, listening, O. found the air around the path quieted after entering the brush. Over their shoulder, O. saw the lights from the complex, the stars high above the ridgeline. The air before the small wood was faintly lighter, the wood itself beyond blue. Dampness chilled the air. O. felt the roughness of ferns as they brushed into them, the oil left on their hands as they held the fronds for balance.

They didn't know how far they went. After some time, O. leaned against a tree, then slid to the ground. They felt their clothes become slightly wet and turn cold. Smells of the soil and groundcover. They stayed for a long while letting things pass through their mind. Then they yawned.

. . .

When O. walked in the door, N. was reading on their handheld. O. quietly closed the door and looked out of the corner of their eyes at N., then went to the kitchen. O. took a glass from the counter and filled it with water from the pitcher beading with condensation, drank until the glass was empty looking at the ceiling, all the while thinking somewhere else, yet aware of N. across the room. Returning around the counter, O. went over to N., who looked up briefly and seemed welcoming but distracted. N.'s hair smelled of them. The feeling pervaded O.'s body for an instant.

Leaning in toward O., N. kept reading.

*

The fifth interpretive essay of Martha C. Nussbaum's *Aristotle's* De Motu Animalium focuses on the explanatory role of *phantasia* (loosely translated as "imagination" and the root of the English word, "fantasy") in understanding how animals, and particularly human animals, come to move after something that they want.[1] Nussbaum writes:

---

[1] Nussbaum, *Aristotle's* De Motu Animalium, 221ff.

[Aristotle's] account of ... *phantasia* ... suggests a very general interest in how things in the world appear to living creatures.[2]

She then proceeds to explore how *phantasia* in human beings is crucial to our thinking, especially to deliberation.[3] Since deliberation concerns the sense of action – where we strive intentionally to flourish[4] – we are left with an interesting possibility: that the striving of human beings involves *imagination*. If we imagine, anachronistically, that imagination depends on its free play – at least to some degree – so that the sense of things is processed according to its various possibilities (e.g., possible outcomes, meanings, relations, etc. in a given act), it could seem that some degree of the positive anxiety of wonder comes *before* – or on the underside of – *phantasia* and so of striving. This strange conjuncture of Aristotle with Kant raises a question: Does the life of our imagination in considering how to live proceed only on the basis of some degree of wondering?

The point here isn't to misread Aristotle but to read Nussbaum imaginatively. That wonder is implicit in imagination wasn't developed by Nussbaum in her early work on Aristotle. She later found wonder to be non-eudaimonistic, unconcerned with promoting our good in the first instance.[5] But if it turns out that coming to terms with the sense of things depends on the free play of the imagination, then it would seem that some degree of wonder is important for striving. A moment in human flourishing would be a moment of letting go of it enough to consider the possibilities that one can imagine around one's life. This would even be to become momentarily lost *so as* to better live.[6] Even more, if such wondering were found *understated* in much of the life of the mind, small acts of wondering would go into moments of daily living. To learn to be momentarily lost in wonder and to let imagination play freely in the midst of daily pressure would then seem virtuous, part of being "finely aware and richly responsible," to echo Henry James as Nussbaum reads his work of "responsible lucidity."[7]

But it isn't easy to show, not simply state, how the mind gets lost in wonder.

*

---

[2]   Ibid., 222.
[3]   Ibid., 234, 239.
[4]   Nussbaum, *Fragility of Goodness,* chapter 10.
[5]   Nussbaum, *Upheavals of Thought,* 74ff.
[6]   In personal correspondence, Rick Anthony Furtak restated, "*[L]etting go* of eudaimonistic pursuits has an importance precisely *for* a virtuous life ... [A] temporary suspension of one's orientation toward plans and commitments, for the sake of accepting one's lostness, ... ultimately has eudaimonistic value."
[7]   Nussbaum, *Love's Knowledge,* 148.

Well, we need a clearer picture of wonder, which means that we might need to get lost. Exploring how wondering is important for considering things imaginatively, my goal is to subtly shift our focus when we come to think of wonder, not to provide an exhaustive account of it. That is beyond the scope of an essay, but it does leave room to wonder. I seek a style of writing that encourages autonomy, i.e., the process of living by what you come to find makes sense to you. So, in what follows, I will slowly circle around an idea, probably raising your anxiety in the process! But please, reader, hang out with me and let's think.[8]

Wondering, like meditation, is especially powerful in drawing down the negative anxiety at the root of reactivity and converting it into responsive relations, including anger as a moral relation without reactivity in it. Think of the story of the night corridor in O. and N.'s life together. In wondering, we open up, draw our minds into, or even cling to or linger on the meaning and sense of things without clarity as to how to go on. We rest in the free play of imagination by which possibilities for the sense or meaning of things might come to light. In wondering, we must be open to what isn't clearly meaningful, what things might not mean, and what doesn't make sense, yet take these negations as givens that lead us to consider further possibilities. Then the moment of being puzzled by the meaning of something is the moment when we must look more closely. The moment of being confused about the sense of something becomes the moment where we must consider it more capaciously or rigorously, even to the point of investigating it.[9]

The point at which we are lost in wondering is the point where our consciousness expands. Toward what? Not knowing, the mind moves out to consider possibilities surrounding the focus of our wonder. This is a phenomenological way to say that in wondering, we remain open-minded to possibilities we hadn't yet considered. In this way, wondering exercises powers of interpretation and of consideration. Genevieve Lloyd, parsing Spinoza on the topic, writes that ""the experience of wonder involve[s] the mind seeing no way forward, yet needing of its very nature to continue the activity of thinking.""[10] I put the point differently: *being momentarily lost is the life of wonder, what makes wondering strive.* Given that the activity of imagination is to develop unseen possibilities, wonder doesn't fixate imagination

---

[8]   On autonomy and its process, see my *Involving Anthroponomy in the Anthropocene*, chapters 1 and 2. Unlike some theorists of autonomy who focus on having choice options (e.g., Sam Sumpter, "Conditions of Empowerment," *Philosophy and Activism*, August 10th, 2021), I focus on being able to live a life that makes sense and being able to come to that life by working it out without threat of domination.

[9]   Anders Schinkel explores an extreme moment of lostness under the name of "contemplative wonder," where we wonder over the fact of the world itself, that there is this "everything" and not nothing or some other thing. Here, the negation of what we make sense of or find meaningful is so extensive as to take in everything that is the case. Schinkel, *Wonder and Education*, chapter 2; see also pp. 20–1, the first example.

[10] See Genevieve Lloyd, *Reclaiming Wonder*, chapter 8, "Political Language and Social Imaginaries."

so much as to activate it. But wondering works off of being lost at the edge of what makes sense or is meaningful.

Being lost in wonder is vital both to wonder and to the life of our minds. Remember O. in the story.

> *Is the sound a bird, a mammal, or a beetle? What does it mean in their code? What does it mean to me that they are here, signaling – or is it simply making noise? How can I interpret them? What kinds of relations matter in this night when the strange beings of the Earth emerge in the darkness invisibly following sounds?*

Wondering involves searching for sense – stretching one's mind and seeking to find sense in things, often in new ways or according to new arrangements. This implies considering things searchingly, often according to their unconventional possibilities as well as to their unexpected or counterintuitive ones. *This path is made for walking, but in a lunar eclipse, it can become something other – a corridor of sound in the darkness leading me to the world I have forgotten.* Such a transformation in the meaning of things makes sense, too. *Because I was lost, I came to consider the strange meaning that appeared in the darkness for how it could make sense in my life. But to allow that strangeness to lead me to a realization, I had to let go of what I expected to see before me and let myself not understand. I became confused and disoriented when losing the light of the moon. In order to proceed, I had to let myself be anxious in a way that considered things, and then – rather than losing my mind in the dark! – I had to search for how things might make sense in this new reality.* If we don't wonder when we're lost as to the sense of things, we won't be open to their unexpected possibilities. But if we're not lost when we think we're wondering, we won't let what we think be transformed.

My understanding of wonder deepens Nussbaum's focus on the centrality of imagination in human striving. This is my addition to her neo-Aristotelian interest in *phantasia* as central to human striving and to her implicitly Romantic interest in the free play of the imagination inside human relations. I'm bringing out the anxiety in human imagination as we search for sense and meaning in order to let us see it in wonder and wondering.

*

My idea is that wonder is basic to the mind and that wonder*ing* is a way of exercising that openness in an active, synthetic mode of attention.[11] A corollary

---

[11] See my "The Reasonableness of Wonder" and Anders Schinkel's commentary on my notion of a "mode of attention" in *Wonder and Education: On the Educational Importance of Contemplative Wonder* (New York: Bloomsbury, 2020), 45ff.

will be that wonder is a form of positive anxiety that needn't be emotional in the instance. Meditation practitioners know this firsthand when they internalize open-state meditation privileging the free play of consciousness.[12] In minds of such forms, one can easily see how wondering needn't be emotional in a conventional sense, especially as enthusiastically expressed within the neo-Humean tradition.[13] Rather, wondering becomes basic to being thoughtfully human in any walk of life at any time when we are responsive, not reactive, to the world. Wondering becomes part of our reflective freedom, something Kant nearly stated in his *Critique of Judgment*. The key to reflective freedom is then that we exist in anxiety as beings who strive for sense and meaning. I will return to this.

This approach to being imaginative is inherently non-narcissistic. To emphasize the moment of being lost in wonder, I will call it by the little word "lostness." Lostness always already takes us beyond seeking to control the world beyond us, accepting our limits in the moment and working within them. In being lost, things are beyond our current understanding and fail to make sense.[14] But acknowledging this gives us the opportunity to question, and any authentic questioning involves openness to the free play of the world's possibilities around what one questions. Perhaps on the surface of things, the confusion of lostness doesn't seem virtuous, and perhaps being anxious seems to be the opposite of being virtuous. Yet I hope that some of what I'll explore might unsettle these impressions should they persist. Being lost in considering things for their meaning and sense, holding to the space around them pregnant with sense and meaning, elaborating on them, filling in a world as one is ready to give up the world to which one is used – in other words, searching to some degree without a definite object – that ends up being excellently human, the very life of our reflective autonomy. Nussbaum wrote in *Love's Knowledge* that "if you are going to see life as it is, you have to be willing to be perplexed, to see its mystery and complexity. . ."[15] In this book, the same goes for ourselves in our world and for

---

[12] Shunryu Suzuki, *Zen Mind, Beginner's Mind: Informal Talks on Zen Meditation and Practice* (Boston, MA: Shambhala Publications, 2011). Thanks to Jeremy Levie for teaching me this practice at Green Gulch Farm in 2005.

[13] Vasalou, *Wonder*, "DELIGHT" and Philip Fisher's *Wonder, the Rainbow, and the Aesthetics of Rare Experiences* (Cambridge, MA: Harvard University Press, 2003).

[14] Late in the process of writing this book, I came upon Zena Hitz's *Lost in Thought: The Hidden Pleasures of an Intellectual Life* (Princeton: Princeton University Press, 2020). I had used the term "lostness" as the title of my paper for Jack Griffith's University of Exeter workshop on wonder in 2019 at the same time as Hitz must have been finishing her book. What a lovely coincidence that lostness was in the air!

[15] Nussbaum, *Love's Knowledge*, 207.

social and political life as they *should* be. But we have to explore how lostness is excellent to get there, and that means getting lost in wonder.

*

Let's keep circling.[16] What does Nussbaum think of striving? She holds that all life strives. It's a basic assumption of the neo-Aristotelian tradition to which her work belongs.[17] That tradition is rooted within Aristotle's biology. To say that all life strives is to say that all life is teleological. It has a form *qua* living being by which its well-being can be assessed and according to which its life cycle can be understood. In the *neo*-Aristotelian tradition, this presumption of teleology is an a priori assumption that is part of seeing some chunk of matter as living.[18] Aristotle didn't see things this way. He thought teleology was metaphysically real, not something we bring to things in order to understand them as living.[19] Modifying this Aristotelian tradition, Nussbaum came to articulate human flourishing with reference to human capabilities understood against the background of our species form.[20]

Autonomy, however, introduces some dynamism within that form since we may then work toward the form "that we prefer,"[21] including biotechnical enhancements. But Nussbaum holds that we are the kind of beings who need to be able to be autonomous in some measure.[22] Autonomy is thus an "Aristotelian categorial."[23] Oak trees grow deep and wide with roots and head for the light, casting off acorns every other year. Corgis, by contrast, grow with a mean meal and then strive to herd. People, by contrast, need to make sense of things. Sylvia Wynter describes this fact about us memorably. She says that we are both *mythos*

---

[16] Each motet in this book was inspired by a piece of music in the background. Steve Reich's *Music for 18 Musicians* draws on Pérotin's twelfth-century redoubling of the polyphonic *organum* cycling in cascading and repetitive waves, each somewhat different than the last, repeating ground, advancing differently.

[17] Nussbaum, *Frontiers of Justice*, "Beyond 'Compassion and Humanity'" and my "From Humans to All of Life."

[18] See Michael Thompson, *Life and Action: Elementary Structure of Practice and Practical Thought* (Cambridge, MA: Harvard University Press, 2008), Part One, "The Representation of Life."

[19] Cf. Henry Allison, *Kant's Transcendental Idealism* (New Haven: Yale University Press, 2004). The argument, of course, needs some nuanced work. That we must suppose a "logic of life" (Thompson, *Life and Action*, Part One, "The Representation of Life") is not, strictly speaking, a deduction to conditions of possibility on experience as such, but a deduction to being able in our life with language to coherently use the category of the living.

[20] See Nussbaum, *Creating Capabilities, Frontiers of Justice*, and *Women and Human Development*.

[21] Giovanni Pico della Mirandola, *Oration on the Dignity of Man, A New Translation and Commentary*, trans. Francesco Borghesi, Michael Papio, and Massimo Riva (New York: Cambridge University Press, 2012).

[22] Nussbaum, *Women and Human Development*, chapter 1.

[23] Thompson, *Life and Action*, "The Representation of Life."

(a story, a set of beliefs) and *bios* (life).[24] We cannot understand being human without exercising our imagination.

Being lost in wondering's mental anxiety is a kind of excitement. There's sense and meaning to consider. We become open to the determination of a world opened up through the shifting of possibilities around the thing being considered. Wondering lives lost in the free play of those possibilities of sense and meaning potentially far-reaching into the world that comes to light in areas and aspects through them. This seems important for human dynamism, foremost through our autonomy. The way we strive would appear to involve wonder, because wondering is important for both imagination and reflectiveness. But we cannot be free to strive without those. Nussbaum agrees.[25]

Once we recognize the importance of wondering in living a healthy human life filled with sense and meaning, human striving gives way to human searching. This point extends the Enlightenment notion of coming of age to mean that we grow up when we come to terms with our searchingness.[26] If we are to flourish as autonomous, reasonable beings, wondering should become an ongoing power.[27]

Learning to strive in searching, anxious though that is, then becomes a matter of learning to be relatively comfortable while being lost. I say "relatively," because even mental excitement is uncomfortable. Still, it is possible to find that discomfort makes sense. Can we find ways to be clear enough while experiencing confusion that we hold open a space to make sense of things and to continue to relate morally? The power of wondering involves this kind of capacity to live with anxiety.

Nussbaum's invocation of wonder has its roots in Aristotelian natural teleology, but the emphasis I am placing on the free play of the imagination comes from Kant's *Critique of Judgment*, the beginning of a Romantic tradition sweeping forward to include figures in Nussbaum's work such as Walt Whitman, James Joyce, Gustav Mahler, and even Winnicottian psychoanalysis.[28] The first tradition is ancient and seems object-centered, if you will. For instance, Nussbaum sometimes writes as though wonder should mainly be a name for a

---

[24] Katherine McKittrick, ed., *Sylvia Wynter: On Being Human as Praxis* (Durham, NC: Duke University Press, 2015), 23. Wynter's claims are "Aristotelian categoricals", too.

[25] Nussbaum, *Women and Human Development*, 78–9; *Creating Capabilities*, 33.

[26] See Kant, "An Answer to the Question: What Is Enlightenment?" and, for searching as a virtue of grown-ups, Susan Neiman, *Moral Clarity: A Guide for Grown-up Idealists*, rev. ed. (Princeton: Princeton University Press, 2009), chapter 10 on *The Odyssey*.

[27] Cf. my "The Reasonableness of Wonder."

[28] Nussbaum, *Upheavals of Thought*, chapters 4, 14–16.

form of biophilia by which the "awe-inspiring" nature of life's striving appears, human life included.[29] But the second tradition is modern – subject-centered. It's not located in life's awesomeness but in the reflective self. What happens if we emphasize this Romantic tradition in the place of the neo-Aristotelian one?

This tension can be found in Nussbaum's work, at least given her literary and musical choices. We would have to accept that wondering is an operation privileging the "free play of the imagination" around most anything eliciting such a response.[30] But it's also not clear how incongruous this is with the older tradition. In the *Metaphysics*, Aristotle locates wonder in the desire to understand anything. Lloyd comments: "Wonder involves a transition – an alleviation of unease or dissatisfaction. We start by wondering at *things* being as they are, but [as Aristotle wrote] 'we must end in the contrary and, according to the proverb, the better state.'"[31] Perhaps it is sense-seeking to make sense of our lives, not biophilia, that explains why Kant's examples come from botanical scenes[32] and speak to our "feeling of life"?[33]

Even focusing on the awesomeness of life-forms says just as much, if not more, about us as it does about them. What does it take for us to find them awesome? For us, it takes wonder. Of course, theorists of wonder disagree whether awe has a place in wonder. Rubenstein, in *Strange Wonder*, appears to think that it does, as does Vasalou (in *Wonder*) at points. Both are theorists steeped in the tradition of thought about the sublime. However, Nussbaum (in *Political Emotions*) is cautious about allying the two, and it is becoming common to disambiguate curiosity and awe from wonder.[34]

But these things are matters of degree, provided that the underlying logic of the relation is the mental excitement of consideration. Curiosity *qua* positive anxiety has a degree of wondering in it, usually framed within intellectual ends that delimit the extent to which the imagination is left open to play freely. On the other end of the spectrum, awe *qua* positive anxiety has so much passive wonder (not wonder*ing*) in it that it can slip over into dread and close wonder down while the very foundations of one's world tremble. Awed, one then stops considering much of anything.

---

[29] Nussbaum, *Frontiers of Justice,* 348, and the analysis in my "From Humans to All of Life." See *Women and Human Development*, 72–3.

[30] Kant, *Critique of Judgment*, section 9.

[31] Lloyd, *Reclaiming Wonder*, 25, quoting *Metaphysics*, A.2, 982b. My emphasis.

[32] Kant, *Critique of Judgment*, section 4.

[33] Ibid., section 1.

[34] Helen De Cruz, "Awe and Wonder in Scientific Practice: Implications for the Relationship Between Science and Religion," in M. Fuller et al., eds., *Issues in Science and Theology: Nature - And Beyond* (New York: Springer, 2020), 155–68. Nussbaum disambiguates the two in her *Justice for Animals*.

I see little difference between Schinkel's nuanced, eerie, and beautiful "contemplative wonder" – dumb-struck at the mystery of the whole of the world – and awe as a form of positive anxiety of consideration. Provided that, in awe, one keeps considering the possibilities of sense and meaning before one, only the categorical focus of Schinkel's concept (i.e., on the world as such) distinguishes it from awe, to which it is qualitatively aligned. Indeed, Schinkel does a good job of showing how something that might appear to be sublime can actually be deeply wonderful.[35]

My view is close to Vlad Glaveanu's perspective. He sees wonder on a continuum involving many different expressions of wonder. I call such a view – my own – a *continuum view* of wonder.[36] It shows us something profound about our powers of constructing a meaningful world in which we can live autonomously. But I have to show you what.

We might begin with the Spinozist lineage of thought about wonder as understood by Lloyd when she writes: "For Spinoza, . . . wonder coexists with and strengthens the pursuit of knowledge, rather than impeding it; and it has connections with other aspects of mental activity which make it an important intellectual resource."[37] This is a point about our striving and how it relies on wonder to give us cognitive agency. The way I put it, our striving and capacity for wonder are interwoven. *Our striving haunts wonder just as wondering is involved in striving.*

"Haunt" is not meant in reference to mourning or to ghosts. It is meant in the sense of "frequenting" and with an ear to the root of "haunt" in "home."[38] Striving brings wonder home as we try to flourish autonomously within what makes sense, while wondering shapes striving. It is only because we strive by seeking to make sense out of the world that wonder has its importance for – and grip on – us, and it is in part only because we wonder that our striving has the particular form that it has involving being lost in and absorbed by possibilities of sense and meaning to consider in the free play of our imaginations.

---

[35] Schinkel, *Wonder and Education*, chapter 1. Schinkel links awe to "greatness" and to the cessation of "puzzlement" (p. 44). The latter especially distinguishes awe from wonder for him. But insofar as awe involves reverence – as the dictionary claims that it does – awe involves consideration. What we don't want, however, is the narcissistic moment when awe becomes dread, i.e., existential insecurity in the face of what is awesome.

[36] Glaveanu, *Wonder*. I had thought that I was operating in outer space around wonder until I found Glaveanu's book in the last sixth months of writing this one. It's a great, modest book.

[37] Lloyd, *Reclaiming Wonder*, 4–5.

[38] "Haunt," *Oxford American Dictionary*. Thanks to Romy Opperman for these connotations in her "Haunting and Hosting," *New School University Gender and Sexuality Studies Institute*, November 10th, 2020.

The search to make sense out of the world is implicit within wonder as its background. At the same time, the way we come to find what makes sense when we are unclear about things involves some degree of the positive anxiety of consideration, even if we do not call it, in conventional English, "wonder." Because striving haunts wonder, being lost in wonder is its life, i.e., its vitality according to our human form of striving. This is so, because being lost is the exact point where we strive *within* wondering to consider the sense of things, reaching out into the unknown or into the confusing.

Understanding such lostness can accordingly help us understand the way striving relates to sense-finding – namely, by illuminating the way *searching* figures in wonder. Wondering's activity intensifies with searching for sense and meaning. But searching often involves stopping our drive to complete things, suspending our desire to control meaning and to make things make perfect sense, and letting ourselves be lost.

Focusing on sense-finding in contexts where we become perplexed and lost in wonder helps us understand the question of why life should be especially wonderful, as Nussbaum – a faithful neo-Aristotelian – holds that it is. *Life should be especially wonderful because it both displays and challenges the sense of our striving as human beings.* All life strives, just as we do. Our striving involves being lost in wonder over the sense of things, including seeking to understand the sense of ourselves. Other living beings display this homology: *they strive just as we do, yet in a way that makes sense differently than we do.* Thus, they both bring up and challenge how we make sense of our own striving.[39] Accordingly, other living beings ought to be wonderful.[40]

Each living form has its own "world." But how can we fill it in? We wonder . . . Being lost in other forms of life as we try to make sense of them thus manifests *our* form of life.[41]

Our life with wonder shows us how much leeway we have in our lives to respond reflectively to how we think that they should make sense. It shows us our capacity for autonomy. On reflection, this shouldn't surprise us, because being lost is at the core of the human condition. There would be no point to the meaning of what does and does not make sense if we were *fixed*. We would not need to figure anything out. We would not need to follow or even register that something does make sense as opposed to not doing so. Because we are *un*fixed,

---

[39] See my "The Other Species Capability & the Power of Wonder" and "The Reasonableness of Wonder."
[40] Cf. Cora Diamond, "The Importance of Being Human."
[41] See my "The Other Species Capability & the Power of Wonder."

we have to seek what makes sense to us in order to find a stable existence.[42] Beings who seek to make sense of things are beings who are not set in stone.

Just so, humans vary in significant ways across generations and cultures, despite commonalities. Even during a person's lifetime, what makes sense for us changes. Even in slow-moving cultures without upheaval, values become nuanced as people make sense of things slightly differently. It's because we relate to ourselves *reflectively* that all this happens.

There is a long and complicated tradition linking our lack of fixity to both our capacity for some degree of reflection and our reliance on normativity.[43] Unless we are self-destructive, when we find what makes sense, we let it determine our world and use it to argue about how our lives should go. Seeing how things make or do not make sense is the general way in which we come to judge the relation of things to our lives and their relation to each other in the world. Sense-seeking is orientation in striving.

(The reason why I am using "sense" as the main orienting concept of striving is that what makes sense encompasses the full range of ways we might consider something, whether as true, good, beautiful, their opposites – or in between.)

Lostness in wonder is the state of our striving that turns to searching. Noting that wonder is open to things as they appear in their own light – considering the many possibilities by which things may make sense and be meaningful on their own – Nussbaum is therefore right that wondering doesn't reduce what we consider to what is part of our already existing calculations or ideological commitments.[44] But it would be misleading to therefore infer that searching isn't part of our striving and so of our human form of *eudaimonia* in the broadest sense. Rather, wonder (the capacity) and wondering (the act) are so much a part of human striving and human striving is so much a part of them that we could not grasp human flourishing without them. Wondering is thus *eudaimonistic* in a more capacious sense.[45] Without it, we cannot *thrive* in our searching.

*

---

[42] Cf. Pico della Mirandola, *Oration on the Dignity of Man.*

[43] G. W. F. Hegel, *Phenomenology of Spirit*, trans. A. V. Miller (1807; New York: Oxford University Press, 1976); Martin Heidegger, *Being and Time*, trans. Joan Stambaugh and Dennis Schmidt (1927; Albany, NY: SUNY Press, 2010); Jean-Paul Sartre, *Being and Nothingness: A Phenomenological Essay on Ontology*, trans. Hazel E. Barnes (1943; New York: Washington Square Press, 1984). More recently, Christine M. Korsgaard, *The Sources of Normativity* (New York: Cambridge University Press, 1996).

[44] Nussbaum claims that wonder is "non-*eudaimonistic*" in *Upheavals of Thought*, 191, and see Schinkel, *Wonder and Education,* chapter 1.

[45] Cf. Jan B. Pedersen, *Balanced Wonder: Experiential Sources of Imagination, Virtue, and Human Flourishing* (Lanham, MD: Lexington Books, 2019), chapter 5 especially.

The set of claims I'm advancing certainly complicates the Aristotelian tradition of which Nussbaum's work is a part even if I am keeping the role of *phantasia* in mind throughout this motet. The question I have is how positive anxiety permeates imagination – even, if you will, "fantasy" (the English descendent of the word *phantasia*). This question reads back "modern" figures into "ancient" thought, not anachronistically and inaccurately, but as a conjecture about how to elaborate ancient beginnings through "modern" perceptions. My interest in the figure of positive anxiety shakes up the space of reason to be open to how other worlds are possible.[46]

One of the interesting things about Nussbaum's philosophy is how it emerges anxiously between ancient philosophy and modern thought. Simply take the Capability Approach.[47] In it, we find a commitment to an Aristotelian orientation to the human good found by looking at our "species norm."[48] This norm shows us how we function as the dynamic kind of beings that we are. The horse runs on four legs, the human on two. The paramecium divides. The human mates and gives a great deal of time bringing up their young. The lilac tree reacts to soil and climate conditions; the human takes things in, learns socially, and reflects.[49] The species norm is a way to talk about the kind of beings we are when we strive in our nature. Applied to humans, it is a way to think about human nature.

To grasp our norm, Nussbaum suggests that we look with wonder at human striving and affirm what capabilities a person needs in order to flourish.[50] At first, this seems straightforward, at least in terms of her Aristotelianism, even if it is vague what flourishing is and complicated by how open to many possibilities of sense wonder is. Yet in *Creating Capabilities,* Nussbaum returns to Vasanti, the Indian woman who was the protagonist of *Women and Human Development* and displays what wondering about our striving means. Nussbaum pays attention to the ways Vasanti comes alive, what she seeks and needs, and how she grows in agency and consciousness.[51] In other words, Nussbaum follows how Vasanti makes sense out of life, how she becomes practically capable in seeking to do what makes sense to her, and how she becomes aware of her world as something that can come to make sense. The things Nussbaum focuses on are wound

---

[46] I.e., it is "pluriversal." Arturo Escobar, *Pluriversal Politics: The Real and the Possible* (Durham, NC: Duke University Press, 2020).

[47] Nussbaum, *Women and Human Development.* Also Nussbaum, *Creating Capabilities.*

[48] Nussbaum, *Frontiers of Justice,* chapter 6, section iv. See also Thompson, *Life and Action,* Part One, "The Representation of Life."

[49] Cf. Thompson, *Life and Action,* Part One, "The Representation of Life."

[50] Nussbaum, *Women and Human Development,* 72–3.

[51] Nussbaum, *Creating Capabilities,* chapter 1.

around the dynamic power of our unfixed condition: the power to search, change our lives and to modify our environment in line with what makes sense to us. Things as basic as health become important because of their capacity (Nussbaum calls it their "internal" capability) to allow us to live a life *that makes sense to us*.[52] Our capacity to flourish becomes wound around our capacity to search and to change our world according to what we find.

Nussbaum's way of searching for how we strive attests to this turn inward to our reflective and unfixed striving for sense, a constituent of which is what she calls "imagination."[53] In *Frontiers of Justice* but also *Love's Knowledge*, Nussbaum names the way she approached Vasanti's life in that prime example of discovering our species norm. She thinks of her method as *sympathetic imagining*. Nussbaum allies it to the "politics of humanity" – a form of respect for human dignity that involves "curiosity" and "imagination."[54] Why imagination? We have to unsettle our fixed ideas to consider what is different in another person's life. In Nussbaum's writing on homosexuality from the perspective of a heteronormative society, this idea of moving inward to a life that may be queer to a "het" person comes out strongly.[55] A heteronormative person might ask, how does another's queer life make sense to them? Is their world my world? How does my sense of the world change when I see how others deal both with my world and their striving for a different one? Human unfixity and the leeway we have in finding what makes sense to us leaves an opening for us to call on our queer imagination.[56]

The point goes deeper, too. Nussbaum explicitly calls on sympathetic imagining to understand other forms of life beyond the human – as she says, "beyond humanity."[57] Yet speaking of going "beyond humanity" is possibly misleading. It is precisely what Nussbaum calls our "humanity" in *From Disgust to Humanity* among other places that involves our power of sympathetic imagination to extend beyond humankind. Nussbaum might merely be equivocal here – using "humanity" in two senses, one to reference humankind, the other to reference a virtue. My own preference is always to use "humanity" to reference a virtue and "humankind" to reference the collective totality of human beings.[58]

[52] Ibid.
[53] Nussbaum, *Women and Human Development*, 78–9.
[54] Nussbaum, *Frontiers of Justice*, chapter 6; *Love's Knowledge*, chapter 14; *From Disgust to Humanity*, preface.
[55] Nussbaum, *From Disgust to Humanity* and *Hiding from Humanity*. Obviously, I am trading on equivocation in the word "queer" here. Both meanings work in context.
[56] Lynne Huffer, *Foucault's Strange Eros* (New York: Columbia University Press, 2020).
[57] This is part of the subtitle of chapter 6 of *Frontiers of Justice*.
[58] See my *The Ecological Life* and Thompson's and my and Thompson's *Ethical Adaptation to Climate Change*, Introduction: "Adapting Humanity."

Nussbaum asks us to find interiority within forms of life that aren't unfixed and reflective like us but that have other modes of making their way in the world. It is a stretch to have sympathy for a spider, yet much-loved children's books attempt it.[59] I take Nussbaum's call to use our imaginations to understand other forms of life as revealing something about *us*, not about "them" (the other animals), to echo Cora Diamond.[60] We need to make sense out of life, including other forms of it.[61] Once again, our sense-seeking shapes how we do what we do, displaying our specific dynamism as the kind of beings that we are in imaginative relation to other kinds of beings. Here *phantasia* shapes our human "imaginary" itself as involving wondering over other kinds of beings.[62]

Nussbaum's reliance on sympathetic imagination and curiosity may seem to stretch the sought-after objectivity of Aristotelian biology. People can be so weird and freaky, as *other to each other* as other forms of life at times. Our normativity may be co-opted by concepts about what is "normal."[63] But the truth is that we are essentially "abnormal" in our range of possibilities and our strange modes of human living.[64] When we imaginatively enter into the lives of other people in order to grasp their striving, we may find that the interiority of a person reveals many idiosyncratic things. At the same time, looking at how we behave doesn't obviously lead us to see our dignity! Varieties of short-sightedness, self-absorption, and selfishness appear as species norms, existing in tension with our cooperative evolutionary inheritance.[65] To put the matter simply, it doesn't seem obvious that what makes sense to people on their own terms is revealing of our species norm, but rather *the way we find* what makes sense.

"Meta" though this formulation may be, it seems correct: *What makes us dynamically human is our sense-seeking itself,* not necessarily our conclusions about what does make sense and the correlative particular ways we come to

---

[59] E. B. White, *Charlotte's Web*, illus. Garth Williams (New York: Harper & Brothers, 1952); see my *Ecological Life*, Lecture 4, "Rooted in Our Humanity."

[60] Cora Diamond, *The Realistic Spirit*, "Eating Meat and Eating People."

[61] I make the argument for this strong claim in "The Other Species Capability & the Power of Wonder" through the argument that *self-reflection* depends on a grammar of living form that necessarily demands some comparisons with other forms of life and that benefits from an ample amount of comparisons.

[62] See Diamond, "The Importance of Being Human."

[63] Michael Foucault, *Abnormal: Lectures at the Collège de France, 1974–1975* (New York: Picador, 2004).

[64] This point raises questions about Emily Anne Parker's use of Aristotelian ablism as the premise of her critique of politics in the Aristotelian tradition, but this is not the occasion to go into this dispute over reading Aristotelianism here. See Emily Anne Parker, *Elemental Difference and the Climate of the Body* (New York: Oxford University Press, 2021).

[65] Philip Kitcher, *The Ethical Project* (Cambridge, MA: Harvard University Pres, 2011); Matt Ridley, *The Origins of Virtue: Human Instincts and the Evolution of Cooperation* (New York: Penguin Books, 1998).

them.[66] Certainly, we eat just as other animals do. But the way we eat manifests our sense-finding not just our nutriment. We have elaborate rituals designed to reflect the sense of the occasion.[67] Certainly, we reproduce as other mammals do and enjoy sex as some cetaceans and primates do without the aim of reproducing. But our sexual orientations and lives are as various as imaginations seemingly go, made up of fantasies wrestling with sense. Certainly, we sleep and dream as many an animal does. But when we wake up, we ask what sense it made and have constructed elaborate ways to interpret our dreams. Being oriented by what makes sense to us is at the core of our species norm, not just or even specific behaviors some people think make sense.[68]

Now the point I've been waiting for is that our sense-seeking is capacious through our capacity for *wondering*. That is one reason why our moral universe shouldn't be circumscribed by potentially autonomous beings like ourselves reading and trying to make sense of philosophy! In Nussbaum's writing on disability,[69] she stresses the dignity of people with – as I like to put the point – *variabilities* (!) that do not fit well into the existing construction of society.[70] People who suffer to make sense of the world in the ways most of us do or who may not be said to make sense of things at all, still turn toward the light that they find – or if they are lacking vision, the sound revealing the world; if they are lacking sound and vision, the touch orienting the come-and-go of life. *The point is that people who have moral accountability can stretch their imaginations to find the sense in many different ways that people end up alive and happy, even when people cannot make sense to themselves in some articulated, elaborated way.* The adjustment of a body to comfort – why is that not a way that anyone who wonders can imagine can make sense? All life strives, and since our orientation

---

[66] On my reading of Aristotle's *Nicomachean Ethics*, the point to take from Aristotle's search for our specific human function is that our striving passes through thoughtfulness in some form. The expression "thoughtfulness" is my translation of the power of reasoning and of speaking that he indicates. Since Aristotle is quite clear that it is bound up with emotional, moral, and intellectual character, "thoughtfulness" is a good translation that gives what Aristotle has in mind some soulfulness and moral consideration. I take Aristotle's focus on virtue as thoughtfulness as an ancient placeholder for the possible construction of what in modern philosophy became called "subjectivity." See Aristotle, *Nicomachean Ethics*, trans. Christopher Rowe (c. 350 BCE; New York: Oxford University Press, 2002), 1.7–8.

[67] Nussbaum, *Women and Human Development*, 72, speaking of Marx's famous play on words between *Fressen* (eating as a wild animal) and *Essen* (eating as a person): "In Marx's example, a starving person doesn't eat food in a fully human way – by which I think he means a way infused by practical reason and sociability."

[68] See McKittrick, *Sylvia Wynter: The Practice of Being Human.*

[69] Nussbaum, *Frontiers of Justice*, chapters 2 and 3.

[70] My *Solar Calendar, and Other Ways of Marking Time*, Study 1, "The Ideas Start in the Kitchen." This phrasing is relevant to disputing Parker's reading of Aristotelianism in *Elemental Difference and the Climate of the Body.*

of striving is to seek what makes sense from out of the possibilities that appear around whatever is meaningful in our lives, we approach the living thus capaciously, too.

*

We are beings for whom the world's sense and meaning aren't simply given, and yet the potential for the world to make sense is evident from the earliest weeks and months we enter into consciousness as infants. This is what Nussbaum observes and takes into her philosophy when she speaks of the mind's "original" joy.[71] Even as we have to learn how to make sense of the world, the superabundance of meaning in the world is a given. This superabundance stays with us in life to a great extent, provided that we are not dulled by deprivation, neglect, or domination and its control.[72]

Within our condition of existing in a world of superabundant meaning and the potential for things to make sense, anxiety itself makes sense. After all, anxiety is the objectless awareness of there being a trembling in the order of things due to unseen possibilities within them. Anxiety is expectant but unclear. It includes the awareness that we might be facing other kinds of sense, even, or that what we take to make sense might be otherwise or have to change to become harmonious eventually (perhaps we realize that we have been living in an unjust society and that we do not know what the implications will be of working out our dim and intuitive sense that justice must be elaborated, even its *concepts* changed).[73] *The centrality of anxiety to being human and the centrality of wonder to working with anxiety have to do with our core orientation toward sense-seeking and meaning-discovery in our lives.*

A way to sum up these assumptions is to say that anxiety is the objectless awareness of our world and our lives in it not making complete sense and possibly making more sense (or some other sense) than they do. We might not know whether our lives not making sense would imply that they will make more sense, because we may not know yet how the difference our anxiety suggests will lead us to make things hang together. The point is rather that the search for a

---

[71] Nussbaum, *Upheavals of Thought*, 189.

[72] In personal correspondence, Rick Anthony Furtak called to mind here Rainer Maria Rilke's *Überzähliges Dasein* which rose up inside him *im Herzen* – from the ninth of the *Duino Eligies*. Rainer Maria Rilke, "Duino Elegies" in *Duino Elegies & The Sonnets to Orpheus: A Bilingual Edition*, trans. Stephen Mitchell (1923; New York: Vintage, 2009).

[73] Cf. Whyte, "Settler Colonialism, Ecology, & Environmental Injustice" and my "Facing Mass Extinction, It Is Prudent to Decolonise Lands & Laws."

new possibility presents itself that sends a shudder through our lives and makes the possibility of having to reorder them obvious.[74]

While anxiety speaks to our condition as beings who make sense of the world, in anxiety the world and our lives in it come into question, open to possibilities we cannot yet grasp. This may be a matter of degree. In some cases, the anxiety takes in the whole world.[75] In other cases, we may simply find ourselves fantasizing around an object that comes to shift in its adumbrations. The reverie is slowly and quietly anxious but modest in its scope.

And anxiety manifests practically, relationally, and theoretically, so to speak – concerning not just what makes sense to our understanding, but what we might do in this life and this world and our social lives and their meaning. All the same, in anxiety, both that one ought to consider – and reconsider – things and that what one has been considering has become indefinite open out into the world (whether "out there" or in our "inner" world) to anticipate unseen possibilities of what could make sense or be meaningful. So, in anxiety we become open to the sense and meaning of the world and our lives in it, increasingly, around whatever our initial focus was, if we even had a focus.

This is what I mean when I say that in anxiety, our worlds and our lives in them become to some significant degree *lost*. There's more sense and meaning to the world than we and our lives can absorb. Things in our lives could truly make better sense otherwise, at least by some new arrangement. Here, the drive to make sense positions alterity – things making sense differently – along the way to clarification – things making better sense. Phenomenologically, the moment of anxiety may involve either alterity or clarification, but the openness to what could make sense in anxiety implies alterity in search of clarification. In this specific way, anxiety's constitutive state is a pregnant form of being lost in the world.

In order to grasp both anxiety generally and wondering specifically, it is important to fathom existing in a world of superabundant meaning and sense. Does this seem hard – even offensive – to do? Being able to be lost in wonder isn't easy in the social configurations of many people's lives. Isn't being able to be lost some kind of privilege? When we are suffering from injustice, our capabilities languishing, dealing with domination, and recurring indignity and humiliation, or at risk for our very lives, it seems wrong to hear that the world is filled with "meaning" and "sense" or that we might learn to become lost so as to strive. There

---

[74] This point was a response to Urszula Lisowska (personal correspondence, February 27th, 2020).
[75] See Schinkel's "contemplative" or "deep" wonder in his *Wonder and Education*.

is a kind of lostness that is removed from being able to make sense of things and from being able to find much meaning in our lives in the world. Within the eye of injustice, the surrounding hurricane isn't "meaning" and "sense." It is their *absence.*[76]

If the oppression of our autonomy, cutting us off from being able to find what makes sense to us, instead produced sense for us, something would be illogical. Evil is senseless because it erases, obliterates, or ignores our basic orientation toward making sense of the world as a meaningful place.[77] Yet the little ones among us – each other's children – don't come into the world finding it meaningless or without its own kinds of sense. That we *object* to evil or oppression, that they are to be *opposed*, indicates that they mean a lot to us. Their presence doesn't prove that our lives in this world are meaningless or that they make no sense, only that the world in which we live confronted by oppression and evil can be a shitty, senseless place. It is the indignation that is *positive* here and that displays how much meaning there should be in *another* world to which we should aspire in our drive to make things make sense. So, the hurricane of injustice or wickedness proves negatively that the world is a place that matters and that demanding that the world make sense goes all the way into the heart of our evaluative language: *This is evil. That is wrong. That system is keeping us down!*

Positive anxiety holds within it a source for resisting injustice. Its form is that *another world is imaginable.* Rather than keeping us in our place as domination would do, positive anxiety implicitly rejects the idea that our sense and meaning are to be fixed in place or our autonomy truncated.[78] Genevieve Lloyd, in her discussion of wonder's political importance in the critique of "social imaginaries," talks about how wonder is bound up with "renewed mental activity."[79] Positive anxiety reflects – as the child's entrance into the world and growth into a life does – the excess of sense and meaning in our world, involving us in a response to make sense of our lives in this world always already by its very eruption of – possibly angry – agitation. When we become excitable that something needs to change *because there is more meaning to this life than the way that things are currently making sense* (!), we have already become involved in the way positive

---

[76] In personal correspondence, Sidra Shahid noted that "some critical theory readers might ask: what if the world makes no sense? . . . Intelligibility in this case is something rare and fragmentary (which is part of why, I guess, Adorno says systematic writing isn't possible)." She is referencing Theodor W. Adorno, *Minima Moralia: Reflections on a Damaged Life,* trans. E. F. N. Jephcott (1951; Brooklyn: Verso, 2006).

[77] Neiman, *Evil in Modern Thought.*

[78] On being kept in one's place as a wrong, see Jacques Rancière, *Disagreement: Politics and Philosophy,* trans. Julie Rose (1995 ; Minneapolis: University of Minnesota Press, 2004).

[79] Lloyd, *Reclaiming Wonder,* chapter 8, "Political Language and Social Imaginaries."

anxiety summons us to both be lost and to leap outward into making sense –
that is, to strive.

*

Against this broad background, wondering is a way that we can structure our
anxieties reflectively and can try to make sense of things. When wondering, we
try to figure out what makes sense while being in some sense lost. It is this
condition of being lost that makes sense ring out in the silence or shine in the
dim light. It is also the way to view being unfixed as something *promising*. We
cannot get a grip on what makes sense without being able to wonder about sense
and, in turn, have moments of being lost. Wondering, being lost, and making
sense of things are linked.

But this may not be immediately obvious if one considers wonder to be an
upsurge of delight or a powerful emotion akin to surprise, as in the Humean
tradition delineated at times by Vasalou's *Wonder* and found within Fisher's
Wonder, the Rainbow, and the Aesthetics of Rare Experiences.[80] For English speakers,
it's extremely hard to shake off the connotations of "wonder" as an upsurge of what
Vasalou calls "delight." Wonder often gets cast as some such dramatic interruption
of our life with considering things. This semantic confusion around wonder
shouldn't surprise us, though. There's a lot going on around wonder.

Recent work on wonder is far-ranging and creative. A good place to locate the
boundary of the "recent" is 1980, with R. W. Hepburn's Aristotelian Society talk
on wonder.[81] Since then, there have been internal debates in the literature
between whether wonder is separate from awe,[82] whether wonder is active
searching, is a surprising experience of the extraordinary striking us, or is
contemplative on the edge of inarticulateness.[83] Authors note the wide-ranging
use of "wonder" or seemingly allied terms in various domains of creativity and

---

[80] See my commentary in "Wonder & Sense." Also within this Humean tradition are Joerg Fingerhut
and Jesse Prinz, "Wonder, Appreciation, and the Value of Art," *Progress in Brain Research* 237 (2018):
107–28.

[81] Hepburn, "The Inaugural Address."

[82] Fingerhut and Prinz, "Wonder, Appreciation, and the Value of Art"; Nussbaum, *Political Emotions*,
331, thanks to a research survey paper by William Watson, endnote 22, p. 430; Mary Jane Rubenstein,
Strange Wonder: The Closure of Metaphysics and the Opening of Awe (New York: Columbia University
Press, 2011); De Cruz, "Awe and Wonder in Scientific Practice"; Lloyd, *Reclaiming Wonder*, where
Lloyd makes the ingenious argument that the late-eighteenth-century notion of the sublime that
became crucial to Romanticism (and, much later, even important to postmodernism) occupies the
space of awe and thereby blocks out the importance of wonder in European post-Romantic culture.

[83] Anders Schinkel, "The Educational Importance of Deep Wonder," *Journal of Philosophy of Education*
51:2 (2017): 538–53 and *Wonder and Education*; Fingerhut and Prinz, "Wonder, Appreciation, and
the Value of Art"; Glaveanu, *Wonder*, on what I call a "continuum theory" of wonder.

research,[84] the prevalence of experiences of wonder across cultures,[85] and also the rich and evolving history about the development of the meaning of wonder.[86] There has also been work emerging on the role of wonder in morality, ethics, politics, and in human flourishing.[87]

Since human beings strive by seeking meaning and sense in the world, it is no surprise, either, that wonder is – in some appellation and form – cross-cultural and that people have developed traditions around it that modify what we are looking at and how the positive anxiety of consideration can coherently make sense – be expressed intelligibly – in a given culture. Our minds seek to make sense of things, thanks to their meaning. Part of what we make sense of is our capacity to make sense of things, including what we call "wondering." Again, it gets that "meta." In so doing, we refine and develop wonder's meaning. Wonder is both cross-cultural and variable because of its nature which drives us to cultivate meaning and sense.

Understanding wonder as the positive anxiety of considering things still subtly shifts the discussion. Soulful excitement is basic to our life with sense and meaning when it has not been beaten out of us. Only in anxiety can we register that the possibilities of sense and meaning in the world exceed sense we've made of things and the meaning that we've found. This condition also makes sense of wonder. While anxiety is dizzying, it's pregnant with meaning. Even angsty dread – a negative form of anxiety suggesting issues with control of the outside world – is intensely meaningful. Otherwise, it wouldn't grip us. There, in anxiety, it's possible to let our minds play freely, even if this may be difficult when the anxiety shades toward the negative. This free play of the mind already approaches wonderment. Doing so is a way of responding to our meaningful and sense-filled condition in a positive manner – i.e., finding meaning and sense in the dizziness of possibilities.

Locating wonder within positive anxiety relocates disparate positions about wonder *along a continuum*. Starting with anxiety, it shouldn't surprise us that wonder can be mixed with awe. Awe suggests being overpowered by one's

[84] Vasalou, *Wonder.*
[85] Fingerhut and Prinz, "Wonder, Appreciation, and the Value of Art."
[86] Daston and Park, *Wonder and the Order of Nature.*
[87] Maguerite la Caze, *Wonder and Generosity: Their Role in Ethics and Politics* (Albany, NY: SUNY Press, 2013); Lloyd, *Reclaiming Wonder,* especially chapters 8 and 9; Pedersen, *Balanced Wonder;* and even Robert C. Fuller, *Wonder: From Emotion to Spirituality* (Chapel Hill, NC: The University of North Carolina Press, 2006). See also Schinkel, *Wonder and Education,* chapters 4 and 5. Lloyd touches upon the political importance of lostness when she writes (in chapter 8, "Political Language and Social Imaginaries") that "experiences of wonder-inducing *aporia* can be a stimulus to revitalising social critique."

experience of the awesome thing.[88] Awe then anticipates a turning toward the negative form of anxiety. Instead of there being only a problem for our mind, now there is a problem for our will. No wonder that awe then becomes the edge along which one can take the mind-opening possibilities of this world and slide – or flee – with them toward fear. Awe's the middle station on that path. Through it, wonder can become dread, moving along the turn from positive to negative anxiety, narcissism kicking up in our wills. At a point, even anxiety itself can become dreadful, passing from awe to fear, leaving its original positive meaning behind.[89] For Kierkegaard (and later, Heidegger), this is a categorical error, for fear has a specific object on which it fixes, but the mistake may be psychologically understandable in that people with negative anxiety already circle the space around narcissism finding relief in projected fears of things outside their control.

Anxiety can be both active and passive, searching and contemplative, depending on the moment when one stops it short – or even depending on its speed. In the *Concept of Anxiety*, Kierkegaard's pseudonym views anxiety as a quickening.[90] This is of a piece with the negatively tinged problems of responsibility and the will that narcissistically haunt Haufniensis's text on "sin." It is perfectly possible to carry on in slow-moving anxiety. This is one thing that open-state meditation habituates its practitioners to do, and it is also something underlying many artists' work practices during spells of creativity. Considering the excitement of sociability, too, it's renowned that states of being in love can manifest slow-moving elation as one's world opens to sense and meaning around the love, resting in the leeway that love gives to everything.[91]

Whereas some scholars view wonder as something that happens to us – for instance, a work of art striking us as revealing something extraordinary[92] – we can make ourselves wonder about things.[93] From this perspective, wonder*ing* is an art of thinking, and it can become virtuous in helping us strive. What's more, in actively considering things for their unconventional possibilities, we are likely

---

[88] Nussbaum, *Political Emotions*, 331. Fingerhut and Prinz, "Wonder, Appreciation, and the Value of Art." Cf. Kant, *Critique of Judgment* on the "dynamical sublime."

[89] See Nussbaum, *The Monarchy of Fear* and *The New Religious Intolerance*. Her *Political Emotions* also views anxiety negatively in relation to fear.

[90] Kierkegaard, *The Concept of Anxiety*, "Subjective Anxiety."

[91] This leeway is also found in being loved truly. See the moment in Andrei Tarkovsky's *Mirror* (*Zerkalo*) (Moscow: Mosfilms, 1975) when the narrator realizes that, back in his childhood home within the care of his mother, "everything is possible." The claim is accompanied by a sense of the beauty and freedom afforded us by being alive. It's one of my favorite sequences in film and helped keep me oriented during graduate school, for my mother was one of the sources of my philosophical disposition. If you have not seen this film and are interested in wonder, please see it.

[92] Fingerhut and Prinz, "Wonder, Appreciation, and the Value of Art."

[93] Anders Schinkel, "The Educational Importance of Deep Wonder."

to be struck by possibilities to which we are not habituated. They will be extraordinary, and some may strike us with their strangeness or surprise.

In other words, the passivity ascribed to experiences of wonder seems to isolate a moment in the process of wondering with that moment itself, in turn, resting within the background activity of the mind being receptive and searching for meaning and sense, trying naturally to make sense of things in our condition's proliferation of possibilities. Recall again how, in *Reclaiming Wonder*, Genevieve Lloyd traces out the ancient Greek and, for her, Spinozist (while for Hepburn, Kantian) tradition of wonder being a background state of positive receptivity to the sense and meaning of the world.[94] Notable also is Vlad Glaveanu's insightful and important understanding of wonder along several axes of qualitative differences and intensities.[95] Slow wondering down enough, and you will arrive at the suspension of meaning and sense marking the arrival of something unexpected, inarticulate, yet pregnant with meaning or sense. This "pregnancy" is the mark of what Kant conceptualized in the *Critique of Judgment* as the meaning of things charged with imagination in the operation going into making judgments of the beautiful. What Kant understands as the "form of purposiveness" is that what we face as striking us as beautiful appears to have meaning and to make sense, but we cannot articulate the content of its sense or meaning.[96]

Why not, then, follow the moment of suspense in wondering all the way to contemplation, where we take in the bare meaning of the world from out of the void? *The moment of contemplation is then the slowest movement of wonder's positive anxiety of considering things.* There, we contemplate the being or nothingness of something. *What if this thing simply were not? What is it for this thing to be?* Here, all the world surrounding the thing about which we wonder becomes wonderful. The world becomes new, as if it had never been ordinary. The entirety of the world surrounding the thing about which we wonder becomes open to question. In other words, *the world itself becomes the question*, with the thing about which we wondered leading us to wonder about the world itself, taking it in as for the first time.[97]

The point remains, though, that in wondering over something, we search into the meaningful space beyond its meaning or the sense-filled space beyond its sense. Returning to the origins of wonder in Greek philosophy, Lloyd traces out

[94] Lloyd, *Reclaiming Wonder,* chapters 1–3, and 6.
[95] Glaveanu, *Wonder,* sections 2.2, 2.3, and 3.3 especially.
[96] Kant, *Critique of Judgment,* section 11.
[97] Schinkel, *Wonder and Education,* chapter 2 and chapter 1, "Some Personal Experiences of Wonder: An Initial Analysis."

the dialectic of knowing and not knowing – and the constitutive *aporias* of this dialectic – in Plato's and Aristotle's philosophies.[98] Wondering is, most precisely, the activity (which involves receptivity!), of going to the edge of things as they are given (or are conventional, expected, ordinary, and the like), and seeing how else their meaning or sense *could* appear.

The subjunctive tense of the modality of possibility – "could" not "can" – expresses this going to the edge of things to turn over their possibilities. It involves holding a meaningful or sense-filled space around them in which consideration can play freely. What makes wondering different than other forms of thinking or attention – say, deducing, inferring, doubting, scrutinizing, inquiring, and the like – is, most precisely, this *holding space* around things for other, more connected, elaborated, transformative, etc. meaning and sense to open up.[99] What I want to underline is that wondering is the part of thinking in which we hold space around the sense and meaning of things, receptive to how their sense or meaning may change by becoming deeper or more elaborate.[100]

And the notion of going deeper is not rhetorical fluff! Wondering fills in the world. Though it may consider things according to their unconventional possibilities, it doesn't void the world of sense and meaning as negative anxiety does. Rather, it goes beyond the given meaning and sense of things to elaborations on or of them.[101] Wondering draws connections. It is synthetic on the whole. It creates a mesh, and it adumbrates things.

Even when wondering involves completely reversing our way of looking at things, wondering leaves us with a world that is renewed in its connections and sense. Wondering draws us into relationship with the world in its subtlety, complexity, and fecundity.[102] In this way, wondering makes us go deeper – or farther. *What would happen if I considered this?* [103]

---

[98] Lloyd, *Reclaiming Wonder*, chapter 1.

[99] This formulation is Scheinfeld et al.'s notation and elaboration of a teacher's wonder over a child's mind as holding "space" around the child's ideas so that the child can wonder. See *We Are All Explorers*, 36–7, "Creating space in [the teacher's] own mind that allows the child's idea to grow":

> The teacher creates a space within her mind that is defined by the child's chosen focus of interest. She then imaginatively puts the child's idea somewhere in that space. The space is larger than the space occupied by the child's idea. This allows the teacher the possibility of imagining directions in which the child's idea might extend/expand outward. The space is now a mutually shared space with the child . . . She creates with the child a model in her mind of the child's emergent thinking.

[100] One analogue to this in phenomenology is found in Jean-Luc Marion's vision of consciousness alive to the excess of meaning and sense around what it finds meaningful and understandable. See Marion, *Being Given*.

[101] Schinkel, *Wonder and Education*, chapter 1.

[102] Hepburn, "The Inaugural Address."

[103] Cf. Ege Yumusak, "The Organizer's Anti-Utopian Imaginations," *Philosophy & Activism*, June 8th, 2021.

Can we get a grip on the sense of things without doing some such thing to some degree? Is some small degree of wonder involved in understanding as such?[104]

*

Even though anxiety for Nussbaum's philosophy is a problem to be resolved or overcome,[105] attention to the relationship between wonder, striving to make sense of things, and the fundamentally positive anxiety of existing in the world with its proliferation of possibilities of sense and meaning suggests that wonder is anxious, that anxiety is basically positive, and that striving depends on anxiety expressed through the mind's original joy.

Accordingly, it should make sense why wondering is a primary way to become responsible for our condition of being awash in our lives' meaning and meaninglessness and the world's sense and senselessness. In wonder, we become open to our condition in the vast array of meaningful things of the world, to the world itself, and to ourselves in it. Then, when wondering, we come to things as they really make – or don't make – sense to us, thereby keeping open a space around the ways we have been taught or expected to follow things. Both the background state of wonder and the process of wondering connect us up to a meaningful world that begins to form around things that make sense to us, in which we recognize things that do not make sense to us, and in which we consider how things might make sense in other ways. Through wondering, we start to become autonomous.

Given her excitement over women becoming liberated in *Women and Human Development*, Nussbaum should be excited about that! But there is more that comes from stressing the relationship between wonder and anxiety, *pace* Nussbaum's views of both. Appreciating wonder's relationship to the positive anxiety of the human mind gives us a nuanced picture of wonder as a capacity that can range – as I've already noted – from a background condition folded incognito into people's ordinary lives to a sudden shock of emotional upheaval, a delight or something closer to apprehensive awe.[106] The important point is that *this changes how striving appears*. Being positively confused but open amid the possibilities of sense and meaning is central to human excellence. Letting things

---

[104] Hepburn "Inaugural Address" and Lloyd, *Reclaiming Wonder*. Glaveanu's position might imply the point, too.

[105] Nussbaum, *Upheavals of Thought*, chapter 4; *Political Emotions*, chapter 7; consider, too, how anxiety is discussed throughout, *passim*, *The Monarchy of Fear* and *The New Religious Intolerance*.

[106] Cf. Glaveanu, *Wonder*, section 2.2.

play out because one has lost oneself likewise becomes important for flourishing. That should interest us because it is non-narcissistic.[107]

In order to live well, people need to be lost at times and to let things play out. To let things play out is to let everything in the set of relationships shift and change – world, self, possibilities, actualities, sense, meaning ... Accordingly, wondering about oneself often accompanies wondering about one's world – and vice versa.

What's so profound is that we can come to change ourselves and our world through wonder, loosening control of ourselves and of our "story" of the world as we grow in our appreciation of the sense and meaning that comes to, and opens, other worlds.[108] Many developmental *and* incipiently political things happen when we prioritize anxiety, wonder, and the centrality of sitting with confusion in order to develop as autonomous people.

*

From the thousand responses of my heart never to cease ...
~ Walt Whitman, "Out of the Cradle Endlessly Rocking," 1871

Can we come to love confusion, provided that we seek sense rather than reinforce domination? Based on my own experience, that could be to take victimhood and turn it toward survival. I follow a tradition – let us call it "the anxious tradition" – in which our being is basically excitable, and that is not a bad thing. It brims with power of spirit. Although one might refer to F. W. J. von Schelling's philosophy of mind in early-nineteenth-century Berlin or (the soon-to-be negatively anxious Nazi) Martin Heidegger's ontology in early-twentieth-century Freiburg, Søren Kierkegaard's pseudonymous tract on anxiety written in Copenhagen near the middle of the nineteenth century is my reference point.[109] But the reason is historical. I came to it from being in love with someone who'd read Kierkegaard and broke my heart. Having the broken heart was good. It showed me my narcissism raised in and against an unloving social world.

The Concept of Anxiety (*Begrebet Angest*) is a text about the moment when people come of age. The tradition also includes such political thinkers as Reiner

---

[107] Nussbaum, *Upheavals of Thought*, 73ff.

[108] Here is where Dipesh Chakrabarty misunderstands and underestimates wonder in his *The Climate of History in a Planetary Age* (Chicago: The University of Chicago Press, 2021), chapter 8, an argument that Urszula Lisowska makes in her contribution to the special issue of *Environmental Philosophy* on Chakrbarty's book. See Urszula Lisowska, "Wonder and Politics in the Anthropocene: Beyond Curiosity and Reverance," MS, 2022.

[109] Søren Kierkegaard, *The Concept of Anxiety*.

Schürmann. He relates the tradition to ancient philosophers such as Plotinus and to early modern religious writers such as Meister Eckhart.[110] In these wider reaches of the apparent tradition, I would also include phenomenologists such as Jean-Louis Chrétien, particularly his *La voix nue* (*The Bare Voice*), a book that understands how words call for songs and where songs are the sensual register of the space of connotative possibilities and tonal adumbrations opening up around words when we give them to others (I mention him because of these motets).[111] But these other thinkers, often murky or diffuse, don't focus on moral responsibility to the extent that they should. The moment of coming of age is a moment of accountability. But around what?

The important point from Kierkegaard's dense, conflicted text is that anxiety involves searching without an object and that responsibility involves growing up to be able to relate to anxiety well for the sake of being a loving, accountable person. It's not easy because anxiety is tricky. Whereas in fear, I anticipate something specifically bad happening, with anxiety, there's no clear object. Fearful, I might worry about the results of a general election in which another four years of inaction on atmospheric and oceanic warming sets in. I have a fairly clear object for my fear: the further irreversible slide into a destabilized climate system and its attendant effects on all living people, future generations, and the world of life already plausibly in the early stages of the sixth mass extinction on Earth. This isn't anxiety, however. In being anxious, *I do not know what I'm anxious about.* When I am not sure what to fear but feel that everything is up in the air *around* (not "about") global warming, then I am anxious.

Operating beneath Kierkegaard's text is an unanalyzed difference between negative and positive anxiety. I am negatively anxious when I sense the proliferation of possibilities while *presuming* that I must fear them, despite my not having clear objects of my fear. In negative anxiety, I cast about searching for an object, but there is none that is clearly what my anxiety is about. *I try to pin my anxiety down, rather than letting it open up my sense of the world and of my life within it. As a result, my anxiety sticks onto things that present themselves to it, casting them in a fearful light.* Just so, it is easy to become irrational when anxious, making something – or someone! – the scapegoat for my anxiety. Searching for an object within anxiety can be a dangerous or self-undermining thing.

[110] Reiner Schürmann, *Heidegger on Being and Acting: From Principles to Anarchy*, trans. Marie Gros (Bloomington: Indiana University Press, 1987).
[111] Jean-Louis Chrétien, *La voix nue: Phénoménologie de la promesse* (Paris: Éditions de minuit, 1990).

Ironically, the pseudonym of Kierkegaard, Haufniensis, true to Kierkegaard's way of making characters who remind us that a book always involves an authorial perspective that can be distorted, seems himself locked up with some degree of *negative* anxiety. There is an absence of love in the background of his tract. The author's inquiry bounces around seeking a way to explain our feelings of guilt and ultimately despair. It isn't safe to be anxious in the world of Kierkegaard's pseudonym. But turn anxiety from a doomed searching closing in on a host of negative emotions leading ultimately to self-reproach. Turn anxiety toward an objectless searching that is open and filled with the possibility of finding how things make sense. Now anxiety is a positive condition.

Elsewhere, Kierkegaard suggests that this involves faith in the power of love to support the sense and meaning to all of our existence.[112] But I wonder if we don't need to become comfortable with anxiety to glimpse what love is. Does so much depend on searching without an object, on not panicking in being lost? Yes, because the phenomenology of positive anxiety is inchoate with wonder and the two are central to our capacity to live with sense and meaning. Positive anxiety, after all, is an openness that always already begins to search about, anything from a proneness to a drive to consider sense and meaning open to their possibilities in various array. This is wonder in some minimal form. We could not have a "possibility" if we were not capable of considering it openly this way and that to some extent. The bare presence of possibility in anxiety indicates the minimal openness of wonder. Anxiety is then the state, and some minimal degree of wondering is its attitude. Since, though, we speak here of a background condition, we might fall in line with the terminology of this book and call this minimal degree of wondering "wonder" while reserving "wondering" for more self-conscious or deliberate exercises of wonder.[113] *The big point is that since wonder is a part of positive anxiety in some degree, to accept anxiety is to accept our lives with wonder.*

What does that life look like when we come of age? Since we're autonomous, it's likely to differ. But I remember how in graduate school I used to walk out into Chicago after taking the "Jeffery Express" (a bus) down from Hyde Park to get lost for the day. I often transferred to the Blue Line or Red Line (subways and elevated lines) to go to different neighborhoods. These walks helped me discover what I was feeling and thinking in my life by way of the city. Things opened up

[112] Søren Kierkegaard, *The Sickness unto Death: A Christian Psychological Exposition for Upbuilding and Awakening,* trans. Howard V. Hong and Edna H. Hong (1849; Princeton: Princeton University Press, 1980).

[113] Cf. Glaveanu, *Wonder*, section 3.3.

by looking at urban life from different vantage points in space and in time throughout the day.[114]

When we make a point of going with the meanings of things to see where they might take us, we bring forward the background presence of wonder in positive anxiety and express the anxiety as an act of wondering, a focus, where the act can be said to be wondering, not just to involve wonder to some degree. Wondering is in this way *an anxious process* that we engage in, whereas wonder engages us more passively with only a minimal degree of activity.[115] Reminiscent of Schelling's brilliant location of consciousness as a pulsing from background receptivity to foreground intensification of attention,[116] positive anxiety involves wonder as a general form of receptivity and can be brought into attention – channeled – as an act of wondering.[117] At times, we may try to remain open with no other point than maintaining a receptive awareness of being. Think of Rousseau's *sentiment d'existence* in this regard. But even in such a state of pure receptivity, as Rousseau notes, the mind seems to wander as if it were searching around, something found as well in many Zen master descriptions of "beginner's mind." Thus, it seems that wonder, to a minimal degree, is the basic form of openness to being as meaningful.[118]

To come of age with anxiety, it's important to get comfortable with the life of wondering and this means with being lost and confused. I've said that "wondering" – the act – is the name we give to a process of mental anxiety by which we consider that, within the parameters of our focus, much else might be possible and make sense. In its most profound form, wondering involves considering that more or less everything on which we've focused admits of much else that might be possible and make sense, and that we might consider, to echo Rilke, *changing our lives.*[119] Wondering involves holding anxiety together in the rigor of seeking what could possibly make sense, often at utterly confusing points in one's searching or daily life.

Leaving the confusion aside, even wondering itself is uncomfortable. To wonder is to consider the sense of things around one's focus as relatively

---

[114] I say more about such walks in *Solar Calendar, and Other Ways of Marking Time,* "Original Academics," "I Want to Meet You as a Person," "I Carried my Teeth in my Heart," and "We Are a Storm in Wondrous Hunger."

[115] Glaveanu, *Wonder,* section 3.3.

[116] Schelling, *System of Transcendental Idealism.*

[117] Glaveanu, *Wonder,* section 3.3.

[118] Jean-Jacques Rousseau, *The Reveries of the Solitary Walker,* trans. Charles Butterworth (Indianapolis: Hackett Publishing, 1992); Suzuki, *Zen Mind, Beginner's Mind.* Thanks to Alex Shakar for the connection to "beginner's mind."

[119] Rainer Maria Rilke, "Archaischer Torso Apollos" (1908; widely reprinted).

undetermined. What does this or that mean? How does that make sense with this? What makes sense around one's questioning isn't settled. Something about it remains up in the air. Perhaps it is what this thing about which one is wondering means. Perhaps it is what this thing implies. Perhaps it is what this thing relates to in a variety of ways. And perhaps it is whether this thing is right, true, adequate, beautiful, or some other evaluation. These are just some of the ways that wonder takes a somewhat determined given and treats it as relatively undetermined in some other way(s).

Whatever the matter, the point to emphasize is that being lost about (some of) these things is the point *in* wondering where we search into and open up our world, trying to determine the meaning and sense of things. This in turn allows us to accept what we find as truly making sense to us from out of alternate possibilities that we find do not make sense when we wonder about them. What we accept may also lead us to seek a different world than our own because it makes sense whereas ours does not. Being lost can open up how we understand ourselves and our society, and it can empower us to change ourselves, come to understand the world better, and be more socially minded. But it takes a hell of a lot of imagination. We have to develop it to do it well and to not succumb to the narcissistic impression that things are so out of our control that we must control them.

Coming of age takes imaginative work that is itself morally responsible. Think about *failing* to accept our anxiety. Negative anxiety closes down the consideration of sense and meaning. According to Kierkegaard's pseudonym, it can even lead to a judgment of oneself as lacking in responsibility and focus as one loses one's self-control. He describes people either searching for an object where there is none or succumbing to despair and finding nothing meaningful or making sense![120] If what one wants is to control the awfulness of the overwhelming condition in which one finds oneself, it is then understandable to move to the extreme. You can turn to self-doubt and self-judgment. Blame it on yourself, on not being focused enough. Control the excessive sense of being lost. Or you can

---

[120] Heidegger followed this negatively anxious path in his inaugural lecture at Freiburg, "What Is Metaphysics?" He notes positive forms of anxiety when he speaks of love and joy, but he takes the path of investigating "the nothing" (*Das Nichts*). A similar focus on negative anxiety haunts *Being and Time*, too. However, Heidegger's insistence on the "ontological difference" leads him to avoid negative anxiety reverting to mere fear, which would be "ontic" (concerned with a specific entity in the world). The result is a systematic ambivalence around anxiety in Heidegger's corpus. Compare Rubenstein, *Strange Wonder*, chapter 1. On Kierkegaard's phenomenology of meaninglessness and senselessness, compare Jared Brandt, Brandon Dahm, and Derek McAllister, "A Perspectival Reading of *Acedia* in the Writings of Kierkegaard," *Religions* 11(2):80 (2020): 1–22.

reject everything, refuse to see sense or meaning in anything, being nihilistic. Either way, that is the narcissistic urge to control the uncontrollable. It's better to let things sit inside our anxiety and to wonder.

In the background of wonder is a lesson that is crucial to being a finite human being who flourishes. *There's more meaning and sense and more meaninglessness and senselessness in the world than one can manage completely.* If to become autonomous is to find what makes sense to us, not simply going along with what we have become used to doing but which no longer makes sense – or with what we are expected to do but which isn't justifiable to us – we have to let go of certitude and of making complete sense *in order to* find meaning and make sense in this life.[121]

Whereas we cannot grasp the totality of things, the very idea of making sense is guided by the idea of filling in the sense of things so that we fill out our sense of the world. To be true to the complicated and ambivalent condition of being human, we can't presume to close down the gap between our limits and that for which we're striving. We have to accept our limitations while being open to making better sense of things.[122]

Usually, making sense of things makes sense. But sometimes, it does not make sense to make better sense of things! Instead, it makes more sense to let confusion be. In accepting confusion to sort our way through it autonomously, anxiety remains open and isn't driven by issues around control.

This is a way to survive. It's more homely than having "faith," and it isn't some romance like being in love. Yet it's some of the *work* that goes into being loving and to having faith that the world can make sense.

How can we grow in wondering? This is a key question for learning how to come of age. Certainly, children have the potential to reflect, and this potential is largely the elemental stuff of wonder. If children aren't terrified by their environment, they do many of the things I associate with wondering. But it is an overstatement to call these things "reflection" or even "wondering" proper. They are the precondition of wondering and so of reflection: including a wild openness to the sense of being, without having any name for it or even any clear sense of sense itself.[123] Yet as children become agents of learning and gradually accountable, wondering practices open up their worlds in every way –

[121] Cf. Ludwig Wittgenstein, *On Certainty*, trans. G. E. M. Anscombe (1969; New York: Harper Perennial Modern Thought, 1972).

[122] Recall Lloyd's focus on this moment in Aristotle's *Metaphysics*, *Reclaiming Wonder*, chapter 1, "Aristotelian Wonder."

[123] Consider Misty Morrison's series "With Wonder" throughout this book.

theoretically, practically, and socially.[124] As they develop more of their capacity to wonder, they deepen as understanding beings. There's a whole project in learning how this can be done.

Much of this motet has focused on aspects of ourselves as we learn to live with anxiety. But learning to live with anxiety through wondering means letting go of one's narcissism and letting things be what they are in their own light and people and lives be free in their own right. Nussbaum stresses this in more than one place.[125] To see how wondering is the opposite of being narcissistic, we have to look and see what is other than us. Still must be features of the thing being considered that can be wondered over or we have nothing to go on when we try to make sense. Even Schinkel's contemplative wonder over the fact of the world focuses on the world's total contingency.[126] These features lead us to exercise wondering in different ways, for instance, by *associating* between a feature and others in other cases, *clarifying* areas of vagueness, *explicating* something implicit in the thing one wonders about, or even *evaluating* the thing in some way so as to figure out how it makes sense when acting in light of it. These are only some of the possible aspects of things permitting wondering over them.

There's also a subtle interplay between wondering and discovering features. The practice of paying attention to something, for instance, is bound to reveal things worth considering. It makes little sense to say that these features would be there *as* features without the wondering. Yet it also makes little sense to say that the wondering has merely projected them there. What is important is that we get good at going outside ourselves and our plans on the world, especially our narcissistic control of things, to really consider other things and people in their own light. And as we grow in our capacity to be open to things and people outside ourselves through wonder, we become more hospitable to the vast meaning of the world and find our cognitive agency in living within its superabundant meaning and sense.

Growing in wondering has a social dimension, too, that is important for the political implications of wonder. A good part of sound reflection is being able to imagine how others (would) make sense of the thing being considered.[127] While it seems too strong for wondering per se to demand that one wondering

---

[124] Scheinfeld et al., *We Are All Explorers*.

[125] Nussbaum, *Upheavals of Thought*, chapter 4, and *Political Emotions*, chapter 7.

[126] Schinkel, *Wonder and Education*, chapter 2.

[127] Cf. Kant, *Critique of Judgment*, sections 18–22, and see Lloyd's discussion of this part of common sense reflection in *Reclaiming Wonder*, chapters 5 and 8, both on Arendt's elaboration of Kantian reflective judgments in the realm of the political where common sense becomes important for preserving what Arendt called "plurality" (differences in viewpoints).

understand the thing in question from the various perspectives of an entire community, it does seem advantageous to one wondering about something to try to do so, and it does seem important that someone who wonders can understand something as others would. To consider the sense of things is in part to consider how they are meant and how they make sense to others. We cannot grasp what makes sense without this minimal social condition, if only to get a bearing on the conventional meaning of things and the premises that are brought to our puzzles. What does and does not make sense as we wonder involves considering how others mean things and how they make sense of them.

By developing habits of attention that get us outside ourselves in wondering and by developing more social minds, we can more readily protect the objectless nature of anxiety and find flourishing ways to live in confusion with some confidence in making sense of things. I guess this is my contribution to the anxious tradition – something down to earth, doable, and social. Paying attention to what one can wonder about in one's mental excitement and opening one's mind to include the polyphony and plurality of others are two ways to accept that there is more meaning and sense to this life than we can master and that, as a result, our lives are never perfectly autonomous. Instead, our autonomy becomes an ongoing process. The negative anxiety that Nussbaum assumes whenever she's used the word "anxiety" doesn't do justice to the openness of our condition to the superabundance of meaning and sense in the world. It also misdirects us away from accepting that openness is a precondition on being capable of living with wonder in the face of our limits. Even Kierkegaard's interest in religious faith belies the stronger importance of developing our always incomplete autonomy through wondering without which, as Nussbaum notes, our love may suffer from our selfish plans and control.

*

> *On the turntable in the back apartment of an old house.*
> *Steve Reich's* Music for 18 Musicians, *1976*

The spiraling of wonder opens up the world, unlike the spiraling of negative anxiety that constricts it.[128] In *Upheavals of Thought*, Nussbaum acknowledges that wonder is unique among the emotions in being "non-eudaimonistic," i.e.,

---

[128] In Schelling, the spiral is the figure of "groundless" freedom – the inspiration for the Kierkegaardian "anxiety of freedom." See Martin Heidegger, *Schelling's Treatise on the Essence of Human Freedom*, trans. Joan Stambaugh (1936; Athens, OH: Ohio University Press, 1985).

not immediately practical with the value of things. Since for her emotions are forms of thought, her view of wonder comes close to viewing wonder as a kind of emotional reflectiveness.[129] Hepburn, in turn, focuses on Kant's distinction between astonishment and a steady state, even mental disposition, of wondering.[130] But Fingerhut and Prinz view wonder as an emotional happening.[131] Even Schinkel speaks of the "trigger" of wonder as separate from its focus, a criterion that could be at odds with viewing wondering as a mode of attention, since once again it makes wonder a form of immediacy rather than of mediation.[132]

But when one practices a meditative art such as sitting *zazen*, one comes to realize that the positive anxiety behind wondering is the basic state of the mind. It is possible to live in wonder – the bare condition that provides the possibility of wondering. Indeed, it is healthy to do so – that is to say, proper to our species form. There's nothing mystical about it, little esoteric. It simply takes practice accepting anxiety and seeing how anxiety is fundamentally positive. While the possibilities of things proliferate around our consciousness, living in wonder is open and clear.

Even so, we may understandably fall into these possibilities as into a pregnant darkness. We may fall deep in thought. How does that go? The positive anxiety of wondering is an active process of being receptive to the *space* around the meaning and sense of things while seeking to deepen their meaning and sense. Schinkel argues that wonder needn't be about something, by which he means an object. To this, he contrasts contemplative wonder which is about the world as such.[133] This, however, is still something. It is right not to call the world an "object."[134] But the world is something and not nothing. Schinkel's careful and intimate phenomenology of wondering leads to contemplative wonder's categorical difference from (what he thinks of as) inquisitive wonder by focusing on the inarticulateness of deep wonder about the world and by the sense of mystery that pervades such contemplation.

Yet one does not need a categorical distinction to understand this depth. The depth is the opening up of the gap (which Schinkel interestingly makes a

---

[129] Nussbaum, *Upheavals of Thought*, 191.
[130] Hepburn, "The Inaugural Address," 3–6.
[131] Fingerhut and Prinz, "Wonder, Appreciation, and the Value of Art."
[132] Schinkel, *Wonder and Education*, chapter 1.
[133] Schinkel, *Wonder and Education*, chapter 1 and 2.
[134] Heidegger, *Being and Time*; cf. Jean-Luc Marion, *Reduction and Givenness: Investigations of Husserl, Heidegger, and Phenomenology*, trans. Thomas A. Carlson (Evanston, IL: Northwestern University Press, 1998).

criterion of wonder) around the sense and meaning of things – and then disappearing into it. In other words, wondering is both articulate and inarticulate to some degree, and at either end of its continuum, it may seem either to be completely lost in inarticulate absorption in the world or proliferating articulate connections as one comes to fill something in. What's crucial to wondering in any form is the space it opens up around the things that we consider.[135]

Even so, the notion of being deep in thought is important for understanding the way being lost in wonder is vital. To be deep in thought is to be completely absorbed in searching for meaning and sense. The emphasis is on the moment of searching, not finding – on following out possibilities that change the thing one is considering and that reorganize the world as seen in its light. These possibilities *stretch* what one has been given. They become hard to wrap one's head around. They may go nowhere. Yet one considers them. Searching is categorically different than what concerns Hepburn in his worries about wonder being anti-epistemic in some way, either as being uninterested in getting things right but wanting merely to stay musing over them, or as given to magical thinking devoid of an interest in reasoning.[136] On my view, both forms of consciousness aren't wondering but are subtly negative forms of anxiety whereby one flees the possibilities of sense and meaning in the world by refusing to consider the connections things have in the world as disclosed by reasoning.

When many scholars describe the things about which one wonders as being especially present or alive,[137] this is the result of being absorbed in them to some degree, whether initially considering them for their unconventional possibilities or becoming lost deep in thought about them. Wondering brings the meaning and sense of things closer while opening up their wider context of meaning and sense – their world – and the possibilities that begin to appear for how to understand and make sense of that world. *As things come closer and open up, they become both more present – our minds filling up with them as they fill out the world – and more meaningful and sense-filled – that is, more alive in their associative possibilities.* They are "alive," because we are beings whose way of being is to thrive when things start to make more sense and become meaningful.

Finding things meaningful and sense-filled is vital for beings like us. This is an assumption also in Nussbaum's work especially when she articulates the need

---

[135] Again, I owe this formulation to Dan and Sandra Scheinfeld during a memorable session at the Erikson Institute for Advanced Study in Child Development, Chicago, circa 2001.

[136] Hepburn, "The Inaugural Address."

[137] Fingerhut and Prinz, "Wonder, Appreciation, and the Value of Art" and Schinkel, *Wonder and Education,* chapter 1.

for the capability of imagination.[138] Since it is vital, going deep in thought is the tendency of wondering. Wondering tends to take us to the point where the world as we know it falls away around that about which we're wondering and we reconsider the world completely, building it up anew as we explore possibilities. This sometimes dizzying process responds to the world, to what gives us reason to articulate something as meaningful in some way and to make sense of it. Yet it also reorganizes the world as we figure it out, for the world is the ultimate horizon of sense and meaning beyond which we know not what. As a horizon, it can be filled in, articulated, and our sense of it rearranged. Moreover, as we discover things about the world, others shift, and we come to see that we were ignorant of the world. Retrospectively, the world as it is always involves things we didn't see. Our sense of the world is incomplete. Wondering has a tendency to get lost in the world because the world is the kind of thing that can be articulated ad infinitum. But so can our lives, and keeping the process open is a big part of our always incomplete autonomy.

We can see why being lost in confusion isn't negative but is positive when we pay attention to being deep in thought. What falls away in confusion is the order of the world as we were conventionally used to it. This is tumultuous. *But what pours into the gaps is the stirring reorganization of the world as one understands one's life in it.* Going deep in thought while wondering amounts to diving into the world and leaving one's old world behind. Searching, then, anticipates meeting, rising up out of the darkness of being lost "into the shores of light," in Lucretius's phrase, *in luminis oras.*[139]

Obviously, this drama that I recount is compressed. Wondering often takes time as one considers things, and the moments of that time may involve profound disorientation. The point that is important to remember, though, is that the disorientation is after something. It is stirred by possibilities of meaning and sense. To speak of depth instead of, say, stupefaction is to underline that wonder does not undermine our intelligence, but displays it. "Being deep in thought" is the name for a disorientation pregnant with reorientation – where it makes sense to come to love confusion.

*

Deep inside thought, what distinguishes wondering from other forms of thinking or even its searching from other kinds of searching? The lostness specific to

---

[138] See *Women and Human Development*, chapter 1.
[139] Discussed by Nussbaum, *Upheavals of Thought*, 182, 189.

wondering is one in which the free play of possibilities around the sense and meaning of things structures and animates being lost. The lostness of wonder is the kind of being lost in thought where the thought is formally structured by its ongoing awareness of the free play of possibilities, the kind of mental anxiety I've been following. *When I've lost my keys*, I think about the possible places that they might be. But *when I wonder about my lost keys*, I think not only about where they might be, but I consider the meaning and sense of them, including the world in which they are used, are lost, and so on. The mental anxiety of being lost in wonder is not, then, a fear of anything or a crippling disorientation by which the meaning and structure of the world dissolves into dread. It is an opening up of the possibilities of the world and of this world's potential to make sense in new ways.

The world plays freely through the free play of possibilities around the focus of my wondering. This is not just any searching around for something, even for the truth of a question. Moreover, since the form of thinking that is wondering is a thinking of the free play of the world's sense, at wondering's limit – its highest degree, if you will – anything and everything is potentially up in the air within reach of the thing about which one wonders in its relatively undetermined sense.

So, it may seem that wondering sits apart from thinking in general. But that is a premature conclusion. It seems on reflection that an intimation of wondering appears in all thinking, searching, and being lost. To think about, search for, or be lost in relation to anything involves at least the possibility that the possibilities we take to be settled in our world come unstuck. Because to discover the sense or meaning of anything involves the potential for the world's sense and meaning to shift, there is some minimal wonder implicit in thinking *simpliciter* whenever we consider what something means or how something makes sense in the world. What wondering in its central cases brings to the fore then appears in hindsight as a mental anxiety humming in the background of thought at all times.[140]

*

It strikes me that wondering is broader than truth-seeking, although wondering must include truth-seeking for wonder to remain an actual form of consideration of what is possible and to remain a mode of thinking.[141] What does wondering seek in addition to truth?

---

[140] Cf. Schelling, *System of Transcendental Idealism.*
[141] Thomas Aquinas, *Summa Theologica,* translated by the Fathers of the Dominican Province (New York: Benzinger Brothers, 1948), first part, question 16, article 1.

One thing that wondering does is to relate things to a world. This need not be our actual world. The world in question could be imaginary or impossible in the terms of our world, but it would still be a world wherein we come to consider what makes sense. Wondering fills out the relations in a world where what makes sense is under consideration for us. In this way, wonder is essentially *world-making* in its imagination, proceeding through setting the world into free play subtly or overtly around the focus of one's wondering.[142] When I then claim that lostness is the life of wonder, this is in part because in lostness we continue to consider the free play of how the world could make sense, driven by our awareness that we have not yet found the world-making sense which we are seeking. This makes us continue wondering – it makes us wonder more.

When wondering is world-making, it involves a kind of transcendence on our part toward the world that we come to see makes sense. One way to understand this is to see how there can be elation in being lost in wonder – even if it is quiet or sometimes uneasy. Being lost while being open-minded exposes us to things. The moment of being lost in wonder prefigures attention:

> *Here I am having lost the meaning or sense of something. I let confusion seep in and the world around this thing fall apart into possibilities.*
>
> *As I do, I focus in more, coming closer to that about which I'm wondering. I attend to its particularities, its details, the way it is related to other things.*
>
> *I give attention to its context and then come back to it again, revising my sense of it, what this thing is before me, what it means, how it makes sense in my world.*
>
> *Looking more closely at it, the conventions I brought to it may come apart. I may begin to see it in a different light, making different connections with other things than I had previously considered.*
>
> *In everything I follow out the details of the thing trying to leave open possibilities of meaning and sense I had not considered and opening my mind widely to make connections to unexpected things.*
>
> *I let the thing come to me in my lost state and fill my world with its world.*

The elation is that lostness bears us out into the midst of meaning to be found and considered. "Elation" suggests rising above and over, being raised over.[143]

Elation is then of a piece with the excitement of wonder. The excitement of wonder holds open possibilities to consider. These possibilities are of meaning – *What is this thing? What does it mean?* – and of sense:

[142] Consider the importance of wonder in constituting the world we can share in my *Involving Anthroponomy in the Anthropocene*, chapter 2.
[143] "Elate," *Oxford American Dictionary*.

How does this thing make sense? How can it make more sense? Where does it stop making sense?

With what can it be connected to fill out the world in which I live?

How can I deepen and broaden my understanding of the world in and through this thing?

How can I go into its world and out of this world around me?

Wondering casts about in slow-motion excitement, and that casting about raises up the world, ourselves, and things in alternate measures and moments. The anxiety is, precisely, elating and – since it seeks meaning and sense – is positive, consisting in bringing forth the meaning and sense of things so that we can flourish. Isn't it exciting to fill in a world while *also* seeking to understand things truly?

That wondering is broader than truth-seeking is something good. What I keep trying to emphasize in this book is that it's a mistake to experience being lost in anxiety as something threatening or scary. Wonder should not even be "extraordinary,"[144] since wondering is basic to muddling through life as a relatively free person with some character as one tries to get one's footing in a given world. Coming to meet the world wherein we wonder, every once in a while, we get elated. We try to be responsive to everything that's going on and to not be reactive about all the stuff that's beyond our comprehension.

*

I think that I became an adult for the first time when I recognized that I was lost. I hadn't just lost my keys, a phone number, or a computer. I hadn't lost a friend. No, *I* was lost.

The experience was different than being lost as a child. I remember losing track of time, missing my keys, having trouble finding home after some wide-ranging day by bike. But healthy kids still seem both self-assured and selfless. They stick stubbornly to what they like, want, think, or they hover in between assertion and denial as if they were a cloud. It is the rare child who says, "I have lost my sense of who I am and my convictions." In that, they would already be grown up.

Saying that you yourself are lost is more troubling than repeating Dante's narrator at the beginning of *The Divine Comedy*:

---

[144] Pace Fingerhut and Prinz, "Wonder, Appreciation, and the Value of Art," and Fisher, *Wonder, the Rainbow, and the Aesthetics of Rare Experiences.*

Nel mezzo del cammin di nostra vita
mi ritrovai per una selva oscura,
ché la diritta via era smarrita.

Toward the midpoint of our life's journey,
I came to myself in a dark wood
where the straight way forward was lost.[145]

This person came to themselves. The verb involves the reflexive. They *found themselves* lost in a wood. They lost their way, but still they were searching. There is someone there, and they are trying to find their way. Midlife has been hard on them, let us say, and they do not know how to go on. This is still not to have lost themselves and their convictions. I can lose my way in life but retain my sense of self.

I realized that I was lost for the first time when I was twenty-two. It was the first semester of my senior year of college, and I was about to plunge into the world. For the first time, I became explicitly aware of my anxiety.

Coincidentally, I was taking an independent study on Søren Kierkegaard's (Vigilius Haufniensis's) 1844 tract, *Begrebet Angest (The Concept of Anxiety)*.[146] In fits and starts and more than once with alarming errancy, I realized that I had no clue where my center was. Myself was the major question. Being lost contradicted what I was supposed to be: confident, purposeful, resolute in the face of my future. Instead, I was a mess.

I was ashamed of being lost. I felt that I barely knew who I was. As a result, I could barely relate to the world and find my way in it. There was little relationship there since I was largely missing.

The world swam. It became fluid. My life became fragmentary and disconnected in parts. Many of my conscious expectations dissolved away.

All I wanted was to find a current by which the world and my life might make sense, regardless of the changes that discovery might produce in my prior reality.

Perhaps because I had become used to it by studying philosophy, literature, and art, and by having developed a habit of wide-ranging conversation with friends and family, I started to consider things that I hadn't ever considered.[147] Then I turned over the sense of the world and of my life in it countless times.

---

[145] Dante Alighieri, *The Divine Comedy*, v. I: *Inferno*, trans. John D. Sinclair (1320; New York: Oxford University Press, 1961), Canto I, lines 1–3, translation modified.

[146] Thanks to Hagi Kenaan for leading it.

[147] Cf. Martha C. Nussbaum, *Cultivating Humanity: A Classical Defense of Reform in Liberal Education* (Cambridge, MA: Harvard University Press, 1997).

In this way, slowly, I became a little clearer with myself and that world in which I lived and then calmer about the life I could live in it. Considering the many possibilities by which things can make sense and trying to find connections new to me between them slowly helped solidify my life through moments of reflection. Eventually, through the gradual accretion of such moments, the fluidity drained out of things, and I momentarily saw my life in the present as on a day after storms.

Then resting back into myself, I felt the world relax around me. By having wondered in this way over a period of many weeks, I became clearer in time. It wasn't that I suddenly understood some things (for I didn't understand much). *It was that I was more comfortable being lost.*

For the world to make sense takes time. What happened to the world and my life in it during this period of intense and prolonged anxiety was interesting. What I did was a mess, but in the times when I stuck with my confusion and considered it, I grew a tiny bit. Once I gave into my mess, it became the way to my maturity. Yes, most everything fell up in the air except the most quotidian of tasks, and even they seemed mysterious. Yes, everything about myself and the world seemed questionable except obvious moral duties, and even they seemed contextless at a certain point. But *considering* things awash in possibilities, opened up the world around me and myself with it. I began to deepen my sense of the world and of myself even as I still felt and found myself lost:

"Where do I find my life making sense?"

"Where does life fit together in this world? Or does it fit together only in some other?"

"Is it possible to make sense in this world? What is this world in which I live?"

The exposure was especially real, more vulnerable with confusion. But once my anxiety revealed that it helped me flourish, it wasn't any longer something to fear. The inversion from irrational, objectless fear to something else, infinite and fecund, wasn't even a crisis. "Crisis" comes from the Greek *krisis*, "decision." In English, the sense of a crisis being a "decision point" arose in early modernity.[148] A crisis implies decision, and a decision supposes someone with a clear enough intention. What I was undergoing was more basic than decision.

---

[148] See "crisis," *Oxford American Dictionary.*

Nothing that I do is perfect, and neither was it back then. I often failed to hold myself steady. But slowly then and as I grew into being an adult, I learned to love pregnant moments of confusion. The love was not romantic, and it certainly wasn't neat. It was a clumsy process of attending to and sticking with the meaning and sense to be found even in a messed-up life.

Now I am in midlife like Dante's authorial voice, and I see the wonder in the act of self searching for the world with itself the major question.[149] Now I consider the world and my life with something other than objectless apprehension.

---

[149] The last phrase is adapted from my "Fleabag, Let Things Get Lost! Wonder, Confusion, and Why Film Needs More of It," *Public Seminar* (September 19th, 2019).

"*In luminis oras* (into the shores of light)," 2020

Infants are driven to make sense of the world. How, then, can parenting contribute to a child's wondering?

MOTET 2 – *HUMANS ARE BORN TO WONDER HOW ANOTHER'S WORLD IS POSSIBLE*

TEXTS: *Upheavals of Thought, Fragility of Goodness*

WORD: "Devotion"

Decades ago, from an open window on Albany St. in Ithaca, New York:
Roscoe Mitchell, "Nonaah," 1977

For Misty and Ellery at the Grayhaven Motel, Ithaca, New York, 2022

Human beings have a need to make sense of the world. The drive to make sense of the world – what in early childhood education might be called "cognitive agency" – is basic to our nature as reasoning beings.[1] The need appears early as wonder over the world. Children frequently do this, lost in the world almost completely and taking joy in its forms and emerging sense. Alternately, poised adults wonder at something, pausing during their day then moving on. Depending on the context, I will speak alternately of wonder "at," "about," or "over." I view these decisions as connotatively nuanced, fitting the phenomenon in question. They do not bely a fundamentally different logic, but a shift in degree depending on the expression of our wonder in practices of wondering. What matters is that in coming to make sense of the world by wondering, humans first begin to establish the conditions for a life that makes sense to them, one that is autonomous. Does the life you lead make sense to you, and do you have the leeway to question?[2] Through wonder, a basic human need is part of the life of autonomy. Nussbaum acknowledges as much when she notes that infants need to make cognitive distinctions, taking joy in letting things appear as they are in their own light.[3]

Although humans are born to wonder, a wondering mind can be denied, even quashed. When that happens, the basic human need – to wonder at the world – goes unmet. Insofar as the causes of the deprivation are social, we are in the vicinity of a prima facie wrong against a person. This moral wrong is often political, part of a system of norms governing how people live together that involves domination to run threat throughout the system. How are wondering minds supported? What kind of social environment is conducive to the mind's original joy? Whereas in the last motet, I explored how we come to ourselves through wondering, here I want to explore wonder *before* we came to ourselves. The reasons why are moral and political. A basic human need is at stake at the origin of autonomy, providing us with an assumption to drive social criticism, shape moral relations, and to approach politics.

---

[1] Compare Scheinfeld et al., *We Are All Explorers,* chapters 2, 4, and 5 and Neiman, *The Unity of Reason,* chapters 2–4.
[2] On leeway ("play-room" or *Spielraum*), Rob Nichols, *The World of Freedom: Heidegger, Foucault, and the Politics of Historical Ontology* (Palo Alto: Stanford University Press, 2014), 46.
[3] Nussbaum, *Upheavals of Thought,* 189–90.

I want to consider the attention a caretaker – let us call them a "parent" – can give to a child so as to nurture their sense of wonder. I am looking for conceptual connections: how the logic of a given form of attention is structured so as to make room for and to support a child's "original joy" in making sense of the world. What I've realized is that by wondering over the child – what I call "finding the child a wonder" – parenting creates important elements of an environment for the child drawing out – "educating" – the child's own capacity to wonder.[4] Having the "image of the child" as a source of proliferating possibilities of sense and of meaning surrounds the child with the affirmation of their own search for sense and meaning within the proliferating possibilities of their world.[5]

While based in a reading of Martha C. Nussbaum's work on child development, my conceptualization involves something exogenous to Nussbaum's work that is consistent with it: something I call "the personal relation." This is the idea of a relation in which we accept another as entering into interpersonal space – what R. J. Wallace calls "the moral nexus"[6] – respecting their being a locus of sense-making and meaning-finding – in Nussbaum's terms, a source of agency, imagination, play, joy, and relationships.[7] Wonder over the child in a personal relationship with the child becomes the conceptual space for creating a "facilitating environment"[8] supportive of their exercising their own mind's excitement.

*

I should show what this means. Not long ago, I was trying to catch up with the birth of my child.[9] With the hours of the day practically inverted, waking at night to feed them, sleeping for the odd hour during the day to rest up, here came discombobulation! I was worn but content in the discomfort, absorbing the excessive meaning of the fact that this one, Misty's and my child, is here.

My sense of life was changing. In *Love's Knowledge*, Nussbaum makes much of the "sense of life" as a holistic, philosophical orientation when reading literature. She emphasizes the philosophical importance of the "active searching of life," something she explains like this:

[4] "Educate," *Oxford American Dictionary*, from Latin *educere*, to lead out.
[5] On the "image of the child," see Scheinfeld et al., *We Are All Explorers*, 35–7, "Valuing the Child's Mind."
[6] Wallace, *The Moral Nexus*.
[7] Nussbaum, *Women and Human Development*, chapter 1, section IV. See also her *Creating Capabilities*.
[8] Nussbaum, *Upheavals of Thought*, chapter 4, sections III and VI.
[9] "He" is here. But we do not know what gender this one will find for themselves. "They" will be raised accordingly. That "he" is here is part of "his" story. But "he" and "his" society can change.

For we do, in life, bring our experience, our active sense of life, to the conceptions we encounter, working through them, comparing the alternatives they present, with reference to our developing sense of what is important and what we can live with, seeking a fit between experience and conception.

As one way to see if I could make sense of Emet's birth, I translated a once-loved poem from high school, Rimbaud's teenage poem of summer. Here "translation" was two-fold – from nineteenth-century French to twenty-first-century American English and from the rough emotional contours of Rimbaud's original to the different and soulful scene of raising a newborn. "Translate" comes from a Latin root meaning to "carry something over," to *convey* something across conditions.[10] And so I did:

Roman / Life Cycle

I

On n'est pas sérieux, quand on a dix-sept ans.

> You outstretched along an arm,

– Un beau soir, foin des bocks et de la limonade,

> Make morning midnight,

Des cafés tapageurs aux lustres éclatants!

> Why sighing air outside

– On va sous les tilleuls verts de la promenade.

> Hums the house with warmth.

Les tilleuls sentent bon dans les bons soirs de juin!

> How's things in the quietest part of the day?

L'air est parfois si doux, qu'on ferme la paupière;

> We've seldom slept them

Le vent chargé de bruits – la ville n'est pas loin –

> But between us in our waking

A des parfums de vigne et des parfums de bière . . .

> Old patterns are shaking.

II

Voilà qu'on aperçoit un tout petit chiffon

> I can't forget this unfitting depth,

D'azur sombre, encadré d'une petite branche,

> Void in memory bearing you as drive

---

[10] "Translate," *Oxford American Dictionary.*

Piqué d'une mauvaise étoile, qui se fond
                                    And darkness wider than the outmost reach
Avec de doux frissons, petite et toute blanche . . .
                                    Where you, unknown, disturb me.

Nuit de juin! Dix-sept ans! – On se laisse griser.
                                    4 A.M. sings the bright room.
La sève est du champagne et vous monte à la tête . . .
                                    Sky suspends the mind:
On divague; on se sent aux lèvres un baiser
                                    What you give without knowing
Qui palpite là, comme une petite bête . . .
                                    Surfaces to the shores of sense.

III
Le cœur fou Robinsonne à travers les romans,
                                    Let's love stories as they are finite.
Lorsque, dans la clarté d'un pâle réverbère,
                                    Having come aground,
Passe une demoiselle aux petits airs charmants,
                                    They rush the brittle wood and vanish
Sous l'ombre du faux col effrayant de son père . . .
                                    Leaving echoed song:

Et, comme elle vous trouve immensément naïf,
                                    Lost familiars
Tout en faisant trotter ses petites bottines,
                                    Kiss in the street all heat
Elle se tourne, alerte et d'un mouvement vif . . .
                                    And later they
– Sur vos lèvres alors meurent les cavatines . . .
                                    United.

IV
Vous êtes amoureux. Loué jusqu'au mois d'août.
                                    You clutch insight as you love to breathe.
Vous êtes amoureux. – Vos sonnets La font rire.
                                    I must thank hindsight or I stop to breathe.
Tous vos amis s'en vont, vous êtes mauvais goût.
                                    Struggle into being without cease,

– Puis l'adorée, un soir, a daigné vous écrire . . .!

There we find you.

– Ce soir-là, . . . – vous rentrez aux cafés éclatants,

I once thought,

Vous demandez des bocks ou de la limonade.

"To care for real."

– On n'est pas sérieux, quand on a dix-sept ans

Then everything mouthed a question.

Et qu'on a des tilleuls verts sur la promenade.

As you cried, we met.

~ Arthur Rimbaud, « Roman, » 29 Septembre, 1870, adapted February–March 2020; May–June 2021, December 2022

*

In that translation across the life cycle, the expanse of what is possible appears through the child, themselves the great unknown. The entire sense of existence comes apart and reorganizes, for parenting is an environment.[11] What role might the environment of wonderment have in developing the child's background condition of wonder, even their incipient ability to wonder? By "wonderment" I mean the *state* – not merely an instance – of wondering. That's how mind-blown new parenting can be.

From early on, Nussbaum was sensitive to parent–child relationships. In *The Fragility of Goodness*, she explored how flourishing depends on caring conditions, emphasizing our vulnerability to the luck of the draw. Did we luck out in this world? Or enter into a scene of domination? What did our parents do? How did they respond – or did they react?[12] Our lives are subject to things beyond our control. But this applies to the parent, too. Their fortune now is bound up with their attachment. "[A]nyone who loves a child makes herself vulnerable."[13] *What can I do for this one? How can I support them faring well in this world?* It's good for the child and part of the parent's good when the parent asks these questions.

---

[11] Here I hear Steve Reich's *Music for 18 Musicians* again, just as much as *Nonaah.*

[12] It's obvious that she develops, deeply, her teacher John Rawls's compassionate attention to fortune in the "Original Position" of his *A Theory of Justice.*

[13] Nussbaum, *The Fragility of Goodness*, p. xxx. This kind of observation is part of Nussbaum's ethical phenomenology of human life, which she discusses through Aristotle's form of phenomenology in chapter 8, "Saving Aristotle's appearances."

The question is, in a precise way, about what is organic in child-raising and in children, here focused on the topic of wonder. "Organic" comes from the ancient Greek *organikos*, related to an organ or instrument.[14] We have to grasp what wonder means for a child and how it shapes their possibilities of becoming within being human. The philosophical context for such questioning involves considering how we function as the kind of beings that we are.[15] As Nussbaum wrote in her preface to the revised edition of *The Fragility of Goodness*:

> We could, of course, set ourselves right without returning to Greek thought at all. But Aristotle's view of nature as containing a rich range of wonderful creatures, each with its own characteristic form of functioning, together with his view that human and animal motions are susceptible of a "common explanation," help us to think better about ourselves and the world.[16]

The passage goes on:

> As Aristotle says: if we have disgust at the bodies of animals, that means we have disgust at ourselves: it is of such parts that we are made. But we should not have disgust: for "in everything natural there is something wonderful." We could do worse than to follow up, and elaborate, the ethical implications of this idea.

This reference to Aristotle concerns *Parts of Animals* I.5.[17] The reference to the motion of animals is to Nussbaum's early project, *Aristotle's* De Motu Animalium. Nussbaum's Aristotelian heritage lends itself to beginning with thought about the human good, but in such a way that our good as humans becomes contextualized within living (not just human) form as such. Here, what I want to do is to "follow up" and "elaborate" on the role of wonder in human flourishing, not just *at* it.[18] For that we can find something wonderful "in everything natural" is a fact about us, about *our* "form of functioning."

Now there are some nuanced differences between the connotations of functioning, flourishing, and striving, and they cause some turbulence when being conveyed in contemporary, American English. At this point, I will move liberally between them, understanding that this can be confusing to readers who seek precision with terms. To ease this concern slightly, I will let Aristotle – or Nussbaum's reading of Aristotle – speak of "functioning" to get at the dynamic form of "work" (my pass at the Greek *ergon*, "function") that living beings do in

---

[14] "Organic," *Oxford American Dictionary*.
[15] Cf. Philippa Foot, *Natural Goodness* (New York: Oxford University Press, 2000).
[16] Nussbaum, *The Fragility of Goodness*, xxiv.
[17] Nussbaum discusses it further in *Frontiers of Justice*, 347–9.
[18] Cf. Pedersen, *Balanced Wonder*.

their "characteristic" form of living. For instance, the "work" of an ant involves roaming for food and returning to the hive. There is also ant-related division of labor here, some ants staying in the hive to work. Not so with human beings, who live socially in various scales of community, at least to raise their young, and whose division of labor is much vaster, attuned to following out the work of human cultures. I will assume that a given ant or a given person may not do their work particularly well, but merely passably – in other words, that there is a noticeable difference between a member of a living kind functioning especially well and merely functioning.

By "flourishing," however, I will presume – drawing on the connotations of contemporary, American English – that we are discussing the work of living going well, well enough that the form of life in question appears to be truly good in its own way. The ant-hive humming, not barely getting by, the human being working in full exercise of her capacities, not stressfully squeezing through another mindless day of weary labor, . . . the old ones among us, for where they are in their decline of powers, still exercising their minds, memories, emotions, and aging limbs. Flourishing is functioning going well, often especially well, and on the whole for where the living being is in life. Nussbaum once taught in seminar that she drew this understanding not only from Aristotle but also from Marx's *1844 Manuscripts*.[19]

The connotations on which I'm drawing do, however, create some tension with Aristotelianism. As Nussbaum writes early in *The Fragility of Goodness*, according to Aristotle "*eudaimonia* consists in activity according to excellence(s),"[20] i.e., virtuous activity. She understands *eudaimonia,* after John Cooper, as "human flourishing."[21] Moreover, functioning in the context of human life implies the work of human virtue, as Aristotle argues in *Nicomachean Ethics* I.7. Someone who functions completely as a human would seem thereby to be flourishing. My use of the "functioning" and "flourishing" is thus particular, emphasizing the distinction between living a recognizably human life and having that life come together completely enough for where one is in life that one can say it really is excellent in its own way.

Against this backdrop, by "striving," I will mean the dynamic work of a living being on the way to flourishing, stretching for it. We can strive without yet

---

[19] Nussbaum, *Women and Human Development*, 72–4. Karl Marx, *Economic and Philosophical Manuscripts of 1844*, trans. Martin Milligan (1932; Mineola, NY: Dover Publications, 2007). The seminar was Neo-Aristotelian Political Thought, University of Chicago, Autumn 1998.

[20] Nussbaum, *The Fragility of Goodness*, 6.

[21] Ibid.

flourishing, but not strive without seeking to flourish.[22] In most cases, functional living beings also thereby strive. With humans, however, the two conditions may come apart, as when someone merely does the work of the day without trying to live well. Of course, one might say that their minds or emotions aren't thereby functioning as they should be. But that seems excessive, even moralistic. In some social conditions, it would be inhumane to say that someone's belabored heart isn't functioning when they run out of drive in the day. That belabored heart gets them through the day, barely, ... with little left to spare. So, they are functional, but not striving. More importantly for our sense of justice, they aren't flourishing yet. Perhaps the fair thing to say is that we can only function for spells without minding what's good for us.

With these many distinctions, we should wonder about wonder in ourselves – about how it shapes our possibilities of becoming as humans. How does Nussbaum think that it does? The obvious place to look is to the passage providing the keystone for this book:

> [W]e need to posit an original need for cognitive distinction-making, and an original joy in sorting out the world, in order to explain why infants get going and pursue projects of their own in the uncertain world.[23]

Nussbaum then continues:

> [A]nimals initiate projects of their own. In human animals[,] the independence from mere self-protection of curiosity, cognitive interest, and wonder is especially apparent, and essential to explain initiative and creativity.[24]

We might ask why these things are "essential" and, among them, what marks out wonder. The original joy of which Nussbaum speaks seems to pertain to figuring things out just as much as it does to wanting to figure them out (e.g., in curiosity), or to the vaguer and more expansive "wonder."[25] But as I have noted, my continuum view of wonder takes these distinctions as involving matters of degree constellating around different intentional pursuits. There is some degree of wonder in curiosity, that is, of considering the possibilities by which things can make sense or mean things through the free play of the imagination around that about which one is curious.

---

[22] In commentary, Rick Anthony Furtak suggested that a comparison with Cavell fits here, cf., Stanley Cavell, *Conditions Handsome and Unhandsome: The Constitution of Emersonian Perfectionism* (Chicago: The University of Chicago Press, 1990).

[23] Nussbaum, *Upheavals of Thought*, 189–90.

[24] Ibid., 190.

[25] See Schinkel, *Wonder and Education,* chapter 1 on distinctions between curiosity and wonder.

Shortly before these passages, Nussbaum reads a gorgeous and somewhat heartbreaking phrase from Lucretius evoking how the newborn enters the world by comparing them with an ocean castaway finally reaching the beach – *terra firma* – in relief and astonishment. Lucretius says that the newborn, like the castaway, enters the world *in luminis oras*, "into the shores of light." Nussbaum comments:

> This phrase lets us see that the world into which the child arrives is radiant and wonderful, claims its attention as an object of interest and pleasure in its own right.[26]

It also lets us see that the child needs this world just as the castaway's bedazzlement intermixes with profound relief at finding firm ground again. Nussbaum claims that the world into which we are born appears as needed and interesting to children and that it must be so in order to explain how the child gets going in the first place, wanting to figure things out. The phrase she states subsequently – "the wonder and interest of the world"[27] – appears even to mark out an ordering, with wonder preceding interest as a first opening onto the world, a first meeting with its cognitive appeal "in its own right." That much makes sense, too, because Nussbaum later points out that wonder is "non-egoistic and even, to some degree, non-eudaimonistic,"[28] so much so that it is "independent[t] from mere self-protection." When wondering, we consider things as they are, not as how we want them to be. Here we are on the strange shores of the world.

Wonder is "essential" to many things such as "initiative" and "creativity" then because it holds open the meaning and sense of things apart from our designs, holding the world in its own right, apart from us, that we must *reach*. This much is structurally needed for "initiative" and for "why infants get going and pursue projects of their own in the uncertain world." The world – as wonder holds it in its independence from us – becomes something to strive for. Wonder allows us to approach our making of meaning and of sense with attention to how things fit together on their own. The relationship between wonder and the "original joy in sorting out the world" thus appears to be that, on the basis of wonder, the world is something that we can meet, something meaningful, "radiant," and promising to enrich the sense of our lives, *and it opens our striving as striving for things that make sense.*

[26] Nussbaum, *Upheavals of Thought*, 189.
[27] Ibid.
[28] Ibid., 191.

All this is visceral as Nussbaum sees it. The world is given in its own right, unclear and full of possibilities. It is also, if we take Lucretius' simile seriously, a great relief to come into sense and meaning again from out of the ocean that, figuratively in the simile, precedes existence as if it were oblivion. What, in this new unknown, do things mean? How do things make sense? Wonder is in these very basic questions. They might even be said to articulate wonder's basic shape: searching for meaning among the world's proliferating possibilities, grasping excitedly (even if quietly) for the sense of things as they fit together and give us a greater appreciation of the world in which we live as something independent from us filled with meaning.

I take Nussbaum in these passages to be implying that wonder is a basic human need that is central to our striving. Wonder here is basic to the human good, because it precedes our grasping of things as good, at least in understanding. Wonder opens cognitive agency. I use the term "cognitive agency" in the spirit of Scheinfeld et al., *We Are All Explorers*, where children are seen as naturally agential in figuring out what interests them in the world. Essential to cognitive agency, wonder is part of us. For the new life, the mind's "original joy" in making sense of the world is a reflex. Wonder, for the child, is a background condition of their mind, and their being in some degree of this state much of the time readily lends itself to untrained acts of wondering at the unknown and intriguing world with all its unclear possibilities of meaning and unknown ways it appears to promise to make sense. Recall the distinction between wonder and wondering and the need for practices of wondering to develop? The child's cognitive agency grows along with wonder and increasingly competent acts of wondering. How could we come to make sense of the world if we did not first wonder at it in its distinct and separate reality?

Wonder is organic in that it is what our cognitive agency in the world needs to start. Wonder is then like a child's hand. Small and strong for an infant, the hand does things. It also moves agitatedly about, comprehendingly, and uncomprehendingly, passing over surfaces, yet also sometimes grasping things as if they were thus conceptualized by that firm grip that the child just gave them.[29] "Agitatedly" implies some randomness, but its root implies doing.[30] This tension between aimlessness and purpose is important for something such as an infant's hand. There is "work" – a "function" – to the child's hand,[31] and there is

[29] Cf. Cavell, *Conditions Handsome and Unhandsome* on the hand and its grip, playing with the German *Begriff* for "concept," but also implying a cognitive grasp of things (from *greifen*, "to grasp").
[30] "Agitate," *Oxford American Dictionary*.
[31] Cf. Aristotle, *Nicomachean Ethics* I.7.

work to wonder: to meet the world in its own right, full of sense and meaning. To consider our organic life from the standpoint of development is not to demand that every organ have only one purpose, but to ask when the child is growing well or ill – capable or incapacitated by the turn of its life – and what the child can do or be with this hand – or with wonder. Through the organic, the capabilities of the being in focus emerge, opening up a range of things that can be done or afforded to the living being. These capabilities have something to do with the form of the being in question – for instance, with what it is to be a human being and not a catbird. When we look at the hand's capabilities – as well as the world the hand opens up – we consider the possibilities of living that come with the hand. So then what capabilities and what possibilities does wonder open up?[32] Just as we come to learn to use the hand, too, we come to learn how to wonder more searchingly and effectively (i.e., through acts of wondering).

All this Nussbaum's Lucretian inheritance suggests. It seems that searching for sense and meaning is bound up with our capacity to wonder. Wonder, as a capacity necessary for our reflection, is thus central to the question Nussbaum asks early in *The Fragility of Goodness* and which she says belongs to the entire problem of the book:

> ... [T]o ask about a conception of human reason. If it is reason, and reason's art,
> philosophy, that are supposed to save or transform our lives, then, as beings with
> an interest in living well, we must ask what this part of ourselves is, how it works
> to order a life, how it is related to feeling, emotion, perception.[33]

Nussbaum does not focus on wonder as part of reasoning in *The Fragility of Goodness*, only beginning to note its significance – albeit still peripherally – in *Upheavals of Thought* and, much later and a bit more centrally, in *Political Emotions*. Her interest in *The Fragility of Goodness*, *The Therapy of Desire*, and *Upheavals of Thought* is with the role of emotions, if any, in practical reasoning. Wonder in *Upheavals of Thought* is given a strange place in this mix as "non-eudiamonistic," whereas every other emotion is "eudaimonistic," i.e., focused on the good of the one who is being emotional. There, she also calls wonder "non-egotistical."[34]

There are several complications to this picture. One is that it is not clear that wonder is an emotion, but rather than it can be emotional. As a basic capacity found in reflection, but even more generally in openness to the ever-shifting

---

[32] Cf. my "The Other Specie Capability & the Power of Wonder."

[33] Nussbaum, *Fragility of Goodness*, 7–8.

[34] Nussbaum, *Upheavals of Thought*, 191.

possibilities of sense and meaning that characterizes the human mind in its positive anxiety, wonder need not be emotional in any given way. That it tends to be emotional in some instances is a result of how considering sense and meaning stirs up what is good or bad for us.

Another complication is that wonder, by being involved in considering possibilities of sense, does concern our flourishing, yet not in an egotistical way. To say that wonder is "non-eudaimonistic" is to reduce what is eudaimonistic too narrowly. Our own flourishing is constituted by openness to possibilities of sense and meaning considered in their own right, as many a human excellence such as thoughtfulness, creativity, leadership, or tolerance shows. This openness centrally derives from our capacity to wonder, and in wondering, we can be said to be open to considering the possibilities of sense and meaning in the world before us. Seeking what makes sense to us, we *are* concerned with that which could make life good – and many related evaluations besides (e.g., calm, reasonable, exciting, creative, related, full of possibility, and so on). It is doubtful, then, that wonder is "non-eudaimonistic." Rather, it opens up *eudaimonia* beyond the narrowly self-interested realm of egotistical concern.

Think about the child again. It is an interesting question what the struggle to learn to make sense of the world involves. Attending to children, it becomes obvious that it is not that there is an absence of sense in the world, as nihilists might think, but that there is an excess of it.[35] This premise is born out in fieldwork within schools where children are allowed to follow their minds.[36] But also look at children who have the requisite basic support: they search instinctively to make out the world, as Nussbaum notes in the passage oft cited here. Yet the excessive meaning and pregnant sense of the world appears especially when our environment is loving. The best illustration I know of this relationship between finding the world meaningful and being loved appears in the opening of Virginia Woolf's *To The Lighthouse* where we meet a child whose attachment to his mother infuses everything with intense meaning whenever he hears her voice or feels her presence around him. Indeed, he is pictured cutting out images from a mail order catalogue of house wares, finding them intensely meaningful as an expression of the possibility he feels in his mother's presence.[37]

---

[35] For the phenomenological deduction of this point, consider Jean-Luc Marion, *Being Given* and his elaboration, *In Excess: Studies of Saturated Phenomena*, trans. Robyn Horner and Vincent Berraud (New York: Fordham University Press, 2004),

[36] See Scheinfeld et al., *We Are All Explorers*.

[37] Virginia Woolf, (1927; New York: Vintage Books, 2005). Cf. Martha C. Nussbaum, *Sex and Social Justice* (New York: Oxford University Press, 1999), chapter 15.

To come to terms with wonder's work is also to begin to be in a position to understand the environment that can support it. Nussbaum has a view on this matter. While, in her early work, Nussbaum doesn't directly take up the background role of love in opening up our striving, she does turn to it when she examines the origin of emotional life in *Upheavals of Thought*. All mammals require the milk of their form's kindness in order to grow. That is part of the mammalian form of life. With humans, the milk of human kindness becomes figurative. For Nussbaum, drawing on object-relations psychoanalysis, human kindness involves being related to personally, not just tended to for food, sleep, and safety. Only in *Upheavals of Thought* is it explicit that an *environment of interpersonal love* is needed to come to terms with human form, that is, with the human good and what human beings need to function humanly.[38] She says quite clearly that there needs to be a good "facilitating" environment wherein people come to be able to be playful and open with the world, rather than closed in with worry and anxieties of control.[39] Moreover, this environment is often political. It allows children to move from narcissistic self-protection trying to overcontrol the world to letting the world be.

We can see where this goes. What is at work within letting be is wonder. Love that lets the child be and relates to the child personally as a source of sense-making and meaning-finding thus becomes an important developmental correlate for wonder, at least insofar as wonder and all that comes with it (the world in its own right, no less!) can grow without being subverted by negative anxieties of control and self-protection. Just so, the question of the form of loving for a being who wonders becomes central to the morality and politics that Nussbaum's concern with the contingent vulnerability of human flourishing involves.[40] *It is hard to think of something out of our control more consequential than whether we grew up loved.* Many things are *as* consequential, including whether we live or die. To die young isn't good, but to live having been unloved is a curse. In other words, it seems that a major form of *tuchē* (happenstance, that which is out of our control) for a human being happens to be whether our caretakers actually cared and related to us personally in love. The past tense use of "grew" seems especially loaded in this context. It happened, it is behind you, and how has it shaped your life?

Hearing these questions allows us to return to Rimbaud's poem. It displays a strange conflict around love in the background. The "loved"-one writes back –

---

[38] Nussbaum, *Upheavals of Thought*, chapter 4.
[39] Ibid., chapter 4, section VI.
[40] Cf. the central concern with moral luck in Nussbaum's *The Fragility of Goodness*.

then she is "ghosted," as some say. The lyric subject of the poem avoids her from
then on. There's an avoidance of love in the foreground of the poem that implies
an absence of love in the background, that is, of trust being a habit for the lyrical
subject.[41] Instead, you narcissistically flee from real contact with someone who
wants to meet you.[42] At the same time, the poem suggests that human striving is
so resilient and powerful that our anxious, erotic potential still involves us in
wonder, that is, in finding the excess of sense and meaning in the world along
with the wave of our being in the world.[43] So there is the versatility of one who
seems unable to recognize the reality of forming attachments. But what
possibilities have they missed?

*

I've met people who survived an unloving environment with enough versatility
that they kept themselves free from overwhelming, negative anxiety. They were
able to wonder. In some, even, their wonder compensated for the unloving
environment. The loving environment cannot be taken as metaphysically
necessary because people's ingenuity and grit are mysterious. If there is a link to
be made between some kind of love and wonder, it must be through how a loving
environment can support wondering. I want to understand how so conceptually
through the logic in the love that coheres with and supports the logic of wonder
and its nascent wondering.

There's a clue in Nussbaum's examination of the kind of love that supports a
child in its emotional development so that they can grow into a being with ample
cognitive agency and minimal narcissism about controlling the world and others
in it. The clue is found through Nussbaum's exploration of how children move
from "infantile omnipotence" to a place where others are supportive, "holding,"
without being fused with the child or controlling.[44] The caring that lets a child
open up playfully meets needs when the child struggles (too much), and is
"relax[ed] into a relationship of trust"[45] oriented by "a real[,] personal relationship

---

[41] Cf. Stanley Cavell's "The Avoidance of Love: A Reading of *King Lear*" in *Must We Mean What We Say? A Book of Essays*, 2nd ed. (1958; New York: Cambridge University Press, 2008), chapter 10. Turning to Rimbaud's biography, one might wonder what role his homosexuality plays in the "novel" he recounts. But that speculation only pushes the matter farther into the homophobia of a poor facilitating environment in heteronormative, bourgeois France in the nineteenth century.

[42] On meeting as basic form of relational – interpersonal – reasoning, see my *Solar Calendar, and Other Ways of Marking Time*, study 4. The idea came from an essay topic, "la recontre," in Anne-Christine Habbard's course on advanced French composition in 1990.

[43] For a teenager discovering *eros* is truly like a wave.

[44] Nussbaum, *Upheavals of Thought*, 192–3.

[45] Ibid., 193.

[where] there is an element of 'subtle interchange.'"[46] The phrase, "subtle interplay," comes from the object-relations psychotherapist D. H. Winnicott, who goes so far as to claim that it constitutes the essence of love, such that "you are experiencing love and loving in this situation [of subtle interplay]."[47]

What is the logic of such a "real, personal relationship" such that it could make sense as the substance of a loving one and in this coherently cultivate wonder? One thought is to consider the logic of interpersonal relationships, at least as a starting place for returning to Winnicott's claims that Nussbaum finds so important. When someone relates to us interpersonally, they let themselves – and they let us – be in a coexisting relationship of respect.[48] Moreover, we *qua* people situate ourselves in a broader network of persons, each of whom deserves respect as being what Nussbaum calls, using Kantian language, "ends in themselves."[49] Between us, then, is accountability to each other as persons. We are accepted and seen as roughly autonomous in our own rights.[50] This much seems a sharpening and concretization of the relative independence and capacity to relate to others outside of our designs that Nussbaum considers in chapter 4 of *Upheavals of Thought*.

Against such a background, consistently developed personal relationships (i.e., relationships where we treat each other as people, not as instruments or extensions of ourselves) involve seeing and accepting the other as a locus of sense and meaning. One might even say that there is a corresponding form of personal attention in relating to another as a person and as one yourself: you would seem to relate to them with something structurally homologous to wonder. *You know not what they will do, but you respect what they can do. You view them as a source of independent sense and meaning in the world.* Moreover, receiving such personal attention, the other should in principle stand within a relationship coming from you in which they are affirmed as having their own, independent being and cognitive agency. The room for their wonder ought to be, at least conceptually, supported.

[46] Ibid., 195.
[47] Ibid., 196. Nussbaum quotes from D. H. Winnicott, *Holding and Interpretation: Fragment of an Analysis* (New York: Grove Press, 1986).
[48] Wallace, *The Moral Nexus*.
[49] See my analysis in "From Humans to All of Life," itself reading *Women and Human Development* and *Frontiers of Justice*, especially. See also *Creating Capabilities* and the discussion of ends in themselves in Jessica van Jaarsveld, *Towards an Environmental Ethic: Revising Nussbaum's Capability Approach*, dissertation submitted to the Department of Philosophy, University of Johannesberg (2002).
[50] Cf. Stephen Darwall, *The Second Person Standpoint: Morality, Respect, and Accountability* (Cambridge, MA: Harvard University Press, 2006), developing Stawsonian insights about autonomy. Technical differences remain between Wallace and Darwall, however.

When love is personal, it comes *from me* personally and is *to you* as the person whom you are. Nussbaum characterizes love as an emotion that is broadly eudaimonistic. In *Upheavals of Thought*, love is given its place in explaining other emotions such as hope or fear, as neo-Stoic accounts typically do.[51] The first mention of "love" in *Upheavals* straightaway assumes that it is an emotion.[52] These matters are complicated somewhat by the many detailed explorations of kinds of loves in part III of the book, where love becomes many things, not all of them straightaway eudaimonistic and some of them pathological. For the most part, love is still characterized as an emotion that, in its infantile form, "underlies all the adult emotion and colors them."[53]

To the degree that love is broadly eudaimonistic, however, it concerns one's good and what one values. That is, love becomes clearly an emotional element involving practical reasoning – considering how to obtain or to do what is good. This comes up against some problems once we realize on reflection that love isn't primarily about calculative, practical reason, but is about *connecting with people in their own right*. Is love primarily about learning how to handle people so as to achieve the good? No! Is it primarily a matter of know-how? Maybe? Is it primarily aimed at a practical goal? Hardly. Or is love primarily about being with people, which involves eschewing manipulating them or plugging them into some plan? *Knowing others*, not know-how to handle others (nor knowing a lot about others), seems the primary logic of love. Yet even here in my disagreement with her work, there is some wobble in Nussbaum's account, for she characterizes love straightaway as having "energy and wonder,"[54] which would imply that love contains some possibility of a non-eudaimonistic core. If love is then wonderful in its form, perhaps love involves something that pulls against practical reasoning when it comes to meeting others? Perhaps love involves the suspension of my schemes and designs on or with others, making way for them in their own right, that *they* are wonders.

An interesting consequence of love being a (potentially emotional) relationship of being-with, not as an emotion in the first instance, is that viewing love as primarily axiological[55] could just as readily interfere with the relationship as support it. To relate to others well, we have to see them just as they are. When

---

[51] Nussbaum, *Upheavals of Thought*, 28.
[52] Ibid., 13.
[53] Ibid., 460.
[54] Ibid., 461.
[55] For instance, as in Furtak's seeing another "in the best possible light" in his *Wisdom in Love: Kierkegaard the Ancient Quest for Emotional Integrity* (South Bend: University of Notre Dame Press, 2005).

someone loves you by seeing you for who you are, they do not have designs on or for you. They are open to your world, even if, on reflection, they will disagree with it at some point. In connecting with you, they acknowledge you as a source of sense and meaning, holding you personally accountable if need be.[56] They see you as a wonder.

Could the personal relation be conducive to cultivating wonder in a child? If so and if wonder is especially important for the human form of striving, separating out the personal relation from other elements of love should help us see one of the ways that our flourishing – our "goodness" in Nussbaum's terms – is "fragile." Whether or not we are loved in a way that is truly personal comes to be a form of moral luck.[57] Remember that Nussbaum understands "luck" not as randomness but in the Greek sense of *tuchē* – that which is out of our control. Randomness is only one kind of such happenstance.[58] But from the side of parents, that we love truly interpersonally in relation to our children becomes an important fiduciary matter. It amounts to whether we create the personal conditions for a child's cultivation of seeking sense and meaning in this life as an autonomous person.

*

The point under consideration here is whether the social environment provided by interpersonal attention in its pure form is conceptually disposed to cultivate wonder. In order to progress in our understanding of the personal relationship for cultivating wonder, it's important to clarify the "subtle interplay" that is central to Nussbaum's view of how a child can grow out into the world, led by their cognitive agency. To clarify that interplay, let's go back to the Lucretian moment in *Upheavals of Thought,* chapter 4, especially the discussion of "original joy." Reading that text from Lucretius, Nussbaum locates three basic needs that infants and young children have: to be fed,[59] to be held and seen in their own right,[60] and to make sense of things in their own right.[61] Of these three needs, the

---

[56] This holds true for bad people, just as "good ones." That a person has turned bad is something that matters to other people as a loss, or corruption, of the social world in which they coexist. The bad person also has the possibility of becoming accountable and turning good. In personal correspondence, Rick Anthony Furtak wrote that "*who we are* includes our striving and our highest ideals of *who we try to be*. In other words, I am both my determinate facticity and the possibilities that I strive to realize."

[57] Cf. Bernard Williams's *Moral Luck: Philosophical Papers, 1973-1980* (New York: Cambridge University Press, 1981), chapter 2.

[58] See *The Fragility of Goodness*, chapters 1 and 4.

[59] *Upheavals of Thought*, 183–4.

[60] Ibid., 185–8.

[61] Ibid., 189–90.

drive to make sense of things – or as she says, "an original joy in sorting out the world" – is discussed the most briefly.[62] As we've seen, she includes in this need wonder, curiosity, and a general expression, "cognitive interest."[63]

Interestingly, although Nussbaum doesn't so much as say it, the first two needs are helpful conditions on the third need being met. If, for instance, the infant has basic "life-sustaining" needs unmet,[64] the new being will succumb to "'hunger storm[s]' at the center of the child's being, which explode[...] within, giving rise to pulsing currents of pain, until the arrival of food calms the storm[s]."[65] Here, "curiosity, cognitive interest, and wonder"[66] are clouded over by the unmet need. Similarly, if parents fail to "identif[y] with the infant," depriving the young being of "sensitive interaction and comfort," then this need to be "held" gives way to a sense of "infinite falling," making room in the child's life for "uncertainty, [negative] anxiety, and rage."[67] These things, too, obviously interfere with the clear and open light of the mind seeking to make sense of things and to understand their meaning.

At the start of the last paragraph, I wrote "helpful conditions," not "preconditions," first, because Nussbaum doesn't make such a strong claim, and second, because the matter is empirically ambiguous. On the one hand, it is hard to imagine an infant being free enough mentally to open wide-eyed to the sense of things if they are stricken with hunger, but I have seen infants trying to make sense of things even when not properly supported. What seems clear is that in this latter case, the sense-seeking is intermittent, overwhelmed at times by the emotional deprivation shutting things down. Still, infants are resourceful when it comes to self-soothing or adaptation, and the unmet need to be held and seen in their own right doesn't seem to preclude seeking to understand things, although it can severely obstruct it. The negligence of parents is as powerful as domination, and the power of children can be as resourceful as revolt.

That Nussbaum notes the "original joy" of a child is a moment when she could be taken to intuit that there is something basically positive underlying the human mind when it is naturally open to life. For beings such as we are who strive by making sense of the world and finding meaning in it, the excitement over the sense and meaning of things is basic to our very being. The word

---

[62] Ibid.
[63] Ibid., 188.
[64] The expression is a translation from Lucretius. Ibid., 182–3.
[65] The expression comes from Daniel Stern. Ibid., 183.
[66] Ibid., 190.
[67] Ibid., 186. The expression "infinite falling" is from Winnicott. Nussbum also refers to Bowlby's psychological work on holding in this long and rich passage.

"excitement" is precisely chosen. It suggests that one is "called out from one's location," or "called forth," from the Latin *exciere*.[68] Here unfettered by negative anxieties, our sense of possibility is originally positive, not negative and closing in on us. Rather, it is open to the "light" of the world, as the Lucretian scene describes. I am led to consider whether the moment when Nussbaum sees the "original joy" of the child is the moment when we can see how wonder is basic to our being, deeper than any negative anxiety. What comes of it by the child being fed, seen, and held?

Wonder is at the heart of our "original joy." As we've seen, shortly after pointing to the original joy of the child, Nussbaum claims that wonder is "non-egotistic" and "even, to some degree, non-eudaimonistic,"

> ... infus[ing] the structure of ... emotions [with] ... a non-instrumental and even non-eudaimonistic aspect from the start, and allowing the child to take its own emotional states as objects of curiosity.[69]

Earlier, she writes:

> The least eudaimonistic emotions, especially wonder, may take a very general object (the moral law)[70] or a highly concrete object (some instance of natural beauty).[71] (Is there background wonder? Or does wonder, as I'm inclined to think, always involve a focused awareness of an object. Wonder's non-eudaimonistic character might be relevant here: for what is especially likely to persist in the background is a structure of personal goals and plans.)[72]

A careful reader will notice that Nussbaum waffles in her characterization of wonder, moving between its being "non-"eudaimonistic and the "least" eudaimonistic emotion – categorically different claims that are incompatible (I see her as feeling things out using her method of reflective equilibrium on everyday beliefs and intuitions).[73] More interesting to me is her uncertainty about whether wonder exists in the foreground or the background of consciousness. I hope that I have answered that in this book. The distinction between background wonder and foreground, focused acts of wondering is one that I have developed, thanks to Nussbaum's remark setting me thinking. As

---

[68] "Excite," *Oxford American Dictionary.*
[69] Nussbaum, *Upheavals of Thought,* 191.
[70] As Immanuel Kant did in the *Critique of Practical Reason,* trans. Mary Gregor (1788; New York: Cambridge University Press, 2017).
[71] As Kant does in the *Critique of Judgment.*
[72] Ibid., 73. These passages are much discussed in the literature on wonder.
[73] Nussbaum, *The Fragility of Goodness,* chapter 48, or *Women and Human Development,* chapter 1.

we've seen, wonder does exist in the background, whereas acts of wondering move to the foreground to consider specific things – or people – over which – over whom – we wonder. Yet contrary to what Nussbaum writes, wonder can exist in the background because deeper than any of our plans is the way that the plans make sense, and deeper than anything making sense is their *possibility* of making sense, something arrived at only when the mind is fundamentally spontaneous and characterized by positive anxiety at the sense and meaning of things. Here, the "original joy" of meeting the world as an excess of sense and meaning, being lost in that "light" of the world, are clues to wonder in the background of consciousness. In such an "original" condition, to be lost is a positive thing, filled with possibilities of sense and meaning.

In the first passage just quoted (on p. 191 of *Upheavals*), wonder makes possible self-reflective curiosity, thereby being curiosity's condition. "Self-reflective" shouldn't be taken to imply a strong sense of self by the child, but rather that the child, in wondering about its own feelings, starts to develop a sense of self.[74] Even more, though, consider what is at stake in an orientation to the world that is "non-egotistic" and "non-eudaimonistic." To say that something is "eudaimonistic" is to say that it is understood in terms of our own flourishing (or good). The expression is linked most commonly in the history of ethics through Aristotle's *Nicomachean Ethics*, where the human good is understood as *eudaimonia*, a Greek word sometimes translated as (objective, not subjective) "happiness" or "flourishing." To say that something is "egotistical" is to say that it is selfish. In both cases, we are talking about the sense of things understood in terms of how they contribute to our lives. That wonder should suspend such self-interest is remarkable and, even more, an obvious condition for understanding things in their own right, without respect to how they contribute to our lives. Wonder, in other words, is a condition on objectivity, rather than being what Descartes worried was a distraction from objectivity.[75] Yet to understand things in their own right is a condition on grasping how they make sense, for I cannot accurately relate things to myself, including to my self-interest, if I haven't understood what they are on their own. Wonder, in other words, is a condition on finding the sense of things, prior to relating them to my interests. That means that wonder, even more than "curiosity" or "cognitive interest," is at the *heart* of the original joy in making sense of the world. It has to be. Wonder is the fundamental openness of the mind. As I put it, wonder is on a

---

[74] On the self as a reflexive operation (the Latin *se* as part of reflexive tensing in grammar), see Charles Larmore, *The Practices of the Self*, trans. Sharon Bowman (Chicago: The University of Chicago Press, 2010).

[75] See Lloyd, *Reclaiming Wonder*, chapter 2.

continuum with curiosity, cognitive interest, and so on – each involving some degree of the positive anxiety of considering things, i.e., of wonder.

Nussbaum is right, then, to claim that our needs as infants are to be fed, to be held and seen in our own right, *and to wonder.* There's a conceptual argument to support her Aristotelian phenomenology. But straightaway we can notice that there seems to be an interesting connection to be explored between wonder and seeing others in their own right. To see another in their own right, I have to wonder over them. The expression, "wondering over," is the right one. Although one often speaks of wondering "about" or "at" things, these expressions lack phenomenological sense for the complexity involved in viewing someone as a whole "in their own right." To wonder "about" someone is too diffuse, and to wonder "at" them is too obtuse. We're talking about the fullness and complexity of a person. Wondering over someone is reflective, personal, and vulnerable. This strikes me as much closer to the rich meaning of wonder than wondering "at" or "about" something. When I see another in their own right, I do not simply direct my mind at them. Nor do I let my thoughts wander casually about them. Both do not take the other seriously, the first turning the other into an object, and the second letting the other go blurry as if they were not the real source of consideration. Rather, when I see another in their own right, I take them into my world and consider them in their own right. Who is this one? How are they? In what ways do they unfold "into the light"?[76] When wondering "over" someone, they become the ground of our world of sense.[77] At least initially, seeing a person as they are suggests that "over" is the preposition to use.

Wondering over a person simultaneously accepts that person in their own way of being – their own "givenness," to use a term from phenomenology[78] – and it relates one's world to that person in a manner that keeps one's world open to – often surprising – possibilities formed out of how that person makes sense of the world and finds meaning in it. This, I think, is implicit in Nussbaum's claim that holding and seeing a child in their own right involves "identification" and "sensitive interaction."[79] "Identification" cannot mean here "being identical to me," for precisely what is at stake is the space needed for a child to become who they are. Nussbaum goes so far as to characterize the way this space is made as a

---

[76] Compare the opening image of Rousseau's *Émile*: a plant reaching for the light, an image found in the great Pindar quotation at the beginning of *Fragility of Goodness.* See Jean-Jacques Rousseau's *Émile, or on Education,* trans. Alan Bloom (New York: Basic Books, 1979).

[77] "Over," *Oxford American Dictionary.*

[78] See Marion, *Being Given.*

[79] Nussbaum, *Upheavals of Thought,* 186.

"dance" – a "balance between indifference and intrusiveness," a "sensitivity to the child's particular rhythm."[80]

Any identification that could be coherent with these disparate qualities of the caring relationship between parent and child involves a keen sensitivity to the way that the child is different than the parent and incipiently autonomous. The parent tries to see the child as a being different than the parent, yet sympathetically reached by the parent's imaginative effort to understand their world. This involves a balance, moving back and forth between self and other:

> As the relationship between child and caretaker(s) develops, it is important that the caretaker(s) show sensitivity to the child's particular rhythm and personal style, which Stern calls a "dance." The balance between indifference and intrusiveness, attention and the giving of space, must be struck in the right way, or the result will be an inability to trust. Winnicott plausibly argues that this balance can be best struck by a person who has a good imagination and who is able to identify with the child in fantasy.[81]

I take this to mean that relating to the child involves letting them be and tending to them, identifying with them as beings who have imaginative lives of their own, and that this identification is premised off of understanding that the child is different than the parent. They are their own being. The openness to possibilities that is essential to wondering is apt – fitting – for taking in the new being's possibilities, considering them through one's own world, yet leaving open that this new being has its own way of being given to things, of growing and of themselves wondering into the world's light.

Here, wondering over a child – identifying with them, letting them be, engaging in a "dance" of attention and giving room – is conceptually fitting to contribute to their capacity to wonder over things, occasionally about them, and eventually at them as their acts of wondering take organic shape. Nussbaum suggests as much, although she also suggests that the relation between wondering over a child and the child's capacity to wonder is indirect. Children who are not attended to in a way that cultivates trust in their caretaking environment have a hard time managing their "infantile omnipotence."[82] They are given to rage and a spiraling negative anxiety that is like an "infinite falling," according to

---

[80] Ibid., 188. Note how different this dance is from the manipulative figure of negative anxiety and narcissism found in Nussbaum, *Anger and Forgiveness*, in the section on the "dance" of anger, chapter 4, section VII.

[81] Nussbaum, *Upheavals of Thought,* 188.

[82] Ibid., 192.

Winnicott.[83] The characterization of anxiety as falling marks it as negative – as a restriction of possibility in the proliferation of negative feelings. This is interestingly close to how Kierkegaard's pseudonym, Vigilius Haufniensis, characterizes anxiety in *The Concept of Anxiety* – something that suggests that possibly Haufniensis simultaneously understood that anxiety is our ground (i.e., is positive in providing a condition for our flourishing) and yet misunderstood it as negative (i.e., as leading us to despair over the sense and meaning of the world).[84] Thus bound up with their own failed omnipotence, how could we expect anything but the exceptional child to "wonder and delight at parts of the world that are not related to [their] own states"?[85]

Perhaps the child's coming to trust that they are seen and held as needed provides room for their positive excitement about the sense and meaning of this world to be worked out. After all, the openness of their "original joy" is part of cognitive agency, and agency is supported in trustworthy enough conditions where our needs are met. But at the same time, what allows those conditions to be attuned to the child in their particularity if they aren't seen in their own right? If to develop trust in their environment an infant should feel the parent "identified" with them – "sensitively" aware of their "particular" being – then it would seem that the parent should come to see the child as they are given, not as the parent wishes them to be. In that case, broader aspects of holding that concern bodily comfort, soothing and that give way to primary needs like food, sleep, and safety all seem to benefit for their thoughtful and attuned realization on the parent wondering over the child!

It is not, then, that wonder begets wonder – that the parent's wonder over the child teaches the child to wonder, although if the child internalizes the parent's way of being, that might be so. The issue is that the parent's wonder is conducive to the child remaining open to its original joy, its excitement to meet with the sense and meaning of the world as in a revelation, and that the parent's wondering over the child attunes them to the particularity of the child's emerging agency. The parent's wonder makes room for the child's wondering, and, even more, brings the parent to a place where the conditions of the child's agency can be trustworthy because the parent is actually seeing the child in their own right. Wondering over the child supports the child's wonder by creating the conditions for their personal autonomy.

*

[83] Ibid., 193–5.
[84] Kierkegaard, *The Concept of Anxiety*, "Subjective Anxiety."
[85] Nussbaum, *Upheavals of Thought*, 191.

Every new human is poised to reconstitute the world according to how it should make sense, especially when their cognitive agency isn't hampered. One thing that is revolutionary about parenting is that parents can hold and support the child's growing to search for meaning and make sense of the world in a way that helps the child to become autonomous, uncomfortable with heteronomy, and likely to chafe at domination. The core of this revolutionary work of parenting isn't particularly doctrinaire, however, for it involves forming a personal relationship with the child formed out of wonder giving room for the child to grow autonomously themselves. Such relatively ordinary work even makes the meaning of what can be "radical" in parenting shift, at once becoming duller and subtler. Perhaps radicals should be rooted simply in care.[86]

We shouldn't say too much here, but also not too little. The love in the personal relationship with a child does involve a perpetual series of new encounters. It's fitting and not at all romantic that relating to the child in a way that encourages subtle interplay centrally involves wondering over the child, the relationship, and even oneself as a parent. Meeting the new life as it grows into sense and meaning occurs over and over as a meaningful, perplexing unsettling – or decentering – even as surprise. Obviously, there are matters of degree here. Yet it seems to be a phenomenological fact of personal relating that there is a moment of decentering, of receptivity in which one's own ego is suspended, even interrupted. In some personal loves, the decentering is world-shaking. The one who loves is "blown away" as a leaf on a gust of wind. In parental love, the moment of suspension is often sustained and involved, even reflected on. Parents often take delight in the fact that they are delighting in the unique striving of their child showing up in the world for the first time, each day, sometimes from moment to moment in the enthusiastic parent's eyes! In the love of a teacher for a student, a nurse for a patient, or of a neighbor for a passerby, the surprise may be barely perceptible, a momentary hesitation in the midst of the work at hand or of the day's ongoing activity. Still, for any of these moments to involve interpersonal relationships, there must be an opening onto the other in which another reaches us as a source of their own sense and meaning, leaving us in momentary vulnerability to what they mean and how we are to relate to them considerately. I hope that my translation of the Rimbaud poem deepened this point, whereas the original may have ambivalently avoided it.

The extent that relating personally involves being decentered draws on and deepens the way in which, in everyday moral life, we each unsettle each other by

---

[86] "Radical" comes from *radic-*, Latin for "root." "Radical," *Oxford American Dictionary*.

virtue of making sense of the world together. The moment that you are a being that makes sense of the world in your own way, and I am to be personally accountable to that, I am decentered by *your* "demand" of sense.[87] Your very presence makes a demand on me that I make sense of my world involving you and how you make sense. Moreover, this positive condition of synthesis – that we are to make sense together even if we disagree (that your world is something that I must consider and absorb as a source of sense and meaning even when it makes little sense to me) – precedes the antagonism that may erupt between us if we begin to try to make sense against each other. In this indirect and minimal way, your very presence calls on me, as someone relating interpersonally, to make sense – as does mine on you.

This bare, moral relationship between us is personal in that it calls on us as persons who make sense and who can be responsible for the sense that we make. To the degree, then, that the personal relation implies some degree of openness to each other's sense and meaning, our basic moral relations to each other are ones of a very minimal (but crucial) degree of wonder, too. This minimal degree of wonder that is implicit in morality – strange as that may sound at first – surrounds us in social life with the ongoing call – sometimes experienced as a demand – to make sense of things together, even if indirectly. This social-environmental condition is so much a feature of the basic condition of our being human that cultures readily relate to the more-than-human world on its basis, that is, personally, trying to make sense of other beings as their own sources of sense and meaning.[88]

Being a person means walking around in the world with other persons and with the world appearing personally to you. To say this is to say that the world does not, from this orientation, appear to us as a field of objects to be cognitively mastered or practically manipulated, but as calling on *us* to make sense in it and of it. Certainly, the demands of sense of others is something that comes to us from having internalized the basic, phenomenological relationship between human beings. As soon as we have a conscience, we have already done this –

---

[87] Cf. Steven Crowell, "Why Is Ethics First Philosophy? Levinas in Phenomenological Context," *European Journal of Philosophy* 22:3 (2012): 564–88. Thanks to Aleksy Tarasenko-Struck for the reference, along with Matt Ferkany and Urszula Lisowska for the reading group.

[88] See Nussbaum, *Frontiers of Justice*, "Beyond 'Compassion and Humanity.'" Going further than Nussbaum does in that book, however, it is reasonable to argue that personification of the more-than-human world is a basic feature of being human. Compare my *The Ecological Life*, lecture 4. Our default personification of everything explains why it makes sense to talk of the more than human world in a way that suggests we interpret what makes sense for its living beings, although we lack a common language.

internalized a way of speaking to ourselves inside ourselves. But as Nussbaum notes, the process begins even earlier than conscience in the child's incipient capacity to wonder about its own feelings.[89] That we must make sense to ourselves already involves the demands of ourselves as another that we find growing up by being held, seen, and made sense of by others, who in parenting us, call us forth into the world that can make sense to them and, they wonder, to us ("How does the world make sense to Emet?"). When we go out into the world – even as we wake up to it (even in our sleep when we dream) – the world bears the traces of this first meeting with our parents.

My love for my child is a highly intensified love on a continuum with everyday morality by which I relate to my child personally in meeting them, again and again. This is to say, by being called to be open to them and to make sense to them, with them (and by virtue of these, to myself). In this way, the personal relation in parental love brings me to become accountable to my child. It accounts for the basic openness to them that is the moral core of my love for them – that I meet them, let them be who they are, and not simply remain in my egotism. The personal relation accounts for how my openness to another is the other side of the relation by which I am left to be accountable to myself, to what makes sense to me.

Wonder over a child isn't an exceptional, lyrical state, but is basic to relating to the child at all. To meet the child depends on the personal relation. It depends on being open to the child as one who is themself making sense of the world, who has their own agency. It depends on not being egotistical with the child. Not only am I to make sense to them, and to myself, but I must let their sense and meaning emerge in their own right, opening up a field of new possibilities in the world, new ways in which the sense and meaning of our world are arrayed. Here I must wonder. To properly see the child not as an object but as a person is to see the child as a wonder.

The child is an unknown, or, when somewhat known, always more than my knowing, for it is the child who determines the personal sense of their world, not me. The personal relation builds mystery into the logic of relationships, and this mystery demands nothing less than wonder in any personal relationship.[90] Such wonder, moreover, need not be an exceptional, exalted state. Indeed, it would be alarming if it often were, suggesting either sentimental egotism on the part of the one who exalts or a lack of attention and wonder during the normal course of things. Rather, the wonder we need in order to relate personally has to be an

---

[89] Nussbaum, *Upheavals of Thought*, 191.
[90] Cf. Zeldin, *An Intimate History of Humanity*.

ongoing state, an orientation implicit in our mature disposition to relate to each other well. As should now be plain in this book, I am arguing for a steady-state, down-to-earth view of wonder and of wondering, so to speak, a day laborer's view.

The orientation of wonder called for by the demands of parenting is clarified by the distinction between enraptured astonishment – *Verwunderung* – and ongoing openness to sense – *Bewunderung* – that Kant made in his *Critique of Judgment*. Speaking of *Bewunderung*, Kant speaks of an "astonishment that does not cease when the novelty disappears."[91] Kant is here discussing judgments of taste – aesthetic judgments. But these are judgments where our imaginations overflow with sense and meaning when considering something. They are moments where "intuition" overflows our prior sense of things.[92] Kant looks to wildflower fields to see such things, but the more obvious place to experience such pregnancy of sense is with a confounding and startling child. Every time we meet them, they are more than we think of them. We have to catch up with them in our minds. Their possibilities are thus not dizzying negativities that engage my narcissism – they are positions of sense and meaning in my world. Theirs is an unsettling that brings with it possibilities of sense and meaning that call on me to make sense of them. If there's any anxiety here, it is positive, an excitement mirroring the child's original joy. But the key thing is: to relate to this child with care and the wonder that makes care personal demands ongoing "astonishment," an openness to how they are given, viewing them as a source of sense and meaning in their own right.

One thing that a child can teach us is that our wonder over them is only an intensification of what must be there at all for us to relate to each other personally. Emet demands my care, and Emet teaches me this. Wonder is at the heart of relationships.

---

[91] Kant, *Critique of Judgment*, section 29, p. 113.
[92] Marion, *In Excess.*

Life Cycle

I

You outstretched along an arm
Make morning midnight,
Why sighing air outside
Hums the house with warmth.

> How's things in the quietest part of the day?
> We've seldom slept them
> But between us in our waking
> Old patterns are shaking.

II

I can't forget this unfitting depth,
Void in memory bearing you as drive
And darkness wider than the outmost reach
Where you unknown disturb me.

> 4 A.M. sings the bright room.
> Sky suspends the mind:
> What you give without knowing
> Surfaces to the shores of sense.

III

Let's love stories as they are finite.
Having come aground,
They rush the brittle wood and vanish
Leaving echoed song:

> Lost familiars
> Kiss in the street all heat
> And later they
> United.

IV

You clutch insight as you love to breathe.
I thank hindsight or I stop to breathe.
Struggle into being without cease,
There we find you.

I once thought,
"To care for real."
Then everything mouthed a question.
As you cried, we met.

~ After Arthur Rimbaud's « Roman, » 29 Septembre, 1870, adapted February–
March 2020, May–June 2021, December 2022

"Jeremy & Esther, 90s," 2020

Getting lost together in making sense of our coexistence allows us to share the world freely.

MOTET 3 – *WONDER IS POLITICAL, HONEST IN OUR RELATIONS*

TEXTS: *Love's Knowledge, Political Emotions*

WORD: "Honesty"

For the Scheinfelds
along with
the Chicago Commons Family Centers,
around the turn of the millennium

0. Invocation

When I was 22 years old, I was lost. But I let myself consider things and my anxiety took shape with wonder. I searched for the world that I avoided, and I searched for who I am. I allowed possibilities to reach out that might make sense even if they seemed strange, unfamiliar, or unhinged. I sought my convictions and how the world could make sense so that I could go on, letting the meaning of things open up as fully as possible and seeking connections new to me between them. By reconsidering the world, I related to it again and found others through it. This moment was developmental, a coming of age.

But how could it be that with something so messy and confused came the threshold of age? By "age," I mean maturity – growing up. By "growing up," I include what Immanuel Kant called *Aufklärung* – enlightenment, the power to use your mind in order to determine what makes sense to you.[1] Authors within Kant's tradition hundreds of years removed have called "maturity" by other names. Michel Foucault called it a "critical attitude": an anti-authoritarian "space" around our norms to reconsider them.[2] Hanna Arendt called it "thoughtfulness," the power to think otherwise when immersed within mass society's "organized irresponsibility" producing the "banality of evil."[3] These glosses on "thinking for oneself" point mainly to forms of autonomy.

But there are also embodied and emotional instances of the attitude that point to other dimensions of the process of autonomy. Sara Ahmed's "queer orientation" or the erotic swerve that Lynne Huffer considers can contribute to ways of "being otherwise," in Sadiya Hartman's phrase, that open up space within our relationship to the sense and meaning of the world, disclosing some degree of the free play of

---

[1] Kant, "An Answer to the Question: What Is Enlightenment?" On the importance of the notion of growing up for Kant's entire critical project, see Susan Neiman, *The Unity of Reason,* chapter 5.V. and her popularized *Why Grow Up? Subversive Thoughts for an Infantile Age* (New York: Farrar, Straus & Giroux, 2015). On my reading of Kant's essay, see *Solar Calendar, and Other Ways of Marking Time,* study 4, "I want to meet you as a person."

[2] Foucault, "What Is Critique?"

[3] Arendt, *Eichmann in Jerusalem.* On "organized irresponsibility," see Jackall, *Moral Mazes,* "*Moral Mazes* and the Great Recession."

possibilities around even the most ordinary things so that we can lose our conventions, discover new ways to be, or rediscover our buried roots.[4] Sure, embodied enlightenments have a more complicated relation to self-determination, thinking, and making sense of things than merely sitting around and thinking do (if that is what Kant mainly did). As Huffer is at pains to point out, the erotic swerve can be devastating and as such can readily trigger negative anxiety.[5] For a scholar of Foucault who distrusts what's "normal," the swerve helps things stop making sense – and this is good, a moment of being lost. But the moment of being lost only backtracks us to wonder, in its anxiety opening up the world to sense and meaning otherwise than we had presumed in it. Both Ahmed's and Huffer's ethics are committed to going into the mystery of what could make sense to us otherwise than by common sense. By setting us searching, they help us get to the bottom of what actually does make sense to us. This suggests, in terms they may not accept but which reference they seem to, what Charles Larmore calls a "practice" of the self and its "authenticity," i.e., to what makes sense in your world being true.[6] Even in a devastating gust of *eros*, when one accepts that one has become swept away in a transformative experience, a "practice of the self" occurs should one face one's desire and make meaning out of it. Certainly, if one isn't careful, falling in love can lead to fixation in negative anxiety and its narcissism when our hearts get broken and we find ourselves devastated by abandonment. But *eros* can strangely ally with enlightenment, even if, in fits and starts, it contributes to a gap-filled, disjointed experience of growing up. Like love, *eros* depends on wonder to reveal the complexity and mystery of the beloved.[7]

What is called conventionally "mental" disorientation exists beside "emotional" or "bodily" disorientation along a complicated continuum whose outline, it seems, is the human range of ways of discovering meaning and coming to find the ways life hangs together. Our entire being is run through with soulfulness, the skin as intelligent as cogitation, albeit differently.[8] But since soulfulness concerns meaning and sense, our being is anxious, a nascent wonder in our relation to

[4] Sarah Ahmed, *Queer Phenomenology: Orientations, Objects, Others* (Durham, NC: Duke University Press, 2006); Lynne Huffer, *Mad for Foucault: Rethinking the Foundations of Queer Theory* (New York: Columbia University Press, 2009) and her *Foucault's Strange Eros*. See also Hartman, *Wayward Lives, Beautiful Experiments*. Unorthodox though doing so is, I read Kant's essay in a decolonial manner.
[5] Sidra Shahid, "Genealogies of Philosophy: Lynne Huffer (part II)," *Blog of the APA*, April 2nd, 2021.
[6] Larmore, *The Practices of the Self*.
[7] Without wonder, love risks being narcissistic. Nussbaum, *Political Emotions*, 277.
[8] See Edmund Husserl's foundational work on "passive synthesis" in *Cartesian Meditations: An Introduction to Phenomenology*, trans. Dorion Cairns (1939; Dordrecht: Kluwer Academic Publishers, 1987), and Maurice Merleau-Ponty, *The Visible and the Invisible*, trans. Alphonso Lingis (1964; Evanston, IL: Northwestern University Press, 1969), "The Chiasm."

things unless it gets beaten out of us. The corresponding openness to what could make sense explains our capacity to take distance on the hegemonic and possibly illegitimate authority of norms, even on the notion of "authority" itself. Our bodies and our feelings can protest against us, wanting to get lost and question or swerve from the norm. The wonder in our soulfulness is, actually, a condition on the possibility of the critical attitude Foucault proposes as well as of being able to accept *eros*'s subversive power. Coming of age is possible only because we accept how our being is awash with meaning and complicated by many modes of making sense. No wonder we are anxious. Or rather, it's wonderful that we are.

Some such soulfulness is what I messily accepted when I felt my world go fluid and my life begin to swim. I let myself be submerged in confusing meaning. What the possibility of wondering brought to my sense of life was the possibility of letting myself be okay in being lost while searching. It led me to see this as an important way of being truly human and being seriously responsible in this life. I now appreciate the way that Martha C. Nussbaum could have used such a broad expression as "the sense of life" to orient our search for wisdom – wondering over stories of this life (and others) with much subtlety.[9]

In "An Answer to the Question: What Is Enlightenment?" Kant famously ends by noting that humans are "more than a machine." In a very different way than Kant's rationally self-possessed process of "enlightenment," wondering makes us more than robotic in this life.[10] Ahmed's and Huffer's embodied revelations of meaning and meaninglessness can be placed alongside Nussbaum's reading of Walt Whitman's poetry and the orientation it takes by loving our bodies for their human vulnerability and need for contact and touch.[11] These approaches can remind us of how people wonder in different ways, disagree with the norms around them by letting wonder be in their bodies and actions, and how wonder stands behind the resistance to being kept in a place that makes little soulful sense. What's wonderful in being human often plays out as anxiety does, as when we go for a swim and find ourselves rhythmically considering the mysterious sense of the world as we lose track of any particular focus.[12] "[I]f [we] are going to see life as it is, [we] have to be willing to be perplexed, to see its mystery and complexity ..."[13] Then let things "'vibrate' in [your] heart, for what [you] see" ("*if* you are going to see").[14]

[9] Nussbaum, *Love's Knowledge,* Introduction, "C. The Starting Point: 'How Should One Live?'," 23–9.
[10] "Robot" comes from the Czech *robota,* meaning "forced labor" (*Oxford American Dictionary*).
[11] Nussbaum, *Upheavals of Thought,* chapter 15, "Democratic Desire: Walt Whitman."
[12] Cf. Lynne Ramsay, *The Swimmer* (London: BBC Films, 2012).
[13] Nussbaum, *Love's Knowledge,* 207.
[14] Ibid. Emphasis mine.

1. Wonder's Power

Our bodies are at stake in the political, although "politics" seems to be so much talk. The idea of a soulful politics would include them, except that "soulful" and "politics" can seem a contradiction in terms! To think about a politics that makes sense to us in our bodies is to consider a politics that won't make us feel negatively anxious but rather excited, open as beings who, when not beaten down, make sense and meaning out of this life freely. In the terms of my argument, it's to consider a politics open to wonder to such an extent that the politics is, in some way to be determined, *of* wonder, drawing on it. Only then could we say coherently that the politics were open to us in our soulfulness as we muddle through this life, no imposition by avoidance or oppression but an extension of our searching, we who are finite beings coexisting in worlds that are so often beyond making complete sense.

But we would have to deal with narcissism. Because so much is out of our control and because we can be lost without letting ourselves be lost and because the environments in which we grow can be precarious, control of things between us is an issue for politics, and domination is a reaction. Is politics an endless cycle of abuse?[15] Yet I've been pursuing this idea from Nussbaum's philosophy, that wonder is important because of its capacity to resist narcissism. To me, that means wonder can resist domination inside ourselves and in the orders of our practices and institutions. It has implications for politics. We have to situate wonder in the life between us.

So, I am going to ask, what is the relationship between wonder and freedom in society?

In the last motet, I showed how wondering over each other opens our striving for sense, giving us room to make meaning as if wonder were a call that recedes as we wake up into the day and go on our way. Here, instead, I'm interested in a politics emerging out of wonder. What is it for relationships to be autonomous in a way that allows us to share the world? How can the sense that orients what we do be truly made in common as moral equals? Since I understand autonomy as depending on each person's soulful consciousness, i.e., their capacities to make sense out of the world in their own ways, I've reserved an important place for wonder. But interpersonal relationships complicate things by calling for a reflective space for wondering within our soulfulness with each other. Aren't we to be free together?

[15] Thanks to Anne-Christine Habbard for suggesting this question, from personal correspondence in 1993.

In this motet, I will pursue politics in light of the space of wonder between us. I will think of this space as a social condition for governance that remains autonomous between us.[16]

The idea is that wonder is important for sharing power with others. Since I accept that

(1) our moral equality implies the obligation to be accountable to each other,
(2) being accountable to each other demands respecting each other's autonomy, in as much as we can be autonomous,[17]
(3) coexisting autonomously demands working out what makes sense in what affects us together so that it can make sense to us together,[18] and that
(4) without wonder we cannot be autonomous,[19]

to respect autonomy in each other involves making room for *us* to wonder around matters of shared concern that affect us together. This has implications for governance, i.e., how we guide collective life. The way that I approach our governing our lives together thus implies a particular form of social power. According to it, governance is built out of relational autonomy between moral equals who are free to make sense of the world in their own ways.[20] I will call this form of governance *isonomy*, governance that is consistent with relationally autonomous "power-with," opposed to holding "power over" people.[21] What I want to follow out in this motet is how, understood through its dependence on wonder, isonomy involves learning to get lost together in the sense implied by wondering and doing so in making sense together of the world we share, often in times of disagreement. In this vision of isonomy, wonder rests at the heart of conflict among moral equals who all have a claim on living as autonomously as can be, given the circumstances that they happen to share.

[16] A project articulated in my "Unacceptable Agency (Part I of *The Problem of an Unloving World*)," *Environmental Philosophy* 18:2 (2021): 319–44.
[17] Cf. Wallace, *The Moral Nexus*.
[18] See my *Involving Anthroponomy in the Anthropocene*, chapters 1 and 2, for my understanding of autonomy as a process of living according to what makes sense to you, giving leeway to question and to disagree.
[19] See Motet 1.
[20] Moral equals may accept social hierarchy in many forms if it is legitimate in their eyes. This is important for decolonial objections. See Thomas Meagher, "Ethics of Freedom, Politics for Decolonization: Thoughts on Devin Shaw's *Philosophy of Antifascism*," *Blog of the APA*, August 17th, 2021.
[21] Lena Partzsch, "'Power with' and 'Power to' in Environmental Politics and the Transition to Sustainability," *Environmental Politics* 26:2 (2017): 193–211; Amy Allen, "Rethinking Power," *Hypatia* 13:1 (1998): 21–40; and Julinna Oxley, "Feminist Perspectives on Power, Domination, and Exploitation" in Carol Hay, ed., *Philosophy: Feminism* (New York: MacMillan Reference USA, 2017), chapter 4. Thanks to Julinna Oxley for referencing Allen's source. The use I am making of "power-with" is not *group solidarity* but a condition on it – namely, the capacity to develop freedom with each other so that any group can be a true community and confront domination within it.

The drive to make sense of things in order to be autonomous has implications for disagreement in politics which wonder between us helps to resolve.[22] This wonder is over the common world that we could share. Here, not even some given world to which we are committed, but a regulative idea of trying to make sense of what is at stake between us emerges, since we are morally responsible, are presumed to all have cognitive agency. At the limit, "the" world – experienced as an aporia between us but projected as the common world that we could share – and not any one of our particular worlds, guides the relationship.[23] I hold that this strange politics of wonder coheres with Nussbaum's outlook and impulses, even as it leads toward a social form of power that may seem more socialist than politically liberal.

Nussbaum's political liberalism is deep and far-ranging. She has worked it out in relationship to her teacher, John Rawls.[24] She accepts much from Rawls's position, especially his emphasis on political conceptions for use in cross-cultural justification (e.g., "overlapping consensus" and "reflective equilibrium"), and his commitment to articulating and providing the social and economic bases of self-respect within a socially stable order that sees the value of social justice.[25] Her contributions and departures include great attention to moral psychology and political or socially powerful emotions.[26] She has also broadened the community of citizens or moral patients to or for whom political justification is morally obligatory to include the disabled, non-nationals, and other animals.[27] Finally, her capabilities approach has greatly expanded how to think about the primary goods, i.e., the basic social conditions that people need to live their lives according to their own plans.[28]

In her work on toleration, religious equality, and the negative emotions bad for justice and human flourishing, she has remained a liberal for whom freedom from interference in what Mill called our "experiments in living" is central and

---

[22] On that drive, consider again Nussbaum, *Upheavals of Thought*, 188–9, and Neiman, *The Unity of Reason*, reading Kant's critical project.

[23] Consider my argument for the regulative idea of "the" world between us in *Involving Anthroponomy in the Anthropocene*, chapter 2. On regulative ideas, see Immanuel Kant, *Critique of Pure Reason*, trans. Norman Kemp-Smith (1781; New York: St. Martin's Press, 1929), and Neiman, *The Unity of Reason*, chapters 2 and 4.

[24] Thom Brooks and Martha C. Nussbaum, eds., *Rawls's Political Liberalism* (New York: Columbia University Press, 2015).

[25] Nussbaum, *Women and Human Development* and *Political Emotions*.

[26] Nussbaum, *From Disgust to Humanity, Political Emotions, The Monarchy of Fear*, and *Citadels of Pride*.

[27] Nussbaum, *Frontiers of Justice*.

[28] Nussbaum, *Women and Human Development* and *Creating Capabilities*.

liberty of conscience is paramount.[29] What she has not particularly explored is relational freedom itself, except in moments in her capability approach where she considers the importance of association for allowing people to realize themselves if they so choose to associate and in a moment from *Political Emotions* that I will interpret later in this motet.[30] Her attention to love and to sympathetic imagination have an ambiguous relationship to freedom that is, it seems fair to say, unthematized.[31]

My approach in this book is not to take on Nussbaum's political liberalism as a whole. There is really too much that is complex should one want to work through liberalism reasonably to support blanket criticisms as have become common in the public sphere among some "radicals."[32] But we can home in on a form of freedom that is unthematized in Nussbaum's work and see what shifts as a result of that. I believe that doing so with the premises and ideas I've outlined about wonder can push Nussbaum's politics – and politics itself – in a fascinating and at times compelling direction. Liberty, as I've argued elsewhere,[33] can be too unconcerned with how things go between us to do justice to the strongly social bonds that we need to be free together in a caring community. It also doesn't account for the social sympathies that suffuse and weave together Nussbaum's picture of social-political life as an environment that could dissolve narcissism and defeat domination as it can be socially reproduced inside us.[34] Liberty doesn't give you good relationships. Moreover, if governance between moral equals implies a form of relational autonomy – that is, if it must be isonomic – then liberty is at best partially suited to governance, just a fragment of the kind of power with each other that we need.

I'm interested in the possibility that the freedom Nussbaum seems at times to develop in her work is much closer to the freedom we have by being in reciprocal and sympathetic relationships of respect and care than it is to the liberty of a laissez-faire attitude beyond non-interference with each other's harmless life-experiments. By focusing on basic moral assumptions about equal respect (or "accountability" as I will tend to think), and by considering wondering as a way

---

[29] Nussbaum, *Liberty of Conscience, The New Religious Intolerance, Monarchy of Fear, Anger and Forgiveness*, and *Political* Emotions; John Stuart Mill, *On Liberty* (1859; Indianapolis: Hackett Publishing, 1978).
[30] On association as a basic capability, see Nussbaum, *Women and Human Development*, chapter 1.
[31] Nussbaum, *Love's Knowledge* and *Upheavals of Thought*.
[32] Cf. Hulsey, "Reconsidering the Aesthetics of Liberalism."
[33] My *The Wind* and *Involving Anthroponomy in the Anthropocene*.
[34] For instance, through "adaptive preferences," Nussbaum, *Women and Human Development*, chapter 2; *Sex and Social Justice*, chapters 8 and 10; *Hiding from Humanity*, chapters 2 and 4; and *Citadels of Pride*.

to govern the world together, I hope to stir into the discussion of Nussbaum's philosophy a more *social* understanding of freedom than she might seem to hold as a conventional liberal.

My suggestion may be counterintuitive to some readers since I translate Nussbaum's focus on wonder in the space of interpersonal life into politics and collective governance. But one can see wonder's social importance when the cognitive agency of people is in trouble. Barring strictly biological causes, the absence of wonder between people plausibly signals a loss in it being safe to consider how things could make sense between them. People have no good reason to stop wondering unless it is no longer safe to do so. Once we take that fact seriously, the idea of a relational power between people comes into view. From the given of each person's basic human need to wonder, each person's autonomy in making sense of the world and their life in it matters. This is how we might first glimpse that a relational autonomy should be at the heart of the processes that constitutes the norms between people, thereby also constituting who they take themselves to be as people in part. If people need to wonder, it seems that they need their relational autonomy supported in society. The human need to wonder leads to a view of the social as having to support relational autonomy.

But the capability to wonder also helps keep things free between people. Autonomy depends on people being free with anxiety – that is, being free to wonder – especially together when disagreements arise or narcissism might rear into view. That being so, remaining autonomous together would appear to depend on people having developed their capacity to wonder. If people are to be relationally autonomous, they need to be able to wonder. Then we should say that the capability to wonder conditions life between people for being potentially free in their relations.

Once we acknowledge that people's minds seek to make sense of things, being originally joyful in just that, so-called "power" that does not proceed by working with people's search to constitute their worlds as making sense to them then becomes problematic. It veers toward domination – a condition in which social relations make it unsafe to follow our minds and to consider things openly as social beings who share life with each other as moral equals. As I noted at the setting to this book, my understanding of domination is indebted to Philip Pettit's old account of it from the 1990s, where what he now calls "the eyeball test" is crucial for the original scene of justice. Can people look each other in the eye without having to look away due to threat?[35] A commitment to securing the

---

[35] Pettit, *Republicanism*. The eyeball test is discussed in *On the People's Terms*.

human need to wonder moves power from being over people to being *between us* as the norms that we can share must make sense between us. The human need to wonder implies that we should form power with each other in ways what make sense to all of us involved. Wonder is a way into a politics that is fundamentally opposed to controlling others, manipulating their interests, strategizing how to influence people as objects, etc. By contrast, any "power" that treats people as objects enters the realm of domination. It thus becomes anti-political.

The implications of this politics more social than liberal are striking, but they are not contrary to much of the spirit of Nussbaum's thinking. Politics governing our lives together in a way that is non-dominating must include the shared capability of opening up between us in wonder. Here would be a non-narcissistic politics, where

> ... we create our lives with one another with ... much subtlety, responsiveness, delicacy, and imagination ... bring[ing] to human beings the material conditions of this life of the spirit, and, at the same time, the spiritual and educational conditions of a loving relation to the world and to one another.[36]

2. Wondering Together

I want to explore wonder's kind of political power, a particularly social power for its complex relationship to relational freedom between people in all walks of life. In this project, I focus on relations between people. But the logic of personification – of what I call "relational reason" – is of course so powerful that relations with other forms of life can follow the analogy to interpersonal accountability to a high degree at times, at least in the projection of other species being patients of our agency and demanding accountability through the way they register our effects. In her work on other animals, Nussbaum notes this form of sociality for us and our relations beyond the species boundary.[37]

---

[36] Nussbaum, *Love's Knowledge,* 216–17. Nussbaum is discussing Henry James's social and political vision. The refined connotations of the appeal to "literary art" in the suite of this passage disappear when one recalls that one of the tests of good literature is whether it brings us close to the infinitely stronger possibilities of meaning and of sense in everyone's quotidian lives.

[37] See her *Frontiers of Justice* especially. See also Van Jaarsveld, *Towards an Environmental Ethic,* chapters 2 and 3. Shiri Pasternak, in her *Grounded Authority: The Algonquins of Barriere Lake Against the State* (Minneapolis: University of Minnesota Press, 2017), also notes the ways in which sociality can be modified to encompass relations with other species, not just regarding them.

Nussbaum's political writings are poised to help the exploration, but one has to read them despite the loudness of "liberalism" in them. Not liberty but *relationship* becomes the focus of the politics of wonder, formed around its distinct kind of power made up of our shared, cognitive agency and ability to be lost with each other. Nussbaum's lifelong interest in the literary imagination and her interest in sympathetic imagination come together to form a politics that is freely imaginative in our relations with each other. Then it becomes possible to read Nussbaum as a philosopher of political imagination with wonder at the center of social-political processes, not just as a "liberal."

My proposition is a stretch, but it is not without textual grounds. There is a moment early in Nussbaum's *Political Emotions* when it becomes clear that she is thinking about freedom in relationships as her guide to the political. From that moment, a little further argument takes us to wonder. Writing of the duet "Duettino-Sull'aria" in *The Marriage of Figaro*, Nussbaum describes a "musical partnership," a "friendly attunement," that is,

> . . . an image of mutual respect, but also a reciprocal affection that is deeper than respect. Neither [voice/person] runs roughshod over the utterance of the other, and yet each contributes something distinctive of her own, which in turn is recognized by the other and carried forward.[38]

> "A partnership based on responsiveness," Nussbaum calls it,[39] involving

> . . . a freedom of the spirit that consists precisely in not caring about hierarchy, neither seeking to avoid being controlled by others nor seeking to control them.[40]

Nussbaum goes so far as to say that with the aria, "this music has invented democratic reciprocity," the "start" of "a politics of equal respect."[41]

> You don't get the right kind of liberty . . . without . . . having this type of fraternity and this type of equality.

What kind of "liberty" is this? It is a "female" type of liberty,[42] by which Nussbaum means one devoid of the male (negative) "anxiety" over "rank" and subordination.[43] This comment should be taken to imply that "rank" is a form of hierarchy that interferes with moral equality. Note the conjunction with

[38] Nussbaum, *Political Emotions*, 36.
[39] Ibid., 37.
[40] Ibid.
[41] Ibid.
[42] Ibid., 41.
[43] Ibid., 37.

"subordination." In the world of eighteenth-century men Nussbaum considers through the presentation of the opera, male "liberty" is self-centered and negatively anxious, preoccupied narcissistically with the insecurities of a world of one-upmanship, vanity, and even domination. Against this, Nussbaum contrasts a form of freedom, available to women and men alike if brought up into it,[44] where our "intense longing ... pursu[es] in a place outside [our] ego" "a good that is outside [one]self."[45] One such male is Cherubino in Nussbaum's interpretation. The positive freedom to seek a non-egotistical good is something Nussbaum calls "love," and she notes that it is "infused with intense wonder," with wonder "driving" the search.[46] The opera delivers Nussbaum's phrase itself – *ricerco un bene fuori di me,* "to search for a good outside of me."

We should recognize the idea by now. In *Upheavals of Thought,* wonder is conceptually differentiated from the intentional consciousness of other emotional states by being "non-eudaimonistic," that is, not focused on what is good for oneself.[47] Such a "liberty" of love, if "liberty" is really the word to use here, is at the core of Nussbaum's philosophical search:

> [P]ublic culture needs to be nourished and sustained by something that lies deep in the human heart and taps its most powerful sentiments, including both passion and humor. Without these, the public culture remains wafer-thin and passionless, without the ability to motivate people to make any sacrifice of their personal self-interest for the sake of the common good.[48]

Yet oddly, though wonder appears often in *Political Emotions,* wonder's importance at the center of public culture isn't brought to the fore, even when the question is how to maintain "stability" in a just society, a question of moral psychology premised off of the instability of human relations and the dynamics of self-interestedness.[49] But it logically should be, since there's wonder in the heart of any free relationship, making them non-narcissistic or "non-pathological" in Kant's sense.[50] Neither in *Political Emotions* nor anywhere else in her extant work at the time of this writing does Nussbaum come fully around to her latent

---

[44] Ibid., 38–43.

[45] Ibid., 40.

[46] Ibid. On positive freedom as freedom to realize ends, see Isaiah Berlin, "Two Concepts of Liberty," in *Four Essays in Liberty,* by Isaiah Berlin (New York: Oxford University Press, 1990), 117–82.

[47] Nussbaum, *Upheavals of Thought,* 73. See also Schinkel, *Wonder and Education,* chapters 1 and 2.

[48] Nussbaum, *Political Emotions,* 43.

[49] Ibid., 5–10. Her question is squarely Rawlsian. But see my "The Reasonableness of Wonder" for why even Rawls should view wonder as part of the "reasonable" in the "Original Position."

[50] Immanuel Kant, *Religion within the Limits of Reason Alone,* trans. Theodore M. Greene and Hoyt H. Hudson (1793; New York: HarperOne, 2008).

insight about the centrality of wonder to free public culture. Yet her leaving open the potential of wonder invites others to develop it. As suggested both by Nussbaum and by the playful back and forth of singing together in the aria exploring the possibilities of harmony and sound, the freedom found in relationships of equal respect involves a spirit involving wonder.

Why should this be so? Let's consider further the freedom in relationships that Nussbaum seeks.[51] Relationships involving wonder tap into the core of our existences in a way that is fundamentally positive and playful. The play of the imagination in wonder and the positive excess of the sense and meaning of the world that is thus involved in wondering are freeing precisely because they lead us to become more autonomous, not alone and apart but together. As we come to work out how life can make sense between us and how the world we share can be found in common, what begins to appear is a deeply social freedom dependent on having the space to exercise our cognitive agency. This interweaving of the social, the cognitive, and autonomy shouldn't surprise us, for Nussbaum recognizes that exercising cognitive agency is a basic human need.[52] Just as sharing food brings us closer together and makes the food more significant, so does sharing meaning. Finding that we can share meaning allows our relationships to become more autonomous, not being arbitrarily imposed on us, but being what they are. Even two people who hate each other and share that meaning become more autonomous in no longer denying what is actually the substance of the relationship, namely, its very breakdown.

The *Oxford American Dictionary* links "politics" to "governance of a country" and to the aspiration to "achieve power."[53] Here, in the conventional meaning of "politics," "governance" and "power" both appear to involve power over others in such a way that there is struggle around it. The emphasis on "govern*ment*" over "governance" could also support this inference. But if the conventional meaning of the political implies a struggle for power over others – or even "status" elevated above others, as some ancillary definitions of the word imply – then what is "political" is not actually so in the sense opened up by Nussbaum's interest in freedom in relationships and the need for free relationships to involve wonder. What, however, is the "political" can be acceptable only on the basis of people

---

[51] Nussbaum, *Political Emotions*, chapter 2, section III.
[52] Nussbaum, *Upheavals of Thought*, chapter 4; *Creating Capabilities*, chapter 1; *Women and Human Development*, chapter 1.
[53] "Politics," *Oxford American Dictionary*, primary definition: "The activities associated with the governance of a country or other area, especially the debate or conflict among individuals or parties having or hoping to achieve power." Alternate definitions focus either on "government" or on "power and status"-struggle.

making sense together as moral equals. Then we ought to look for relationally autonomous forms of governance, at the least alongside – if not besides – liberal government.

One question inspired by Nussbaum's invocation of non-narcissistic orientations toward others in the duet is what a politics of autonomy that resists domination down to its roots could be. What would it be for the spirit over which Nussbaum enthuses to reach into the depths of our souls as the very music can? A scholarly distinction from a different tradition than Nussbaum's might help us see the point. We might say that with wonder as a basic human need among moral equals, the political cannot be a domain of subjection. Instead, it must be a field of "subjectivation," of becoming autonomous together as people. The French term *subjectivation* should be contrasted with *asujetissement*, being formed as a subject, or even subjugation in a broad sense. "Subjectivation" refers to practices by which people become free and maintain their freedom. By contrast, with subjugation in the broad sense, we aren't just focusing on people submitting to rule, but more broadly on the way people can be socially constituted before and against their wills. Because free relationships centrally involve wonder and wonder's spontaneity and trembling of convention, they fall on the side of subjectivation.

I came to the terminology by way of Jacques Rancière's work, himself modifying work by Foucault in his last period of the ethics of the self. Rancière's concern predates Foucault's terminology, however, and appears when he excoriated his erstwhile teacher, Louis Althusser, for his authoritarianism.[54] For Rancière, politics as "the police" in *Disagreement* is the subjection of putting everyone in their place, found in Rancière's early Vincennes lectures of the time of *Althusser's Lesson* and included in the volume translated into English.[55] In *Disagreement*, Rancière contrasts politics as "the police" with politics as an event of collective agency when it becomes possible to reorganize how we share the world, that is, with subjectivation.[56] He thereby de-individualizes subjectivation, because for him, the process can remake what we might even think of as selves, subjects, etc.

For Rancière, this process is collective, and it does not encompass the totality of people's lives. Rather, it is a way that people affiliate around a cause of social justice that challenges everyone in a society to reorganize some of the basic norms and arrangements of that society to the extent that what the common

---

[54] Jacques Rancière, *Althusser's Lesson*, trans. Emiliano Battista (1974; New York: Continuum, 2011).

[55] Ibid. That notion of politics, it seems, led Althusser to create the concept of "ideological state apparatuses"!

[56] Rancière, *Disagreement*.

world is changes its order and meaning. The movement to abolish slavery is a good example, as is the civil rights movement or for Rancière the student-led uprising against education and all things fascist in French society in 1968. My usage of the term "subjectivation," however, is not meant in this narrowly collective sense, although it could be expanded to include it. I am interested in the idea that subjectivation is a process that can belong to the self just as much as to a relationship between two or a few people, from a small group to a micro-public to a public. In this process, the norms that have been common sense are suspended because they do not make sense to those affected by or involved in them and the drive to make sense emerges in people as a soulful wonder, a moment of suspension in which people become lost alone or together and introduce a swerve into their life with inherited norms. The opening discussion in this motet (of Ahmed and Huffer) speaks to subjectivation as I understand the idea.

The reason that the term seems pertinent to me is that it is an extreme term – as many French philosophical terms have been since the time of Descartes – that in being extreme underlines how revolutionary Nussbaum's tacit politics of wonder can become in some areas of our life. The French term, odd for its association with an anglophone philosopher who has conspicuously avoided French philosophy in her writings, shows on a number of connotative levels the potential in Nussbaum's philosophy to go somewhere out of her control, so to speak, beyond what might seem conventionally evident from reading her works. To see how the politics of wonder implies a politics of subjectivation from the self to the collective shows us how soulfulness is at stake in Nussbaum's philosophy alongside and even besides liberalism. To put it bluntly, there's a *social romanticism* latent in Nussbaum's work that should be heard just as much as the high-minded liberalism that she avows. She did not grow up imagining the French Revolution for nothing.[57] This social romanticism, as I put it, implies a dynamic governance emerging out of moral relationships centered around an openness to the positive anxiety, the soulful excitement, of coming to make sense together about things of common concern such as the norms that guide our lives together.

The implications for autonomy are significant. "Subjectivation" is a reverse or counter-process against subjugation in which people search out for themselves what makes sense to them and enter into processes of living accordingly against anything that puts them in their place, and this is foremost domination. To

---

[57] In personal correspondence (January 2022), Nussbaum clarified that in high school she wrote a play in French about the Revolution that her drama club later put on. At the all-girls school, she played Robespierre. I first heard this story in the early 2000s from an interview or talk.

protect room for subjectivation in our politics is to demand *leeway* in our practices, institutions, and our lives together to swerve in the many ways that human souls do seeking to find their idiosyncratic meaning and to make personal sense in this life and world, even throwing into doubt the meaning of the world in the process.[58] Following John Haugeland, the leeway in our understanding of practices is found in the possibilities permitted within the governance conventional to the practice, i.e., the rules.[59] But I depart from Haugeland's understanding of the space of possibilities in a crucial respect to note that since in anxiety as Heidegger himself held, people exist within practices and may reject them as not making complete sense to them,[60] there is always already the possibility of finding a possibility that departs from the practice's rules. This is what subjectivation always involves, the possibility of being otherwise, found by the trembling of our practices that Rimbaud's poem first suggested impressionistically.[61]

The autonomy of subjectivation isn't a once-and-for-all state of rational self-regulation or of independence from social constructions as "autonomy" is sometimes characterized.[62] Rather, autonomy is a process involving moments of *disidentification* from convention – from how one has been socially formed – just as much as moments of sense-making that are more Kantian in their drive to find what makes sense of the world and of our lives in it. Such a process is also iterative, not absolute, turning our understanding of things over and over again as we disidentify and get lost. The politics of subjectivation is a politics of people discovering what makes sense to them out of possibilities that stretch, personalize, or contest the conventional and that transform their identities. As such, it is a politics of wonder.

What I'm suggesting at the least is that Nussbaum's location of wonder at the heart of the political appears to drive toward the conclusion that "politics" as both subjugation and convention is to be contrasted with "politics" as relational autonomy and subjectivation as found in our getting lost together in wonder. Or,

---

[58] On leeway, compare Nichols, *The World as Freedom*, 41–9, in his interpretation of section 31 from Heidegger's *Being and Time*.

[59] John Haugeland, *Dasein Disclosed: John Haugeland's Heidegger*, ed. Joseph Rouse (Cambridge, MA: Harvard University Press, 2013), "*Dasein's* Disclosedness" and "Being-in as Such." See also Nichols, *The World as Freedom*, 46, interpreting p. 145 of *Being and Time* (German pagination).

[60] Heidegger, *Being and Time*, section 40.

[61] See the Setting to this book. Cf. also Jean-Luc Nancy, *The Experience of Freedom*, trans. Bridget McDonald (Palo Alto: Stanford University Press, 2004), and, on trembling, his *The Birth to Presence*, trans. Brian Holmes et al. (Palo Alto: Stanford University Press, 1994), "Identity and Trembling."

[62] Samuel Bagg, "Beyond the Search for the Subject: An Anti-Essentialist Ontology for Liberal Democracy," *European Journal of Political Theory* (published online, 2018): 1–24.

in Nussbaum's terms from *Political Emotions*, the Rousseauian strand of public culture formed through subjugating uniformity is to be contrasted with a "Herderian" public culture emerging through the playful differentiations of active relationships, with wonder involving others at the relationships core.[63] In this way, Nussbaum's suggestive reading of Mozart's opera reveals the political as a social field of interpersonal agency and freedom in thought as we organize our lives together. At the center of it is wonder and it is oriented by making sense of our lives together, but only in the radical soulfulness suggested by both the song's reach into our depths and the swerve into uncontrol that wonder always implies – that is, only in disidentification, the trembling leeway around norms that would simply keep us in our place without the room to play and remake them. One can see how Nussbaum might lose this behind liberty and its experiments in living but it is, I think, actually more profound and social. In any event, it demands cognitive agency in ways that completely surpass the potentially private carelessness of liberalism, the lower pleasures that haunted Mill's liberalism consistently.[64] Liberals give leeway within the state, but the politics of wonder demands leeway *in our minds* for the sake of making sense of the world together, that is, of a collectively created world that is isonomic.

Now, my reading of the importance of wondering together is surely a stretch, as should be fitting for a book on this topic! Nussbaum's tendency in *Political Emotions* is to seek a public culture formed of sympathies and attachments but not explicitly of wonder-filled movement, unconventional possibilities, and the capacity to let others be themselves. She doesn't put her emphasis on wonder, giving it passing importance.[65] Yet at the same time as I've noted, she points out that there is wonder at the center of free relationships.[66] Wondering allows us to relate with each other through our differences from each other as separate and particular people, often with different histories, circumstances that have brought us together, and cultural coding that we carry or assert.[67] By contrast, sympathies are moot as to their relationship to our differences from each other. Sympathies are just as easily identifications. The result of Nussbaum's emphasis is a tendency to emphasize the emotions of likeness over (positively) anxious relating through differences. But the approach I am arguing for here is "anti-identitarian."[68]

---

[63] See *Political Emotions*, 44–9, 54–5, also my "The Reasonableness of Wonder."
[64] Mill, *On Liberty*.
[65] See Nussbaum, *Political Emotions*, 457 – the index entry for "wonder."
[66] Ibid., 88, 171, 174–7, 182, 397 (the ultimate question and point of the book).
[67] See my "The Reasonableness of Wonder."
[68] Cf. Katia Genel and Jean-Philippe Deranty, eds., *Recognition or Disagreement: A Critical Encounter on the Politics of Freedom, Equality, and Identity* (New York: Columbia University Press, 2017).

The problem goes deeper, too, because Nussbaum turns to political liberalism to produce a justification for government, not more broadly govern*ance*, that can legitimately step in to ensure the protection of liberties for when people are of different minds and ways of life.[69] Here, the protection of liberties takes the place of the soulful drive to work through and to make something together of differences relevant to sharing life with each other around matters of common concern. But both of these tendencies in Nussbaum's search for a free, related, political culture are symptoms of not forefronting what wonder reveals about the political. Relying either on sympathetic identification or governmental management of possible schisms in a polity misses the potential of centering politics in governance practices of wonder between us.[70] It seems to me, by contrast, that wonder reveals that cognitive agency, including disagreements between us where we feel free to disagree, is the path to public culture, and that positive anxiety in instability, not "stability," ought to be our guide to persistent, not "enduring," social justice. The politics of wonder would then take us to a politics of unsettling, not of settling,[71] a politics not of "my kind" but of both "why do you feel - or think – that?" and "how is another world possible for us together?"

Early in *Political Emotions*, Nussbaum explores the late-eighteenth- and early-nineteeth-century European idea that a civil religion is needed to provide the "social glue" for free people.[72] One of the disputes she visits is the dispute between the positivist rationalism of August Comte and the romanticism of John Stuart Mill concerning ritual.[73] Comte's vision of a religion of humanity is, as Nussbaum says, robotic.[74] The rituals within it are rigid and leave no leeway for "quirky, idiosyncratic [people] who might deviate from the prescribed course."[75] They are even humorless, leaving no room for the free play of wit and foolishness. Mill, by contrast, chafes at all ritual as inauthentic.

We might call the disagreement set up between Comte and Mill a disagreement about what social processes allow people to find the life between them intensely meaningful and structuring while keeping open people's freedom in those processes. One of the things that's missing from the discussions is wonder,

---

[69] Nussbaum, *Liberty of Conscience*.

[70] Thanks to Ben Mylius (personal correspondence, July 2021) for emphasizing the expression "wonder between us" that he underlined in his reading of an early draft of this book. He was perceptive. The title for this book (from 2019 to 2020) was *Between Us*.

[71] See my *Involving Anthroponomy in the Anthropocene*, chapter 2.

[72] Nussbaum, *Political Emotions*, chapter 3. I owe the expression to David Keymer.

[73] Ibid., 64–7.

[74] Ibid., 66.

[75] Ibid., 66–7.

although Nussbaum almost mentions it.[76] Nussbaum criticizes Comte this way: "Thinking of himself as complete and final, not imagining that life has surprises to offer, Comte has a hard time laughing." It seems that Comte lacks an appreciation of the ways in which human striving involves searching and wonder. Another thing that's missing is an explicit focus on domination. Yet social processes constructed around wondering are neither rigid nor arbitrary, and they have a role in surfacing from – or the least locating – domination. They are structured ways for people to keep on growing freely, coming up against the threats that keep them in place against their will. Especially in a society involving domination at pervasive points in its reproduced social order (such as policing around race or reproduced misogyny), we should look for social processes formed around wonder. At best liberating, they can at least be resistant.

When one rereads Nussbaum in the way that I am suggesting, some interesting possibilities reveal themselves. The repeated use of the word "space" to describe the world of free relationships and free minds Nussbaum seeks in *Political Emotions* is especially intriguing. Nussbaum is interested in preserving a "space" for subversion and dissent, "and that space will be a major topic throughout [the book]."[77] The book seeks to fill the "space" left open by Rawls "for a reasonable moral psychology" stabilizing justice,[78] and that moral psychology will seek to underscore relationships between people where there is "a sense of free space within which people can live and be themselves."[79] Even within reasonable minds, Nussbaum acknowledges following her reading of both Kant and John Stuart Mill, there is "an untouched free space, a funny unevenness that is both erotic and precious."[80] "Space" is used in these three instances in different senses, and yet if we add in wondering, they become remarkably linked. The "space" in the mind finds freedom in the "space" between people, and the psychology of such relationships steps into the "space" Rawls left open.[81] Some basic space of wonder seems involved in sharing the world, beginning with coming to make sense of and in it.

To get to such a point, however, we have to rethink politics by taking seriously the mind's original joy and the human need to wonder. If we really need to

---

[76] Ibid., 67.
[77] Ibid., 7.
[78] Ibid., 9.
[79] Ibid., 45.
[80] Ibid., 46.
[81] On the notion of the "space of freedom," see my *Conscience and Humanity*, dissertation submitted to the Department of Philosophy, University of Chicago (Ann Arbor: UMI, 2002), chapter III.2.2.3. There, when discussing the sense of humanity, I was indebted both to Jean-Luc Nancy's vision of freedom and to Nussbaum's and Sen's discussion over the Capability Approach.

wonder in order to be free, what are the political implications of being free and wondering together?

One thing that should shift is how we think about our conflictual relationships with each other. By looking closely at the role of wondering in bringing people to be free with each other, we can articulate a politics "preserv[ing] space for dissent and for different human experiments."[82] What wondering together does is to forefront how our conflictual differences in how we think we should live must be seen as, at the least, disagreements over the world. This shifts conflicts to questions of interpretation of the world, that is, to questions of learning how to live together here in this world in a way that makes sense to us. This shifts conflict from being primarily a battle over control to being a tangle of freedom. It moves us from the domain of narcissism to the domain of morality, wonder, and understanding.

In conflicts that are disagreements, the world becomes contested between us, and each of our worlds is questioned by the other's. If we then become accountable to each other's minds, as we must as moral equals respecting each other's cognitive agency, we must try to consider the sense inside the way we each make sense of the world, even as we disagree with it. Since the other world is disagreeable to us, not making sense, we will have to wonder over it in order to consider its possibilities and it *as* a possibility. But if we then wonder together around the disagreement, we will expand our understanding of the world and of how it can be misunderstood. Seeking to fill in the world with our newfound understanding of what is possible in another's world gained by disagreeing *and wondering*, we are positioned to change our understanding of the world, even if slightly, in a way that includes another's world. If this, then, is mutual as it should be, we come to share the world if only by including the history of our disagreement and our expanded understanding of there being many interpretations of the world – many worlds each on their own – in our society. Honestly disagreeing while holding moral accountability to others opens up worlds in this way – activating the various modalities of our world (i.e., the world, a world, my world, your world, our world, etc.), and giving us a history of worlds as we come to difficultly share our world in disagreeing over it.[83]

---

[82] Nussbaum, *Political Emotions*, 55.
[83] On worlding understood through disagreement in this manner, see my *Involving Anthroponomy in the Anthropocene*, chapter 2, and also my "Unacceptable Agency (part I of *The Problem of an Unloving World*)," where I discuss Cristina Yumie Aoki Inoue, Thais Lemos Ribeiro, and Ítalo Sant' Anna Resende, "Worlding Global Sustainability Governance," in Agni Kalfagianni, Doris Fuchs, and Anders Hayden, eds., *Routledge Handbook of Global Sustainability Governance* (New York: Routledge, 2020), 59–72.

I just focused on what happens with worlds in disagreement, but what I am intent on is what happens with relationships. One important thing that rearticulating conflicts as disagreements does is to forefront how we have a relationship by virtue of disagreement. The moral accountability that is obligatory in moral equality is preserved around the cognitive agency that joins the disagreement over the world. When people disagree, they are disagreeing about or because of something. The real disagreement shapes the relationship, setting many of its terms and conditions. These terms and conditions, however, are not a contract as when we speak of a contract's "terms and conditions." They are prior to any contract, continually negotiable, and exceed the narrow focus of a contract. They are the terms of disagreement – what we don't understand of each other's worlds in our disagreement, the meanings in and over which we disagree. They are also the conditions only in which we have a disagreement and by which we might resolve one. Within our moral accountability to each other, the terms of our disagreement set up a social relationship by serving as obstacles to it, stones jutting out of the stream of life between us, detouring the flow. We do, then, share the world in disagreeing but only, for the moment, as a world of disagreement. It is not a world either of us is comfortable with, not a world that we take to be our own. It is positively anxious in its very structure, opening up possibilities around what we had taken for granted and unsettling ourselves. And here's the thing: if we seek to make sense of things in this unsettling world, as humans with the need to wonder do, we have to seek the world *between* us where the conflict locates the perturbation of what makes sense for the things we share in common. With each disagreement between us, like ripples around a rock in moving water, multiple modalities of what could possibly be *our* world emerge.

Still, what makes sense to me may not make sense, and what makes sense to you may not make sense. What makes sense is "outside ourselves"[84] – not in the sense that it is external to human life but that it is outside the way we have made sense of our world so far. Since we anchor our freedom in what makes sense, when we disagree about what makes sense – or when it disagrees with us – we have to consider *the* world again or we fail to search for sense thoroughly and with conviction.[85] Moreover, in disagreement, we consider the world each from our *own* worlds. Then to make sense between us we have to consider *each other's*

---

[84] Recall Nussbaum, *Political Emotions*, 40 – *fuori di me*.
[85] See my "Autonomous Conceptions of our Planetary Situation," *Studia Wratislaviensia* 15:2 (2020): 29–44.

worlds as they bear on the problem of the world arising between us. If, though, we have to consider *the* world as best as we can outside ourselves and our worlds, we can do no other than relate with each other *around* the world between us. In this way, the *world* brings us together by way of disagreement. Shifting conflicts to disagreements not only habituates us to the constructions of interpreted worlds, it joins us in relationships to each other around the disagreement and ultimately grounds *our* relationship in something outside our control that we must consider as best as we can on its own terms. Like I said, conflicts become spaces of learning.

When we are honest with ourselves and with each other, we should find that we often disagree.[86] Honesty is interesting. It is an expression close to wonder that isn't wondering yet should readily lead to it. When we are honest, we are open about what we think, even refusing to be closed. When honesty moves through resistance to become open, it appears to tremble the sense of things that have been closed off from consideration, introducing possibilities to consider. Honesty would appear at times to act as positive anxiety with regard to considering things. Then honesty draws on wonder and leads to it.

These ideas about wondering aren't found in the wonderful duet Nussbaum so loved from *The Marriage of Figaro*, perhaps because it is not a duet of disagreement. But through honest disagreement, we get outside of ourselves to consider what makes sense to others, become lost together, and in this very lostness find that we share the world at least through the process of trying to make sense of the world and our lives in it. Honest disagreement is important to isonomic politics. This is something that the politics of wonder shows. To be honest is to be open that something is such and so. Honesty is a way of getting outside ourselves, of being not about ourselves. In saying "I" – "I think this" – the "I" and the "me" separate. I don't focus on myself but on what I have to say. Honesty is, formally speaking, not about me. Its formal expression is "not-me," but rather *this thing that I have to say in being open*. In honesty, what we really think, feel, or intend is our focus between each other interpersonally or with ourselves intrapersonally. In such a simple way, in honesty, the truth sets us free by bringing us into focus with what we actually think, how we actually feel, what we actually are doing insofar as we can tell. What I show may not be convenient for me, but it is what and how it is. I have to let go of constraining what I think

---

[86] Compare Larmore *The Morals of Modernity*, chapter 7.

makes sense to acknowledge what actually does, of controlling how I feel to instead see how I do feel, and of fooling myself or others about what I actually intend to be forthright about what I do intend. Like wondering, honesty leads me beyond narcissistic control, and so, with honest disagreement, one doesn't need "social glue" (e.g., sympathy) the way that Nussbaum's project in *Political Emotions* gets framed. The tension within Nussbaum's writing on and around freedom leads beyond liberty and sympathy to being honest with each other in times of conflict about what our disagreements really are and to wondering in the spaces of and beyond our disagreements. The space opened up between us when we are honest and wonder, or wonder and are honest, is a space given to disagreement but *in moral and educational relationship.* Being accountable to each other, we "lead each other out," and what makes sense comes to guide – or "steer" – us.[87]

Wondering together in honest disagreement, the space between us is both a space of "protest" testifying before each other about what we think ought to be considered, and it is a space of learning.[88] Such a politics is grounded in honestly being lost together. To say that it is so "grounded" is not to say that there is a complete and total justification that serves as our ground, as may seem the case when focusing on deliberation in ideal political theory.[89] Rather, it is to say that what makes our relationship justifiable even in conflict is our searching together – the process of wondering, not some rational content. This could be a way to reinterpret Kierkegaard's pseudonymous claim that "truth is subjectivity" – i.e., the search to make sense is "the Truth."[90] Ironically, this search to make sense of the world out of our disagreement together grounds us precisely by loosening the hold of our separate worlds. This is something that is subtly revolutionary about getting lost together.

---

[87] "Educate," "govern," *Oxford American Dictionary*, where the Latin roots imply that to lead someone out is to educate them, and to steer them is to govern them.

[88] Contrast this with the "protest" of strategic manipulation of others as I discuss in "The Neoliberal Radicals." Also see my "Reconsidering the Aesthetics of Protest" and "How to Do Things without Words: Silence as the Power of Accountability," *Public Seminar* (June 28th, 2018).

[89] Samuel Bagg, "Can Deliberation Neutralise Power?" *European Journal of Political Theory* 17:3 (2018): 257–79.

[90] See Søren Kierkegaard, *Concluding Unscientific Postscript to* Philosophical Fragments, trans. Howard V. Hong and Edna H. Hong (1846; Princeton: Princeton University Press, 1992).

3. Social Power

Almost two decades ago in a small apartment at night
in University City, Sharjah, UAE:
Windy & Carl's "Balance (Trembling)," 2000

Let us say that governance is the process of guiding the way we live in the world together and let us situate governance in a society pressured by the premise of moral equality. Then only the politics of wonder can loosen the hold of identity on us and generate free relations while being structured by accountability to each other. The word "guidance" may seem strange in the context of the political. Guidance is the inner idea of governance, which derives from a long line of Old French, Latin and Greek words meaning to steer things.[91] Steering, however, is guidance, and the guidance involves everyone and everything in and affected by a given society. Those "with" or "beyond"; "inside" or "outside"; "to be let be," "to be protected," or "to be ignored" within the society – everyone and everything affected by the society – are part of the logic of guidance, for it is concerned with the organization of society as a whole. The guidance shows and presumes what is supposed to make sense for that society. Of it, we might ask, was the "steering" arrived at through searching? Does it make sense? Is it open to people being involved in finding sense and guiding the society together?

Even coercion is a particular species of guidance. For instance, when people are to be left alone and how to handle situations where people fail to share life respectfully are part of the logic of guidance. What is done or omitted, conceived, misunderstood, or avoided in the organization of life for the society as a tenuous whole (with its "wholeness" also part of its scheme of guidance) pertains to the society's guidance, to its order of what is supposed to be sensible. Moreover, its guidance affects people together insofar as some rule and others are ruled – begrudging, subversive, or not – while still others have to bear the brunt of the society's ways of life. The realm of governing depends on tacit acceptance of norms and lays out much of the parameters of subterfuge in reaction to them, as when a classroom with rigid rows of seats lays out the subversive reaction of trying to pass notes between them.

When things that are supposed to make sense between people in the guidance of common life no longer do make sense to those involved, governance comes

---

[91] "Govern," *Oxford American Dictionary.* See also my "Unacceptable Agency (Part I of *The Problem of an Unloving World*)."

into difficulty, even crisis. Questions of governance then raise questions of guidance. Both the subjection that those who are excluded from governing together come to recognize and the subjection that is hidden beneath conformity to what is supposed to make sense but which has somehow become senseless begin to tremble. Is a world other than this senseless one possible? Surfacing such lostness is important for surfacing crises of governance without which we cannot have autonomous societies. Interestingly, the matter of finding subjection hidden within the supposedly acceptable order of what a society holds to make sense is an issue Nussbaum considers in her capability approach especially under the matter of "adaptive preferences."[92] Becoming lost is important for surfacing adaptive preference. As the tradition of "power-in" developed especially by Foucault emphasizes, simply giving people the space to make sense together does not translate to freedom, for the norms of discourse and the positions of people in social hierarchies and networks can simply speak through people as what they apparently avow.[93]

There is no way to start from a blank slate here in a crisis that is always part historical. Rather, the question is one of orientation. What becoming lost does is to bring out the search for sense, opening up a soulful and unsettling process wherein we begin to have space on what is supposed to make sense and is taken as authoritative. Foucault called this space a "critical attitude," and it was important for "subjectivation."[94] The process is something present that we can have the responsibility to undergo by accepting our anxiety and maintaining moral accountability, but it is not historically abstract. Because history is involved, to come to terms with what eventually does make sense while introducing a trembling inside what is supposed to make sense demands a robust genealogical approach to the world in which we are lost, and for this one still needs space on norms as one assembles a genealogy of normativity in the present.[95] That is, one needs to wonder about them, even to the point of suspending the seeming necessity of what one calls the "world" so that its sense and meaning appear strange and possibly contingent.[96] The strangeness of the world we have inherited is a mark of what Schinkel calls "deep" or "contemplative" wonder.[97]

[92] See Nussbaum, *Women and Human Development*, chapter 2 especially.
[93] See Bagg, "Beyond the Search for the Subject" and Oxley, "Feminist Perspectives on Power, Domination, and Exploitation" on constitutive power. Cf. Berlant, *Cruel Optimism*.
[94] See Foucault, "What Is Critique?"
[95] Nichols, *The World of Freedom*, and Shahid, "Genealogies of Philosophy: Lynne Huffer (part II)."
[96] Huffer accepts this. See *Foucault's Strange Eros* and Shahid, ""Genealogies of Philosophy: Lynne Huffer (part I)."
[97] Schinkel, *Wonder and Education*, chapters 1–2. Cf. Heidegger, *Being and Time*, section 40.

Crisis in governance is important for society and essential for our political autonomy, but what must guide it is a truly social power that is structured around emergent learning of how to make sense of the world together. It's this notion of what I consider *emergent social governance* that I want to consider in the last half of this motet. Especially in protest and during times of disagreement, the moment of becoming lost together troubles common sense and raises doubt about whether we can share the world in our society. But at the same time, it does raise the possibility of sharing our society in terms we can all accept. By unsettling both common sense and society, becoming lost together renews the expectations we bring to society so that it could make sense between us. Becoming lost together turns things over and over, and in so doing it opens up a space for us to seek what could make sense. The sense and meaning of things become unstuck, in motion. How can we guide our lives together?

Here, the process of governance emerges between us as *emergent learning*. The term comes from early childhood education and curriculum design. It refers to learning that emerges through dialogical challenge.[98] Since becoming lost together is a crisis of collective guidance seeking orientation through what comes to make sense across contestation and wondering, we must be open to learning something together about how to share the world. The moment is crucial for dispersing governance between us. While it isn't enough all on its own to disperse power, it is needed, since without collective soul-searching we risk continuing normalized subjugations.

What can we learn of social power by focusing on emergent learning? I want to begin with a plain example that doesn't concern a crisis in governance yet solidly shows what emergent learning is within the conventional space of schooling. We will see that a form of collective governance appears through it by following how those involved get lost together in wondering about what they are learning. The matter at hand takes over and guides them to the world that their minds want to share in the play of their imaginations and the leeway of their questioning. I am thinking here of an early childhood educational program in Chicago that was woven into a set of municipal family centers in the 1990s and early 2000s. These centers exist to this day, although I will be speaking of the time in which they were documented and analyzed in a landmark study. The study was the first in the world to show how "Reggio principles" work well in

---

[98] See Scheinfeld et al., *We Are All Explorers*, chapters 2–5 especially. Chapters 2–4 present the building blocks of chapter 5's "emergent curriculum": "Listening, Observing, Reflecting, and Responding," "Co-constructions of Understandings with Children," and "Children's Representations."

low-income communities dealing with structural racism from colonial history.[99] The Chicago Commons Family Center Head Start programs for young children were inspired by the municipal school system of Reggio Emilia, Italy, itself a public educational response of "Never again!" to the crisis of governance that was Italian fascism. Since "Reggio principles" are ideas and there is no institutionalized dissemination of them (such as there has been with Montessori or Waldorf schooling), and this is deliberate, the Chicago Commons *and their neighborhood communities* created their own version of the approach that drew inspiration from the municipal pre-school system in northern Italy.

There are many moving parts to what made the Chicago Commons Family Centers work as community schools, and a great many of them were unconventional in the context of American society. Perhaps the most important, however, was the use of what is called "emergent curriculum."[100] In the context of the rich aesthetic and communal environment of the schools, emergent curriculum was the single most powerful and clear way in which wondering became the dynamic core of a well-articulated, social process that both drew on and cultivated collective guidance of shared life through what makes sense to people. It is worth considering it as a social process in which disagreement and wonder about the world were intimately joined in a way that expresses freedom in relationships.

The core idea of emergent curriculum is that what we learn should not be planned in advance but should unfold from our interests, challenged to grapple with the world.[101] In the emergent curriculum chapter, Scheinfeld et al. emphasize the process of listening to children's interests and building learning plans from them, including hypotheses to be collectively considered. The role of challenges through dialogue is underemphasized. Yet chapter 2's section on listening for underlying interests makes it clear that a form of active interpretation considering children's expressions critically is taking place on the part of adults.[102] Chapter 3's emphasis on the ways adults can "facilitate thoughtful dialogue with and among students" further shows the ways in which the education of students by adults involves challenges, perspectives we might reconsider and so on.[103] To call this "disagreement" may seem puzzling, but disagreement needn't be angry. In

[99] Ibid.
[100] Ibid., chapter 5.
[101] Ibid., 59ff.
[102] Ibid., 22ff.
[103] Ibid., 27ff.

the Reggio Emilia municipal school systems, challenge is a much more explicitly discussed part of dialogue.[104]

The surrounding ethos of the classroom becomes honest inquiry, curiosity, and even searching. I saw this firsthand, and I know it to be true by the study. What's called the "image of the child" in the school system was of a human striving to become part of the world of sense and meaning. That made it conducive to locating wonder at the heart of education. Children were presumed to have agency and intentionality. In these classrooms where the design was meant to accept children's agency and where an emergent curriculum was the learning process, children displayed interest in many, idiosyncratic things. They were not like Auguste Comte's robots, but like the quirky people Nussbaum thinks a culture of freedom brings out and respects.[105] Emergent curriculum became the social process by which children unfolded in their grasp of sense and meaning while becoming accustomed to searching. They did so together, side by side. Their autonomy was formed in relationships with each other as they learned, and their direction and needs guided the direction that the school took throughout the year, even the form its environment took as the *children* helped co-construct it.[106]

The Dinosaur Study, 1998–99

One good example of emergent curriculum became known as "the Dinosaur Study."[107] Teachers at one family center were working with the kids as they explored monsters. Some children had been afraid of them, and so the teachers began a sympathetically imaginative exploration of how monsters live, feel, dwell, and so on. This led to the 3- to 5-year-old children drawing various kinds of monster faces up close, dressing up as monsters, and speaking as monsters into tape recorders. An entire ecology of monsters unfolded.[108]

The teachers – who regularly went around the classroom listening into children's conversation and noting them down – began to hear mention of "dinosaurs." Children were fascinated by the long foot of Godzilla – the monster

---

[104] See Carolyn Edwards, Lella Gandini, and George Forman, eds., *The Hundred Languages of Children: The Reggio Emilia Approach to Early Childhood Education,* 3rd ed. (Santa Barbara: Praeger Publishing, 2011).

[105] Nussbaum, *Political Emotions,* 64–7.

[106] Scheinfeld et al., *We Are All Explorers,* chapter 6, "The Learning Environment."

[107] Scheinfeld et al., *We Are All Explorers,* 65–9.

[108] Some of these details are not included in *We Are All Explorers.* I was a research assistant on the project and so saw more of the picture than could be included in the book.

dinosaur modeled after a Tyrannosaurus Rex – that stretched along Chicago busses that year. The sign showed the foot and read, "HIS FOOT IS AS LONG AS THIS BUS!" The sign belonged to the advertising campaign for the film *Godzilla*.[109] Noting all this, the teachers challenged the children to learn about Godzilla and then, when the kids became excited about dinosaurs, to learn about dinosaurs generally.

What followed was an in-depth study of dinosaurs. Children learned about many different kinds of dinosaurs, how they looked, how big they were, where they lived, what they ate, and how they interacted. They even learned their Latin names. After several weeks of study, the class journeyed to the Field Museum of Natural History to study dinosaur skeletons, 4- and 5-year-olds carrying clipboards with drawing paper on them which they used to depict the actual remains of pre-fifth-extinction life. The study ended with teachers challenging children to recreate the dinosaurs they'd seen at the museum, but this time *inside the classroom*, attempting to capture the immensity of them. Using light projectors, the kids' drawings from the museum were projected onto walls on which were hung floor-to-ceiling pages of white paper. Children then outlined these drawings on the paper with the help of their teachers. One night, the massive drawings were cut out around the lines and backed with cardboard by the teachers so that they could be positioned around the school as interactive beings when children returned to school the next day. Surprised and overjoyed when they entered the building, the children finished the dinosaur study with a sense of wonder at the virtual presence of these ancient creatures among them, no longer monsters in the least.

The story of the Dinosaur Study gives us an example of how emergent curriculum can evolve and serves as an allegory for how negative anxieties and fears can become – through the positive anxiety of wonder formed around challenges to our sense of the world – genuine relationships with each other and to the world. An emergent, structured process of wondering kept open what was wonderful about the sense and meaning of the world's strange and unexpected life.[110] The children began with fears about monsters. They ended with a sense of how living beings strive in their ecologies within an ancient order of life bound up in the geological history of life before the last mass extinction.[111] Along the way, they were challenged to come to terms with aspects of the lives they had

[109] Roland Emmerich, dir. *Godzilla* (Culver City, CA: Tri-Star Pictures, 1998).
[110] Cf. my "The Other Species Capability & the Power of Wonder" and "The Reasonableness of Wonder."
[111] See Schinkel, *Wonder and Education*, chapter 1 for a relatable example of wonder and paleontology.

studied that they hadn't considered. They discussed dinosaurs and disagreed with each other. They had to pull together a world – the world of the dinosaurs – across fragmentary evidence, insights, and perspectives. They wanted to do so, because they were taken by the surprising possibilities of the new forms of life that appeared before them. Coming to approach their fearful fantasies as parts of a world where all life strives to flourish in its own dynamic ways changed those fears to wonders. By working on their fears together, they began to make sense of the world together and to experience some degree of collective autonomy.

I want to just say this simply but with as much soul as I can. The Chicago Common (community-staffed!) Family Centers in the early 2000s were models of institutions that incorporated wonder and fostered it through the entire educational environment of their schools and programs. In them, emergent learning and emergent guidance were joined together. They are to this day the single most wondrous educational system that I have ever seen in the world.

But what can they show us about wonder in politics? By seeing our fears of the world as sources of learning and by coming to terms with the unknown world we share little by little over time in a long process, we can take things between us and move them outside us so that they are not about you or me. Provided that we are honest and sincerely try to understand how we have gotten where we are and how the world we share has come to be such that we are both lost in searching our way through it, we can become open to possibilities for how we might be in the world separately and together that we hadn't anticipated. We can learn that the world and ourselves are more complex and stranger than we had thought.

Then what makes sense in the world is not something right by me and wrong by you. It is something articulated and complex that joins us in it. What we come to find makes sense of our world resituates us in it and so makes our disagreements part of the complex story of how we live here. Such a synthetic accomplishment cannot happen without being honest with each other and with ourselves, and certainly not if we aren't accountable to each other as beings who search for sense and meaning, in this way being equally intelligent.[112] We have to respect that, while we strive to make sense out of life, we are free in the world we co-inhabit only together. Guiding our lives together through wonder is intensely liberating, because its possibilities of the world appear according to what comes to make better sense, and because they appear only between us. The world is not me or you. It makes sense to us.

---

[112] Cf. Jacques Rancière, *The Ignorant Schoolmaster: Five Lessons in Intellectual Emancipation*, trans. Kristin Ross (1987; Palo Alto: Stanford University Press, 1991).

The classrooms of the Chicago Commons schools were a good guide for how to become lost together. However, imagining the Chicago Commons schools as a guide to politics seems to rest on a weak analogy. But if we were to see the things that we bear witness to between us – the things that we think must be considered lest we lose track of what makes moral sense in this life – as challenges to guide our learning to find sense in this life together, emergently, then your being lost in the senselessness of a society that must be protested would become my being lost in trying to understand you and the cause you protest. With some honesty and some wonder, we could fill in the world together by working through our fears and our lostness together on the basis of our cognitive agency. *The social form of power in the Chicago Commons schools, grounded in cognitive agency, is the promising part of the analogy.* Even exercising our cognitive agency to remain as autonomous as we can be together in the face of overwhelming structural injustices is potent for giving people some faith in social and moral progress.[113]

At the same time, the family centers were relatively harmonious in that parents came to trust their children to them, and the professional staff were devoted to making the schools a safe and wondrous place deserving of the trust placed in them. But the disagreements that transform conflicts into matters of cognitive agency aren't such harmonious affairs. I have been characterizing them as potentially world-shaking moments of dissensus. This raises questions that challenge my allusion to the Reggio-inspired schools: How can emergent learning be constructed in social processes of protest and in the conditions of deep unsettling dissensus in our world? How can emergent learning be found in scenes of domination where we rise up against our collective insecurity? Is there a category of social processes constructed *for wondering* that are built around collective guidance of shared life and that come against domination in our systems? We could call such processes *conflictually emergent governance processes* – signaling the opposition to domination that autonomy necessarily implies. They might help us imagine what a politics of wonder could be.

A possibility comes from "social practice art."[114] Now social practice art is often limited by its institutional framing in a contemporary art economy.[115] The

---

[113] Susan Hawthorne, "Philosophers Fight Climate Change: Jeremy Bendik-Keymer," *Engaged Philosophy*, July 21st, 2021; and Philip Kitcher, *Moral Progress* (New York: Oxford University Press, 2021).

[114] Scholette, Bass, and Social Practice Queens, *Art as Social Action*. Cf. Wolterstorff, *Art Rethought*, for a different understanding.

[115] My and Misty Morrison's "Trauma-feeding," *Cleveland Review of Books*, September 16th, 2019, and Claire Bishop, *Artificial Hells: Participatory Art and the Politics of Spectatorship* (Brooklyn: Verso, 2012).

art form easily becomes a mere gesture rather than a transformative process of learning to share norms anew and to reject ones that no longer make sense.[116] But the ideas it uses are not constrained by galleries, museums, or funding applications. They can in principle be extended beyond the frame of the so-called "art" institution and used to imagine shared governance. That's what I'd like us to do now as an addendum to the Chicago Commons example.

Social practice art intervenes in common social practices or constructs new ones so as to lead people to reconsider the sense of these practices, the sense of the world, and the sense of themselves.[117] Social practice art solicits the involvement of people in the reconsideration of the practices in question and in the consideration of what the constructed practices of the art bring about. What emerges through the process of participating in social practice art is that the norms we share become open to decision. In many ways, the art form is mainly about the norms we share and about what it is to share norms in common life, often tacitly embedded in practices we take for granted. In other words, social practice art uses power-with to dislodge and question power-in.[118]

Social practice art both stimulates and depends on honesty. By confronting participants with a strangely constructed practice or by intervening in practices in such a way as to make what seemed normal become strange, social practice art challenges people to open up about how they relate to the practices in question and to whatever the practices concern and involve. Often, practices of self-reflection, intentionally open communication, and imagining how practices could be otherwise are part of the rituals involved in the artwork. Social practice art projects thus involve multiple modes of reflection – not only self-reflection, but communal or group reflection, and the concrete experiences of doing things otherwise. In these modes of reflection and displacement – from journaling and letter writing to difficult discussions, dinners, and experimental performances done by ordinary participants – people are encouraged by the practices to renegotiate their understanding of norms and to become both more critical of them and autonomous within them. Social practice art projects thus tend to be communicative projects joined with room for self-determination as an explicit concern. This is how the work on "power-in" involves "power-with" – mainly through communicating around the experience and imagination of how the world could make better sense.

---

[116] See my "Beyond Gestures in Socially Engaged Art: Community Processing and *A Color Removed*," *Public Seminar* (September 6th, 2018).

[117] See, for instance, Chloë Bass, *The Book of Everyday Instruction* (Brooklyn: The Operating System, 2018).

[118] Cf. Bagg, "Beyond the Search for a Subject."

A Color Removed, 2013–18

Since social practice art projects tend to be situated at points of normative difficulty in the world,[119] working through an example from social practice art can help in thinking about emergent governance. From 2013 through 2018, I was part of a socially engaged art project that was, at its heart, a work of social practice art. The work was, ultimately, flawed due to the failure of moral accountability of its main artist and by the status maneuvering of its artistic director in the context of a brand-new urban triennial explicitly created to rebrand my city for seed investment and gentrification.[120] But the project's process was promising. Its concerns were vital and prescient, dreamlike, but ultimately garbled by the conflicted selfishness at the heart of the art economy.

The social process in question began before the project in 2010, when I began setting up a biennial public lecture series at my university as part of my professorship in ethics. The first speaker gave a lecture on the power of conscience and questioned how a university could contribute to social conscience, including beyond its classroom walls.[121] Reflection on the first lecture led to inviting the next speaker to give a talk on working through historical crime in the United States of America by learning from what Germany had done as a state to work through its Nazi past.[122] Decolonization was in this way in the air. How could the university work to contribute to the social conscience of a society, the institutions and practices of which maintain the injustices of a colonial history?

To respond to this question raised in 2013, I invited a socially engaged artist to change the norms of the next lecture slated for 2015 and to continue the process of engaging with the past critically. The artist was fascinated by a discussion group organized through the professorship called "The Ethics Table" that met biweekly at the university, acting as a sort of externalized conscience within the community where people's moral and political concerns could be aired freely. Without a preset curriculum or speaker series and using a rough form of emergent curriculum as developed within the Chicago Commons Reggio Emilia family centers, the Ethics Table gathered in the Cleveland Room of the student center on Case Western Reserve University in Cleveland, Ohio, to

---

[119] For several examples, see my "Democracy as Relationship," *e-Flux Conversations* (April 30th, 2017).
[120] See my and Morrison's "Trauma Feeding."
[121] Simon Critchley, "The Powerless Power of the Call of Conscience," *Beamer-Schneider Lecture in Ethics, Morals, & Civics*, Case Western Reserve University, April 12th, 2011.
[122] Susan Neiman, "Learning from the Germans: Tarantino, Spielberg, and American Crimes," *Beamer-Schneider Lecture in Ethics, Morals, & Civics*, Case Western Reserve University, April 11th, 2013. This lecture became the start of her book project, *Learning from the Germans: Race and the Memory of Evil* (New York: Farrar, Straus & Giroux, 2019).

discuss any issues of moral or civic concern that participants wanted to work through or to consider. The Ethics Table was open to the community and included students, staff, faculty, and community members from outside the university from retirees to a janitor, a lab technician, a doctor, and a nurse at the University Hospital across the street.

In August 2014, Michael Brown was shot and killed by the police in Ferguson, Missouri.[123] Civil outrage ensued over the lethal injustice of the police perpetuating a pattern of oppression against the descendants of people subjugated by slave owners and institutions and practices of slave ownership as chattel slaves. When school began again in September, the Ethics Table began talking about the militarization of the police, structural racism, and related matters that fall broadly under the postcolonial work of confronting the ongoing inertia of the once institutions of slavery in the United States of America. These discussions occurred throughout the Fall of 2014 when two further injustices beset Cleveland, both ultimately failures of law in the deepest way. The first is that former Cleveland police officer Michael Brelo, the main shooter of the 137 police shots fired to kill Timothy Russell and Malissa Williams in East Cleveland, began a trial that ended in his acquittal.[124] The second is that on November 22nd, former Cleveland police officer Timothy Loehmann recklessly killed 12-year-old Tamir Rice who was playing with a toy gun at the Cuddell Common Recreation Center playground.[125] One of Tamir Rice's cousins, R., who worked across the street, was a participant in the Ethics Table.

At a meeting of the Ethics Table, R. broke down in grief. Tamir Rice was to be interred that week. When the artist heard of the meeting, he was moved and came up with the central idea of the social process art project that would be called "A Color Removed."[126] Responding to the police's initial claim that Tamir Rice was killed because the orange safety tip had been removed from the toy rifle he had been handed by a playmate, the artist challenged everyone who cared about social justice in the city of Cleveland to remove the color orange from their lives and deposit it in a central area where an evolving, community-driven space of outrage, mourning, and healing would accumulate like orange stacks of bags of dates (*tameer* in Arabic, pronounced like "Tamir") that the artist (who is

---

[123] Larry Buchanan et al., "What Happened in Ferguson?" *The New York Times*, August 10th, 2015.

[124] Patrick Cooley, "Everything You Need to Know about the Michael Brelo Verdict," *The Cleveland Plain Dealer / Cleveland.com*, May 23rd, 2015.

[125] Tom McCarthy, "Tamir Rice: video shows boy, 12, shot 'seconds' after police confronted child," *The Guardian*, November 26th, 2014.

[126] I discuss the art project from this point on in "Beyond Gestures in Socially Engaged Art."

Arab on his mother's side) had once seen in Dubai sending off an aura on the
walls of a storage hanger. The artist's maternal lineage is Iraqi and Jewish. Many
of his artworks refer to or use dates in them, such as his community-based
dinners made from maternal recipes involving dates, the syrup of which the
Iraqi Jewish community used in place of honey for holy rituals. He was making
a link between his past, the sacred fruit for Iraqi Jews during Passover, the name
"Tamir," and postcolonial violence on a global scale. The artist proposed this
project as a form of resistance to the norms of our society that deny everyone the
equal right to safety. That was what his lecture in the spring of 2015 was about: it
was a project proposal.[127]

Out of respect for the family of Tamir Rice that was dealing with bringing
charges against Timothy Loehmann, the project was put on hold for a year.[128]
When the newly branded Cleveland Triennial – oddly called *Front* – began to
seed-fund local arts organizations, a contemporary art gallery's director became
eager to take over the project. The irony of calling a neoliberal branding exercise
Front seems to have been lost on its creators. *Front* was a front for capital, an
afront to serious artistic motives, and a front – like a storefront – to the city.
There were several layers of irony.[129]

The project then began making its way toward the summer of 2018 when it
occupied the gallery of the local arts organization for the summer. Sadly, along
the way, the artist didn't fulfil his obligations in a timely manner and neglected
to come to Cleveland to do much research. When he came, he tended to insert
himself into the spotlight. The project gained speed only at the end when the
Rice family became involved after much handwringing by myself and the gallery
owner about the project going on without them. With a fore-gallery staging the
work exclusively of Black artists from Cleveland and the participation of Tamir
Rice's mother, Samaria Rice, the project came to fruition as a collection of

[127] Michael Rakowitz, "A Color Removed," Case Western Reserve University, April 7th, 2015. See also
Chloë Bass, "An Artist Embarks on an Impossible Project for Tamir Rice," *Hyperallergic*, April 20th,
2015.
[128] In her article "An Artist Honors Tamir Rice, One Orange Object at a Time," *The New York Times*, July
29th, 2018, Jillian Steinhauer claims that the project went dormant and was "revived" by the gallery
to which it was handed over. But this is a falsehood since the project continued with organizing
during the intermediate time and was deliberately withheld as a form of solidarity so as not to
become a vain distraction without the Rice family's guidance. Steinhauer knew this but chose to
present a narrative that spotlighted the gallery, thereby erasing some of the community work behind
the project. This was immoral, bad journalism, and aesthetically compromised from the standpoint
of the goals and form of the art project, something that was to be ongoing and community-based,
not primarily art-institutionalized.
[129] Front International, "Read More: First Edition of FRONT Generates over $31 Million in Economic
Impact," *frontart.org*, December 17th, 2018.

community-gathered orange objects in the gallery space within which various teach-ins and discussions were held.

A troubling amount of these gatherings were facades, thereby throwing into doubt the sincere efforts of many participants. When the project opened, it was staged with objects that seemed unlikely to have been donated randomly. This may have been the result of the artist's delay in getting the donation bins up and running and the need for a staged presence. Many of the events were also staged in a way that limited discussion or, even worse, were exclusive. Particularly fake was the dinner composed of equal parts Black and white participants that was closed to the public. It became a photo opportunity and actually an exhibit for the front cover of the arts organization's annual report. Events in the report described as "community driven" were not. They tended to involve panelists talking at audience members.[130]

Both the problems of the project and its potentials are instructive for the possibility of making *a social process that brings people to become honest and wonder about the norms that structure even the worst and most recalcitrant of historical injustices* such as colonialism and ongoing structural racism conducted through police brutality and the reckless killing, including murder, of Black people. The project's explicit intent was wonderful. It wanted to make the everyday look of the city strange by removing a much-loved color from it and repurposing that color for the sake of protests carried out one by one by people from out of their daily lives, like a slow-moving ritual of condemnation of injustice and love for the innocent child killed during the Cleveland Police Department's history of brutality and neglect. For example, the Cleveland Browns football team's colors are orange and brown. One suggestion, by Cleveland artist Elaine Hullihen, was to repurpose the Browns' stadium with its almost 68,000 orange seats as a repository for the protest. Basketballs are also typically orange, and Cleveland is a city that held dear the 2016 NBA World Champions, the Cleveland Cavaliers. That color removed would in turn raise questions about who has safety in the United States of America and draw attention to the precarity of Black people in the American police state.

By making the space of protest also a space of mourning and healing, the project intended to speak to the registers of sense and meaning that go beneath abstract rationalizations. It tried to get real with people as soulful, beings who strive for sense all the way down to their depths. Finally, by seeking discussions

---

[130] See SPACES Gallery, "SPACES Is 40 and Fabulous: 2018 Annual Report," SPACES Gallery, 2018; and my "Beyond Gestures in Socially Engaged Art."

of how society should be organized, the project sought to generate momentum for reflective, social change – linking community realizations about how the world could make sense otherwise to proposals for social justice and reformed policing, urban planning, education, and public health.[131] In short, the social process of "A Color Removed" sought to open up people's social and political possibilities. That is, it strove to make people wonder in and about a society still structured by racial domination institutionalized through property and policing regimes of collective insecurity.[132]

Disagreement was central to the social process's aspirations, too. During the buildup to the project, it interacted and drew on the community-based spinoff of the Ethics Table named The Moral Inquiries. Comprised of around two hundred community members, that group was a safe space for complicated disagreements that met biweekly over four and a half years. In that space, compassion was joined with critical thinking, the adversarial nature of the latter dissolved by the notion that the disagreement was held between people who were in a relationship of moral accountability, solidarity, and civic trust.[133] "A Color Removed" aspired to be like the Ethics Table and the Moral Inquiries, even including in its gallery installation space for a table – like the table found in the Cleveland Room from whence the project originated in fall 2014.

In the Moral Inquiries, especially, the core way by which disagreement opened up people's sense of what is socially possible was through bringing people together to realize that everyone has a different take on the world. Often, we live in different worlds, but the disagreement makes us realize that we both have to be accountable to each other and to the world. That makes one think, even wonder. Were such disagreement to be joined with the luminous, monochrome environment of "A Color Removed" and allied with the intention to confront a wrong so deep it shows that core aspects of our society's basic structure is just plain wrong, it would take on new depths, foremost by stirring people's imagination and the soulful dimensions of our searching for sense in this life.[134] In Fyodor Dostoevsky's "The Grand Inquisitor," the killing of one child is said to make all of existence questionable, rendering its Creator a moral monster.[135]

---

[131] Some of what it would have taken to realize this intent is discussed in my and Morrison's "Trauma-feeding."

[132] Cf. Táíwò, "Who Gets to Feel Secure?"; Hartman, *Wayward Lives*; and Whyte, "Settler Colonialism, Ecology, & Environmental Justice."

[133] See my "Beyond Gestures in Socially Engaged Art."

[134] On basic structure, cf. Rawls, *A Theory of Justice*.

[135] Fyodor Dostoevsky's "The Grand Inquisitor," *The Brothers Karamazov*, trans. Richard Pevear and Larissa Volokhonsky (1879; New York: Farrar, Straus & Giroux, 2002). We discussed this story in the Moral Inquiries.

Around that challenge, disagreement – held in a considerate relationship between us surfacing sense – would lead us to try to guide our lives together in ways that could recognizably make sense to us. That is how the project succeeded at times in developing community-based governance. In its call for people to actually break property laws when, e.g., taking orange safety cones from the road, and in its focus on direct action, albeit in an aestheticized form, the project aimed to rework governance. The art-institutional, neoliberal framing of the project and the various personal and professional vices of the artistic director and artist, however, hampered this intent.

Perhaps the simplest mistake by both the artist and the arts institution was to distrust the slow and emerging work of community discussion. The artist didn't put the time in getting to know Cleveland, and the arts director micromanaged everything, since the gallery had staked everything during the triennial on the project's installation and, ironically, spectacle.[136] At the same time that both individuals acted in ways that were either self-absorbed or overcontrolling, they made the collective work about them – images of an art star, staged meetings of an up-and-coming arts organization. Narcissism predominated. But if everyone involved had made the work so that it were not about themselves – if their mantra had been "Not about me!" or *ricerco un bene fuori di me* ("to search for a good outside of me") – they would have been able to engage honestly in the emerging process – and let it go where it made most sense.

Nonetheless, the failures clarified several conditions needed for conflictual emergent governance grounded in wonder to work:

(1) Ways to open up people's relationship to sense-making and meaning-finding,
(2) Ways to let the process go where people collectively think that it should go,
(3) Ways to center the process in what is communal, not in what is egotistical, and
(4) Ways for people to disagree with their whole hearts, to protest, while remaining in relationship.

The project ultimately lacked the second, third, and fourth things, but it did involve the first. In spirit, it was originally designed to let things go where both community processing and disagreement took it. Problems with the art world inhibited these things, but they also made it clear how to imagine a process that

---

[136] In *Artificial Hells*, Bishop singles out spectacle as corrupting participatory art works.

worked. "A Color Removed" wanted to give people the possibility of protesting in slow motion, coming to terms with a society that often makes no sense. In the process, it wanted to give people the chance to reconsider their own agency, to withdraw tacit consent from contingent and unjustified social practices and institutions, and to demand a better world, one in which everyone can feel safe. So, the project meant to take back the meaning of the word "safety" from policing. It took up people's "right to safety" from a world where safety is filtered through public safety officers, i.e., the police, and where coercion comes across as domination, not as collective guidance:

> Can Black people in the U.S.A. be safe from the violence of the police?
> Where in this world can we count on being protected equally?
> Why do the police in Cleveland seem to care more about property damage than Black people's lives?
> Can we imagine a world where everyone is equally safe and has the freedom to play in the park?

The project pointed toward a better meaning of "safety," a world of collective security, community trust, and emotional intimacy, not "the protection of goods with guns"[137] in a society where people are collectively insecure. The redirection of safety toward such an orientation in community relationships was one concrete way in which "A Color Removed" contained the possibility of involving emergent and collective guidance through a slowly shared "sense of life."[138] Perhaps, in some small way, too, it did, contributing to Cleveland's own culture shift that supported Black Lives Matter's critique of the police becoming common sense for the mainstream of American culture in June 2020.[139] Writing then in *The Guardian*, Ed Pilkington reported on what he was seeing across the United States of America:

> The New York Times writer Jelani Cobb captured best the sense of wonder at what is happening in America. He posted a tweet from Mitt Romney, the Republican senator from Utah, which showed the former presidential candidate marching alongside demonstrators under the banner Black Lives Matter.
>
> "Ladies and gentlemen," Cobb remarked, "This is what you call uncharted territory."[140]

---

[137] Thanks to Misty Morrison for leading a conversation to this expression.

[138] Nussbaum, *Love's Knowledge*, chapter 1.

[139] See Jose A. Del Real, Robert Samuels, and Tim Craig, "Black Lives Matters expands into movement embraced by the masses," *The Washington Post,* June 9th, 2020.

[140] Ed Pilkington, "After 15 days of stunning antiracist protests . . . what happens next?" *The Guardian,* June 10th, 2020. The Tweet is at Jelani Cobb, "Ladies and gentleman, this is what you call uncharted territory," *Twitter,* @jelani 9, June 7th, 2020.

4. Honest in our Relations

Any politics concerned with establishing a culture of free relations must be concerned with the power concentrations that lead in effect to the control of one part of society by a dominant elite.[141] What it takes to establish free relations through breaking up wealth concentrations, the hegemony of the state, and completing decolonization on Earth is a task as large as planetary justice.[142] Let me just be clear. I am for that. The social world we've inherited in the United States of America and within the international order of post-Westphalian nation states is profoundly unjust and wrong in so many ways. The politics of wonder is not sufficient for taking on empire. But it is needed. I would not write this book if I did not believe that something subtle was profoundly missing from politics.

Without seeing what free relations mean in our lives together and what they could be in society, without developing modes of governance that *are* free, we risk socially reproducing domination as many a revolution and many a revolutionary have done. The topic of the politics of wonder began in 2007 when an idea that Nussbaum used in her work on other animals – an animal politics of wonder – put me in touch with something profound that I had been missing in my upbringing into American politics. In my experience growing up in Reaganite Amerika, national politics has always been narcissistic, domination-recycling, and deeply unequal and precarious. But things only got worse. In the last decade, as Nussbaum herself has discussed, narcissism became an entire "politics."[143] When in 2016, I engaged in legal observing with the National Lawyers Guild to protect the civil rights of protesters during the 2016 Republican Convention in downtown Cleveland, Ohio, I came to view the politics of wonder more profoundly than I ever had, for I saw how narcissism had come to structure civil society to an unbelievable extent. This intensified after the 2016 presidential elections in my country. This book on the politics of wonder began then, and as I write, it hasn't become less relevant. We are still strange, seeking beings who become dynamic in getting lost together, trying to figure out how we can all be free and secure. But would you know it?

The subtle thing about politics as it should be is a particular moment in the process of sharing the world together as moral equals who seek mutually

---

[141] Thomas Piketty, *Capital in the Twenty-First Century*, trans. Arthur Goldhammer (Cambridge, MA: The Belknap Press, 2014); Whyte, "Settler Colonialism, Ecology, & Environmental Justice."

[142] I.e., justice that concerns the Earth as a planetary system inclusive of global justice. Cf. Chakrabarty, *The Climate of History in a Planetary Age*.

[143] Nussbaum, *The Monarchy of Fear*.

acceptable and participatory self-governance. This is what I have been exploring all along in this book: the moment when, wondering, we together find what makes most sense or, failing that, remain lost in thought – together, all of us having cognitive agency. A collective process of wondering constructed around this moment is a relationally autonomous way for people to find what makes sense to them in and through disagreement. The disagreement continues when someone remains lost and when another's sense of things does not find its way to the world of the one lost. The disagreement resolves when things make sense to everyone there or when those who still remain unsure decide that the disagreement makes enough sense in the way that it is going to share a world with those with whom they disagree. Whether people reach consensus or trust in the ongoing disagreement, the world nonetheless becomes open to people's different worlds, since it began in disagreement and wonder between different people's different worlds and since it is capable of persisting there. To speak of worlds becoming "plural" is a stronger claim than that *a* world becomes "pluralistic." "Pluralism" often refers to differences over how to live the good life within reasonable and shared constraints of a given institution or society.[144] But worlds becoming plural to each other suggests that people may become profoundly lost together, struggling to make sense of a shared world at all.[145]

Such a situation should be seen as "isonomic," where everyone disagreeing about what makes sense knows that the condition of sharing the world is that it be open to making sense to everyone with leeway to question. What I mean by "isonomy" is unconventional, however. "Isonomy" was traditionally understood, for instance by Herodotus, as equality under the law especially with respect to distributive justice.[146] But some modern reinterpreters have stressed a different meaning.[147] Isonomy has also been dubbed "no rule."[148] Kōjin Karatani focuses on the joining of economic equality with freedom. However, he understands that there are wider normative conditions of isonomy, found, for instance, in his exploration of natural philosophy and the critique of religion within Ionian society and among Ionian thinkers. But by linking isonomy to the conditions of the world making sense as I have done, *isonomy becomes involved with the*

---

[144] John Rawls, *Political Liberalism* (New York: Columbia University Press, 1993).

[145] See Escobar, *Pluriversal Politics*.

[146] Josiah Ober, "The original meaning of 'democracy': capacity to do things, not majority rule," (Princeton/Stanford Working Papers in Classics, version 1.0, September 2007).

[147] See, for instance, Hanna Arendt, *On Revolution* (New York: Penguin Classics, 1963), 20, as cited in Kōjin Karatani, *Isonomia and the Origins of Philosophy*, 14.

[148] See Karatani, *Isonomy and the Origins of Philosophy*, 14–17, who appears to take the expression from Arendt.

conditions of autonomy, where the social world should make sense to those who act in it and not be an imposition of senselessness. Structured by wondering, isonomy involves something different than mere opinion-giving. At issue is whether we who disagree can figure out what makes sense and, if not, whether we can be true enough to ourselves to remain lost so that the world we share becomes co-constituted by the search for what could make sense between us. Such an understanding of isonomy prioritizes relational, imaginative engagement with each other and our worlds and does not leave anyone out who honestly tries to make sense of things. On my reading, isonomy is a form of social power fit for the world in conditions of deep contestation between worlds.

Here is a particular understanding of democracy, where the power to act legitimately as a polity comes from collective autonomy.[149] Governance is immanent to the norms that make sense to those who are governed by them. This is because, through wonder, we become lost in thought or find what makes sense to us. Imposed rule falls away. Being lost is the life of this searching, the location from which our cognitive agency strives, drawing on the mind's original joy. When we can get lost together, such freely imaginative relating leads us to seek mutual governance by what makes sense to us, rather than to rule over each other or push each other around. That is what became ultimately revolutionary to me about Nussbaum's politics of wonder. It suggested a revolution in ways of relating, not more strategy and narcissistic control.

One of the things that confirmed my subjective path during this inquiry is that I came to realize that my understanding of isonomy prioritizes honesty. In other words, the politics of wonder was taking me to a more honest politics. This was like water for my parched earth. We may think that the person who spouts off their reactive views on television or the internet is being honest, but they aren't truly concerned with what honesty means in life between people and how it relates to wondering. When we are truly honest with other people or inside ourselves, we must come to terms with our discussion being able to get lost and sometimes with ourselves being lost. I am sorry, but no human is God. Our beliefs get lost somewhere, and our believing something does not make others believe it so. To share the world by what makes sense to us collectively takes getting lost together at times. At the same time, to get lost in searching for what makes sense and what is meaningful demands that we be honest. We cannot

---

[149] Cf. Ober, "The original meaning of 'democracy': capacity to do things, not majority rule." *Kratos*, the Greek root of the suffix "-cracy" suggests the power to act. Thanks to Timothy Wutrich for help on the history of this word.

wonder without honesty with ourselves, and we cannot wonder together without being honest. To explore the possibilities opening up around the focus of our questioning or astonishment demands that we acknowledge the space between the meanings we take for granted (one of the reasons paintings and music make this book an entire sensorium is to surface that space!).[150]

When we think about isonomy and the politics of wonder, we can see how honesty is important for it. Honesty was a condition on emergent learning as seen in the Chicago Commons family centers, and it was ultimately missing in the staged events of *A Color Removed*. Honesty opens up people's relationship to sense-making and meaning-finding, lets social processes go where people collectively think that they should go, and centers such processes in what is communicative and thus at least minimally communal, not in what is egotistical and closed. Honesty keeps the space for people to disagree with their whole hearts, even to protest, all the while remaining in relationship precisely through the honesty. When I am honest with you, I am opening up to you and I am open to you. Of course, this sounds nuts to anyone who has built their life around a cynical "politics." But of all things involved in the politics of wonder beyond wonder itself, honesty might be the most important.

Recall Nussbaum's interest in "Duettino-Sull'aria" from *The Marriage of Figaro*.[151] She described what she heard, read, and saw as a fluid interchange between two people of different social classes who treated each other in the task they shared as of equal intelligence.[152] What characterized their interactions was a frank sharing of their views and a conjoint intention focused on the matter at hand. Their minds were open to each other in this. Without such honesty, what they thought makes sense wouldn't have flowed between them. The ampleness of the world as a place rich with sense between them by virtue of their different lives coming to terms with it would have been closed to some extent. But with their honesty, the world as a place where multitudes of people make sense of things was momentarily in the room. Sense, we might say, was free to play between them then – and they could consider it. They could see that more is possible in the sense and meaning of things than either one of them sees. Being honest opened their position in the world, giving them some room to be responsive to the sense and meaning of things.

Of course, this fantasy didn't take seriously the dependence of the servant on the master and what differences of class can mean in employment contexts

---

[150] Cf. Nick Wilson, *The Space that Separates: A Realist Theory of Art* (New York: Routledge, 2019).
[151] Nussbaum, *Political Emotions*, 35ff.
[152] I borrow this expression from Rancière, *The Ignorant Schoolmaster*.

where precarity is a structural feature. There is nothing easy about honesty in a society with domination cycling around in it.[153] Domination casts a shadow over things, moving back behind honesty between each other and into one's capacity to be honest with oneself.[154] Under threat, people understandably no longer find themselves at ease to follow the mind's original joy and to wonder. A profound gap settles in between minds that is at bottom expressed in the fact that people have lost the actual freedom to wonder together. When people cannot openly disagree – or as Philip Pettit memorably said, look each other in the eye[155] – the mind's original joy does get curtailed. Having been raised without severe neglect or abuse and having been left without threat of abuse, humans will wonder of their own accord. But in dominating conditions, someone putting their own lostness forward to seek a common world is a form of forthrightness that can be foolish and is likely to be unreciprocated. People have their loved ones to protect. The vulnerability of opening up about being lost is a kind of honesty that, within conditions of domination, could be a supererogatory virtue. Yet it could also be a vice, since it carries forward the human excellence of being lost in wonder into a space fraught with often great risk to oneself and one's loved ones. I don't think that it is moral to make honest wonder into a superhuman virtue in the often unsafe conditions of this world where poor facilitating environments reign.

Although they don't examine the extent to which their participants live in a society of collective insecurity, some studies of democratic micro-publics have found that it can be very difficult for face-to-face conversational encounters between people to lead anyone to suspend the commitments that make up who they are.[156] Someone might argue that even without immediate social conditions where domination remains a threat, we have "power in" us, having been formed and having been forming ourselves in ways so intimate and profound that the sense of our world tends to be laid out strongly in our identities.[157] Then, someone

---

[153] E.g., Sidra Shahid, "Understanding Academic Precarity with Iris Marion Young: Who's Responsible?" *Blog of the APA*, December 31st, 2021.
[154] Dotson, "Tracking Epistemic Violence, Tracking Practices of Silencing."
[155] Pettit, *Republicanism*.
[156] Bagg, "Can Deliberation Neutralise Power?" Bagg speaks of deliberation being "expensive," rather than difficult. With some organizing and some (social practice) art, "rhetorical bridges" can cross the "deliberative pathologies" that lead people to seem unable to see eye to eye enough to consider the world between them together. See John S. Dryzek and Alex Y. Lo, "Reason and Rhetoric in Climate Communication," *Environmental Politics* 24:1 (2015): 1–16, and Simon Niemeyer, "Intersubjective Reasoning in Political Deliberation: A Theory and Method for Assessing Deliberative Transformation in Small and Large Scale," *Centre for Deliberative Democracy and Global Governance*, University of Canberra, no. 4 (2019), especially pp. 15–17. Thanks to John S. Dryzek for his perspective on Bagg's challenge and for the citations.
[157] Bagg, "Beyond the Search for the Subject." Oxley, "Feminist Perspectives on Power, Domination, and Exploitation."

might say, when people face each other and try to make sense of things together, they are likely to interpret the world by their own lights and in ways that protect their identities or, they may think, their very being.[158] But now add domination and the negative anxieties and fears that we internalize and confront in living under it, and disagreements so profound that they go all the way down into our identities, purportedly our very being, seem understandably precarious and worth avoiding.

I don't think that this objection has untangled having hardened identities as a result of living in a precarious world with domination in it from some purportedly existential, even natural, commitment to being closed around who we are. I just don't see that hardening in children unless wonder gets scared out of them. Nussbaum's instincts are right here, that human beings love to playfully grow and to relate when they are secure from injustice and healed from histories of violence. But we can take the objection on face value and still show why honesty is important in the isonomic politics of wonder *precisely because* honesty is needed to confront domination and to work through it. Identities aren't so deep that they are inaccessible to sense and meaning. They are formed of these things! Even when we confront each other vexed by actual pathologies – the kinds of things Nussbaum draws on when she discusses the object-relations psychoanalysis of Winnicott to make a broader point about our capacity for narcissism as human beings[159] – these things still are worked on through "talking cure[s]."[160] Humans are highly plastic beings who, in the words of Giovanni Pico della Mirandola, "fashion" our "form."[161] What honesty contributes to the massive anti-imperial, de-colonial, anti-capitalist, anti-racist, anti-sexist, anti-homophobic, anti-ablist, etc. . . . work of countering our inherited histories of domination is the understated thing – the "small axe"[162] – of opening up cracks in distrust so that wonder can flow in.

There is no honesty without saying what we think, acknowledging what we intend, expressing what we're feeling.[163] In doing these things, we have to remain

[158] Bagg, "Can Deliberation Neutralise Power?"

[159] Nussbaum, *Upheavals of Thought*, chapters 3 and 4; and *Political Emotions*, chapter 7.

[160] On "talking cures," see Sigmund Freud, *Five Lectures in Psychoanalysis* (New York: Penguin Books, 1995), 8–9. "Anna O," one of Breuer's patients in the early days of the invention of psychoanalysis, described the process with that expression.

[161] Pico della Mirandola, *Oration on the Dignity of Man*.

[162] The Wailers, "Small Axe," on *Burnin'* (London: Island Music/Tuff Gong, 1973).

[163] Cf. Larmore, *Practices of the Self*, and the closing paragraph of Søren Kierkegaard, *Either/Or, Part II*, trans. Howard V. Hong and Edna H. Hong (1843; Princeton: Princeton University Press, 1987), "Ultimatum [a Final Word]: The Upbuilding that Lies in the Thought that in Relation to God We Are Always in the Wrong."

Nussbaum's Politics of Wonder

in touch with our being in the world as ones who are striving to understand the meaning of things and to make sense of them. Yet as we have seen in an earlier motet, the very condition of seeking sense and meaning involves being in touch with the possibility that meaning and sense could be otherwise. So, searching must then involve the background presence of positive anxiety in considering things. Honesty rests on the possibility of wondering, just as wondering, as I've noted, demands honesty. The two are siblings whose parents are sense and meaning.

Honesty and wonder open up "power-in" to new kinds of world-making. Once we see this, we must realize that it's not that talk – and more importantly relating – can't work to help dislodge our barriers to each other and each other's worlds. It's that we often don't *organize* the social processes that allow us to do so. That takes art. But we are also not looking for the political moment in social life honestly enough, and we are not wondering about it searchingly enough. A social understanding of freedom as the dispersion of governance between us takes politics to the street and into the quiet of the everyday where we learn to become lost together and have the world we can make sense of together guide us in our living. Free, isonomic relations where we become lost together emerge in a collectively guided world. This is utopian on the big stage of big "politics," *but it is eminently possible in the communities that people build out of moral accountability and against narcissism.* It's not that politics starts in the home or only in small communities, but that it arises whenever people can make a form of it seep through the cracks in the day. One of the things that an anti-narcissistic politics implies is that it is a moral and existential error to assume that "politics" – or matters of political importance – happen only when there is power over many things, as in some grand strategy. The politics of wonder asks us to disabuse ourselves of such tastes as being adaptive preference for what we think are more palatable forms of domination in a deeply narcissistic world of collective insecurity.[164]

For there to be a common world that makes rough sense and that we each share and where what is supposed to make sense in the world isn't imposed on any of us, we must eventually work to articulate a world that makes sense that we can share, working through disagreements around the chaos caused by histories of violence and ongoing domination. Such work is incredibly hard because our beliefs are strained in it and because the ongoing effects of domination in a given

---

[164] Cf. Nussbaum, *Women and Human Development*, chapter 2.

setting can lead us to silence questioning as either agents of domination, those privileged by its persistence, or those dealing directly with its insecurity and threat. But all guidance of common life depends on the articulation of common sense enough that people are organized through it, whether fitting it or falling outside it.[165] Since honestly becoming lost together surfaces this condition, often against the presumption of a world that is supposed to make sense and often out of people's quiet oblivion in that world,[166] *I see no choice but to insist on the moment of the politics of wonder and demand that we make room for it in our lives as a basic task of politics.* What really makes sense for us in matters of common concern – *all* of us? Then, to those who would disabuse us of the politics of wonder for being naive or sentimental, the answer is that we are morally responsible to pursue it. What's naive is to think that cynicism is morally satisfying. What's sentimental is the unacknowledged sadness that drives such a position.[167]

In its communicative approach to life with others and toward oneself, honesty opens up the free play of sense and meaning – an open responsiveness – between us. This free play between us is something Nussbaum states is at the heart of non-narcissistic relationships.[168] What might make sense? What is revolutionary about honest, isonomic wonder is what is revolutionary about water: it finds the cracks, any space where it can stream through. One reason why this motet looked to early childhood education and to art is that these are areas of social life that allow a space for honest wondering, even if the space was corrupted in the latter. That space was still possible, just not as SPACES in Cleveland, Ohio, in 2018. Against the spectacle that that gallery and its artists eventually sought, we should remember that sometimes "the revolution will not be televised"[169] because it is happening out of sight. Part of creating the next world is building spaces for another world that is possible.[170] In the spaces where we can come to hold them, honest, isonomic disagreements bring us together, creating a dispersion of power between us for the co-creation of the world we learn to make sense of together over and over again as we disagree. As John Dewey suggested, the most important thing about learning in this political situation is to learn how to go on learning

---

[165] Rancière, *Disagreement.*

[166] Ralph Ellison's *Invisible Man,* 2nd ed. (1952; New York: Vintage Books, 1995), and Margaret Atwood's *Surfacing* (1972; New York: Simon & Shuster, 2012).

[167] "Sentimental," *Oxford American Dictionary;* "... prompted by feelings of ... sadness."

[168] Nussbaum, *Political Emotions,* 176.

[169] Gil Scott-Heron, "The Revolution Will Not Be Televised," on *Small Talk at 125th and Lenox* (New York: Flying Dutchman Records/RCA, 1970).

[170] This is one of the points of Sadiya Hartmann's *Wayward Lives,* and also of the late work of Foucault on subjectivation through practices of the self.

together.[171] But the key to that is to learn how to honestly become lost together. Then, we can loosen up hardened identities that we adaptively try to preserve.[172] Being anxious in honestly being lost, we must also loosen our grip on what is actual to make room for what is possible. This eases us back from strategic manipulations of each other as well.[173] Honest, isonomic wondering is slowly transformative – as the Moral Inquiries showed over its five-year life.

Finally, there's this. Societies traumatized by domination need reparative work so that identities can soften between people and people can find ways that make sense to them to become more fluid in the relationships they have with each other in society.[174] This is a precondition on coming around soulfully again to politics. Honesty is important here, too. Contrast being honestly lost together with being lost and being *dis*honest with oneself about that, suppressing one's lostness and trying to control it through some form of projection, displacement, delusion. Arbitrariness then characterizes us – appearing certain while avoiding moments when coming to terms with things or with each other would surface the extent to which we are lost about the sense of things.[175] Contrast the honest lostness that appears between us with the state of affairs where people are negatively anxious, distrustful, and *alone,* even next to others. People then live sunken in their own confusion, orbs of oblivion passing by each other in the day and night – or subjecting each other to the force of their lives like volatile projectiles careening off of walls, striking bodies. But as I hope that both Misty and I have shown throughout this book, honest consideration is important with ourselves and for others, given that we can gloss over the ways in which our own world does not actually make sense or is merely given without being critically examined and given how hard it can be to see and to hear others. Since in honest attention, as I've noted, being honest must bottom out in wonder, we must suspend the fixation on our own identities – on ourselves as an object – and become more open – less "me" and more "I," "you," and – possibly – "we."[176] That

[171] John Dewey, *Experience and Education* (1939; New York: Touchstone, 1997).
[172] Bagg, "Can Deliberation Neutralise Power?" and Jordan E. DeVylder, "Fixity of Thinking and the Foundations of Identity: An Argument for the Evolutionary Adaptiveness of Illusions," *Early Intervention in Psychiatry* 13 (2019): 720–1.
[173] "Strategy" is a word historically rooted in the idea of leadership in warfare, and it still maintains some of that bellicose logic. Strategy is primarily calculative, rather than interpersonal in its logic. "Strategy," *Oxford American Dictionary.*
[174] Murphy, *The Conceptual Foundations of Transitional Justice.*
[175] On arbitrariness, see my "'This Conversation Never Happened'," *Tikkun*, March 26th, 2018.
[176] In personal correspondence, Sidra Shahid correctly noted that I am providing a modified and circumscribed use of the ancient skeptical *epoche* – suspension of judgment – in this book through the figure of getting lost in wondering.

is, we must become *more relational and less egotistical.* In societies traumatized through domination such as mine, still structured by it and by narcissism, and where people every day recycle the ridiculous reactivity of commercial and public culture, honesty is important in these two fundamental ways. It says, *Less me. More us and the world.*

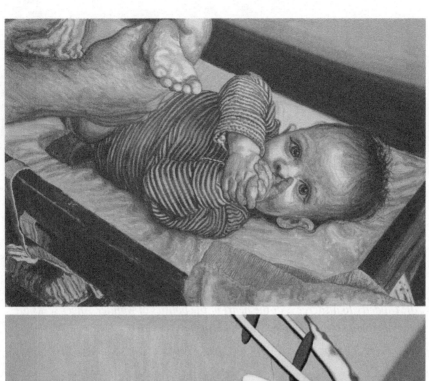

"Changing," 2021 / "Mobile," 2021

The capacity to disagree is at the heart of the politics of wonder. Anger seeks the moment when a wrongdoer gets lost with us in reconsidering what makes sense in the world we share.

MOTET 4 – *CAN ANGER BE WONDERFUL? IT CAN SURFACE MORAL WRONGS*

TEXTS: *Anger and Forgiveness, Therapy of Desire*

WORD: "Vulnerability"

& for the Moral Inquiries,
Mac's Back's Books,
Cleveland Heights, Ohio, 2015–19

Long ago on the CD player at 53rd & Kimbark:
Fela Anikulapo Kuti & Africa 70's "International Thief Thief (I.T.T.)"

To talk about anger in this book, we're in the best position. The book is at our backs.

It's easy to think of wonder as a happy affair. But nothing in the nature of positive anxiety requires that wonder be pleasant. Excitement is more soulful than that.[1] As I've stated, one of my contentions in this book is that, in some forms, even anger can be an expression invoking wonder. Political thoughtfulness can likewise involve protest. These things push against Nussbaum's view of anxiety and anger as mostly bad emotions. But I argue in the spirit of the main idea of her work as a whole: to confront and counteract narcissism in all its expressions in moral and political life.

When anger arises in moral relations where it belongs, it is a vulnerable expression of a perceived wrong, decrying the contravention of our relationship while appealing to it. *Anger should be primarily communicative.* In demanding that we reconsider the sense of our actions, even of our lives, anger calls on wonder. It's a protest! When the apparent wrongdoer gets lost in reply, searching for sense, they begin relational repair in a moment that is isonomic.

This flies in the face of convention and opposes Martha C. Nussbaum's view on anger.[2] But let's look at anger differently. This book is about the unconventional politics of wonder, where insight by insight, relation by relation, another social world than a narcissistic one becomes imaginable. Wonder then is revolutionary, but with wonder, the connotations of being "revolutionary" themselves "roll back" from reactivity and control over others to thoughtfulness emerging between us.[3] This applies to anger, too.

*

Moral wrongdoing is the greatest disruption of the sense of things. This is not because we cannot wrap our heads around it by abstracting away to a place

---

[1] Cf. Rubenstein, *Strange Wonder.*
[2] Nussbaum, *Anger and Forgiveness.* Her recent *Justice for Animals* uses the language of "outrage" more sympathetically, allying it with the one, practical form of anger that she supports. But her basic account of anger has not changed in the latest work.
[3] "Revolution," *Oxford American Dictionary.*

where people's motives are corrupt or their characters fallible. We can do that. Moral wrongdoing is disruption because what makes moral sense is bedrock to how grown-ups live, and because its sense is supposed to be shared between people. But the apparent wrongdoing has torn you from that home in the world.

Morality speaks to both of these things at their heart, that *we are in relationship* and that *we have lives that matter to us unto death*, including when we sacrifice our lives for who or what matters in it. The way morality gets at both existential concern and social relationship is through the core notion of accountability.[4] Accountability is the "fact or condition of being accountable." Being accountable means being "required or expected to justify actions or decisions."[5] A moral person is accountable *before* any wrong that they do. As moral people, we are expected to be accountable to each other concerning the ways in which we relate to each other's lives, including even the ways in which we see them. We each and all have lives, and to fail to mind them is to fail to be accountable.

To commit a moral wrong is therefore to negate, in the instance, accountability to each other regarding the lives that we lead. By appearing not to be accountable, an apparent wrongdoer doesn't seem moral in the instance. This momentarily suspends the existential and relational structure of our lives with the wrongdoer and what was supposed to be *our* shared world. Given what we honestly think is a moral wrong, the apparent wrongdoer, our lives with them, the surrounding context in which the wrong appeared, all these things are thrown out of joint and don't make sense, viscerally. We have to call the wrong a wrong for sense to return, even wounded.

Perhaps the worst thing is that being wronged conveys that one is, in the instance, *not relatable*. Wrongs alienate those wronged from the accountability relationship they must expect and that structures sense, in the instance, as lived and as social. The one(s) who wronged you did not find you considerable in the instance. "In the instance" is an important qualification. The wrongdoing may have occurred in a momentary moral failing. Still, by focusing on moral wrong, we aren't discussing excusable mistakes. Someone may be inconsiderate without morally wronging another. When someone wrongs another, it isn't covered by excuses, and under no circumstances is it ever excusable to ignore the moral considerability of someone. Wrongs act as though those wronged are *out of*

---

[4]   Darwall, *The Second Person Standpoint.* See also Wallace, *The Moral Nexus.*
[5]   "Accountability," "accountable," *Oxford American Dictionary.*

relation, not deserving of accountability in the eyes of the one(s) who wronged them. Even in an instance, this is jarring, because it suggests that your considerability is conditional.

In this way, morally wronging others truly is the deepest form of inconsideration. In the moral wrong, lack of consideration opens out. As social beings, we relate to each other, and as beings who are in relation with each other, the way that we relate to each other positions us relatively in the world. When we are wronged morally, the one(s) wronging us take us out of relation. In the moment, they abandon us to a relative position in the world that is conditionally devoid of accountability. From that void-position, the life of shared sense comes unmoored, because we are not in that instance, relatable. The qualifications "in that instance," "in this position," etc. mark the *phenomenological environment of being wronged and of wrongdoing.* Thankfully, in any situation where there are others who are moral or where a strong moral imagination can be used, we can remind ourselves that the instance of wrongdoing does not speak beyond itself. Wrongdoers do not have that much power over us, but phenomenologically speaking from within the interpersonal ("I–you") standpoint of the relation, moral wrong is sharp in what it – even momentarily – conveys to another. *How can something make sense to me when I am erased?*[6]

The issue isn't simply that one has not been recognized[7] – or that one's capacity for leading one's life by one's own lights has been eclipsed.[8] These are just part of the story, a story that includes the entirety of interpersonal – or as I will say "relational" – life. Relating is a fundamental mode of being human, as central to our being as thinking and as doing. Moral wrongdoing undercuts relating by making the considerability undergirding it conditional. So, it undercuts human community in the instance. This throws being human out of its sense-filled order, for we are social beings.[9] Moral wrong contravenes the basis of social relationship.

---

[6] In *Anger and Forgiveness*, chapter 2, Nussbaum considers anger as a response to "down-ranking," a way in which we are relatively positioned in status hierarchies. But the relative positioning provided by moral accountability is non-hierarchical, consisting of moral equality. Anger that should arise in response to its negation through moral wrongdoing is not therefore about down-ranking and isn't subject to Nussbaum's criticisms of that (amoral and status-conscious) expression of anger.

[7] Axel Honneth, *The Struggle for Recognition: The Moral Grammar of Social Conflicts*, trans. Joel Anderson (Cambridge, MA: MIT Press, 1996), here concerning the most fundamental "first" form of misrecognition.

[8] Darwall, *The Second Person Standpoint*, who follows Strawson on this matter.

[9] Nussbaum, *The Fragility of Goodness, Women and Human Development*, chapter 1, and *Upheavals of Thought*, chapter 4. See also Marx, *Economic and Philosophical Manuscripts of 1844*, "Estranged Labor."

Human beings are not practical robots. Nor are we cogitating computers. We must be people to each other if we are to have a social life. When we are not, social life breaks down. We then treat each other as facts (i.e., as things to know about), or we manipulate each other. Either way, we stop being social. Strictly speaking, a person who comes across as a threat is being reduced to a calculus *of practical reason.* This is, precisely, to erase the person as a person. Once we speak precisely of people as people, we are in the realm *of relational reason,* where moral accountability is basic. This point may seem semantic, even if it is put forth as logical. But it speaks to a deeper problem beginning with what Marx called an alienated view of human beings – namely, one in which our fundamentally social dimensions are already eclipsed by the practical logic of instrumentalization.[10] The elimination of interpersonal acquaintance from the picture of us eliminates our humanity by making social life opaque.[11]

A good way to see the space of relational reason in the human heart is to consider loveless – merely practical – marriages. For instance, in Mati Diop's film *Atlantique* (*Atlantics*), Ada is locked in by her family's custom to marry Omar, who does not love her and whom she does not love. Instead, he views her as one of his many possessions. Even Ada's friend, Fanta, argues that Ada should marry Omar because of the access to things she will get. Ada cannot do any of this because she loves Souleiman. The contrast marks the loss of humanity that occurs when we conflate the intimate with the practical. When Ada insists on identifying intimacy with relating, the gorgeous, profound poetry of the film attests to all that is human *thanks only* to relating.[12]

Loss of "humanity" points to our relational nature. It doesn't mean that one is no longer part of humankind. People often use "humanity" to mean "humankind" (the collective of all of us). It helps to keep the moral term "humanity" separate from uses of "humankind." "Humanity" is a name for the potential of human beings to connect with each other.[13] This capacity for connection – our humanity – is crucial for our life with sense and meaning, and it depends on moral accountability.

---

[10] Marx, *Economic and Philosophical Manuscripts of 1844,* "Estranged Labor."
[11] On relational reason, see my "'Do you have a conscience?'"; "The Moral and the Ethical;" *Solar Calendar, and Other Ways of Marking Time; The Wind;* and *Involving Anthroponomy in the Anthropocene,* chapters 3 and 4. In *The Wind,* I argue against Kate Manne who, in *Down Girl: The Logic of Misogyny* (New York: Oxford University Press, 2018), argues that being a person to another person can just as easily be a threat as a moral summons. Manne's account conflates practical and relational reason.
[12] Mati Diop's *Atlantique* (Paris: Films du Bal, 2019).
[13] Zeldin, *An Intimate History of Humanity.*

There are two general ways that sense-making between people depends on interpersonal relationships grounded in moral accountability. The first is that what makes sense to us depends on our being able to make sense of things. The point is almost tautological: if we cannot make sense of things, things cannot make sense to us. But to affirm the capacity of people to make sense of things is first and foremost to relate to people as people – leading lives, striving, getting by, and searching for sense. If you fail to treat people as people, you deny an important dimension of how they can make sense of things, and this erases – even if momentarily – their capacity to make sense. Hence, it interferes with the sense of things reaching them – even if momentarily – like a chilling wind. That is the coldness of being treated as if you weren't a person with a mind and will of your own. At best, you must protest. But even so, the wrong has shuddered the sense-making between you both. Interpersonal relationships are needed so that people can make sense of things between each other. The relationships, however, depend on moral accountability. Only in moral accountability are people conceived of as striving to make sense of things in the ways that people do, i.e., including personally by acquaintance.

Second, sense-making between people depends on interpersonal relationships also because sense-making is intrinsically public.[14] To determine that something makes sense is to be able to share it for why it does. Even figuring it out oneself, reflectively, depends on it being out there in the world enough for one to be able to consider it. Sense-making between people is intrinsically sharable. It is meant to be shared in some way. Even a person who kept something to themselves shares it with themselves over time. Accordingly, sense-making between us depends on social life – on the space between people where things can be shared in common. If we close down that space by negating people's capacity to make sense in the instance, we divorce sense-making from the people who make it and thus treat what makes sense as if it were not public, open to interpretation. But interpersonal relationships hold open the space for sense-making between people by holding open the space for sharing it – the space between us.

To negate someone's person in the instance by wronging them morally has a knock-on effect on the life of sense-making. It momentarily jars the world of sense-making by negating social space and the way that sense-making opens a shared world for people who strive to lead their lives, thanks to meaning, and for what makes sense. Inversely, to open up the life of sense-making between people is, indirectly, to open up relating and thus, again indirectly, to open up the

---

[14] See also Ludwig Wittgenstein, *Philosophical Investigations,* trans. G. E. M. Anscombe, P. M. S. Hacker, and Joachim Schulte (1953; Malden, MA: Wiley-Blackwell, 2009) on the critique of private language.

thickness of moral space by making accountability between people around what makes sense more meaningful and sense-filled. In contravening interpersonal relationship, moral wrongs contravene our sociality. It's proper to feel that they make "no goddamn sense!" in the instance. *How could that person do that? How could they relate to you that way?* Agnes Callard articulates the core expressive complaint of anger in ordinary American English as "How could you *do* that?!" One might even more precisely see it as "How could you *relate* to me that way?"[15] Moral wrong sits in relationship *as the breaking of it.*

It is therefore reasonable that people who honestly think that they have been morally wronged should get angry at the one(s) who wronged them. Anger is a protest. Anger is a form of relationship with a moral core than is often emotional. To conceive of anger not, in the first instance, as an emotion but as a moral relation that can be emotional contradicts convention. But since anger has a moral core – i.e., involves moral responsibility – it is fundamentally a thing of *freedom*, not of involuntary reaction. That its freedom is among the most difficult things to realize doesn't change this fact. Once we grasp that anger is a part of moral relations, however, it no longer makes sense to identify it with a set of feelings or autonomic reactions. Instead, we should identify it by its normative space, in which feelings and gut reactions are subject to moral responsibility and, as is actual in some cases and so possible, one may be angry without being emotional. Anger can be emotional, but need not be, and is itself not an emotion, once one takes seriously that to which moral responsibility commits us, i.e., to seeing as authoritative what should be, not simply what is given.[16]

Although the emotional display of anger, too, can draw on visceral, autonomic reactions that charge the body with aggression, the moral core to anger shows that anger is to be considered in light of moral demands, not in light of reactive force. *The moral core of anger always already moralizes it and the discussion of its emotionality.* To think of anger as an emotion or as a disposition of bodily reactions and feelings (say, to defensive aggression) is thereby to ignore anger's morality. When Jesse Prinz understands emotions through their formal objects and singles out basic emotions by basic relations that they express on the basis of these formal objects, Prinz might seem to be acknowledging the moral relationship within, say, anger.[17] But the formal objects are not moralized. Moral

[15] See her "The Reason to Be Angry Forever," in Myisha Cherry and Owen Flanagan, eds., *The Moral Psychology of Anger* (Lanham, MD: Rowman & Littlefield, 2019), 123–37.

[16] Cf. Neiman, *Moral Clarity*, on this last point.

[17] Jesse Prinz, *Gut Reactions: A Perceptual Theory of Emotion* (New York: Oxford University Press, 2004).

accountability isn't presumed in them, and this allows Prinz to distinguish them from sentiments (cultivated emotional responses).[18] At the same time, much work on moral sentiments doesn't grapple with the fact that the core moral notion of approbation or disapprobation already *assumes* a relationship involving accountability between people, not merely an eudaimonistic sense that something bad has been done to "me" and "mine."[19] But it is this relationship that is the core of morality, not the approbation or disapprobation.[20] There's wobble in these moments.

We mustn't overlook that anger's morality already draws anger into moral responsibility and freedom of response. In her discussion of anger, Agnes Callard faults philosophical accounts of anger with picking out the moral possibilities in anger and purifying anger of its immoral possibilities. She says this "carves away the dark side" of anger.[21] "Everyone [in the philosophical debate] assumes that we can retain the moral side of anger while distancing ourselves from paradigmatically irrational phenomena such as grudges and vengeance."[22] She then makes a second claim, "[W]hat if we humans do morality by way of vengeful grudges?"[23] – and goes on to suggest that holding people accountable by "forc[ing] my own thinking down your throat" where "your bad is my good," "'teach[es] [you] a lesson.'"[24] There are two issues here about the nature of morality, the first being about whether morality is a given. But of course, it is not, since it involves how we *should* act, not how we happen to want to act. So, in principle, it is the stuff of morality to distance aspects of our dispositions from how we should act. That's what moral self-determination is.

Callard knows this, and so she makes the second set of claims. But they simply internalize the first problem. If the way we "do" morality is by doing something that seems to be *im*moral, then on moral grounds of self-determination we can criticize what we think is the way to "do" morality and actually make more sense. This is the main point, of which the suite of other claims simply repeats the problem: Is it accountability if a person is "forced"? No. That's submission. Can

---

[18] Jesse Prinz, *The Emotional Construction of Morals* (New York: Oxford University Press, 2007).

[19] Thanks to Rick Anthony Furtak for emphasizing Prinz's eudaimonism.

[20] In technical terms, the issue is the moral nexus, not the interference with what is good for us. See Wallace, *The Moral Nexus*, particularly in differentiating "desirability considerations" from moral reasons for action, a distinction traceable back to Strawson, as Darwall also developed. The term "desirability characterization" comes from Anscombe's practical logic from G. E. M. Anscombe, *Intention*, 2nd ed. (1957; Cambridge, MA: Harvard University Press, 2000).

[21] Agnes Callard, *On Anger* (Cambridge, MA: MIT Press, 2020), 15.

[22] Ibid., 16.

[23] Ibid.

[24] Ibid., 19.

someone come to account on their own (i.e., "be accountable") by having their voice choked out? No, again. That is submission. Can someone "learn" to see something as making sense by being made to submit to something by force? No. Their limbs submitting don't translate into their minds believing. Callard's tactic is to keep hiding what happens to be a disposition inside of what is called "moral" (or "educational") and to then argue that we accept it as moral or educational, when it contradicts moral responsibility and autonomy, interpersonal consideration, and other moral relations (like compassion). Her approach urges us to give up striving to find what makes most sense in things in order to settle for what is given.

There's a reason why people who are angry needn't be reactive or convey heat, even agitation. Moral autonomy lives at the core of anger as part of moral relationship. By contrast, Callard views moral wrong as a fact that a *norm* was violated rather than that a *relationship* was broken. Her account of moral wrong speaks of relationship but has a strangely self-focused character about it. Wrongs, for Callard, are instances of norm violations. This, in Michael Thompson's terms, is a "monadic" concern, not a "bipolar" – relational – one between two people or agents.[25] Anger is therefore technically an *ethical*, not a moral, matter that just happens to be occasioned by another person.[26] Callard seems to short-circuit the second personal nature of the wrong by focusing on the instance of a violated norm, a perfectionistic misdirection of the fundamentally communicative and relational nature of anger.[27] She paints anger as a reactive desire to return the bad to the wrongdoer by making them suffer a wrong in some way similar to what they caused. This fails to see the relationship *in* anger as, at least in part, working through damage done to the relationship that *preceded* the anger. Even her discussion of holding onto the wrong forever while moving ahead to practically value what might be possible for your future relationship misses the point.[28] Her view might be summarized this way:

---

[25] See Michael Thompson, "What Is It to Wrong Someone? A Puzzle about Justice," in R. Jay Wallace, Philip Pettit, Samuel Sheffler, and Michael Smith, eds., *Reason and Value: Themes from the Moral Philosophy of Joseph Raz* (Oxford: Clarendon Press, 2004), 333–84.

[26] See my "The Moral and the Ethical" and Wallace, *The Moral Nexus*, distinguishing prudence from justice, desirability considerations from the moral nexus.

[27] On the second person standpoint, see Darwall, *The Second Person Standpoint*.

[28] In "The Reason to Be Angry Forever," Callard argues against the idea that a moral wrong can be repaired, although she does argue for anger as the beginning of the practical repair – she calls it "co-valuation" – of a relationship. Callard's view depends on a misunderstanding of morality caused by conceiving of morality *primarily* through practical reason. She reduces morality to ethics (to desirability characterizations or "values").

1. Anger reflects the fact that some *wrong was done*. (Perfectionism 1: "You must uphold the norms!")
2. That fact can never be changed. It is "eternal." (Perfectionism 2: "You have failed forever at this thing!")
3. Turning the wrong against the wrongdoer is the way to make them face what they did. (Obedience training 1: "Feel the norm by feeling the norm violation!")

By contrast, consider this view which focuses entirely on relationships, not on norms, in the first instance:

1. Anger communicates that *you or others were wronged*. (Relationality 1: "We must maintain moral relationships.")
2. The fact of the communication shows that the relationship matters. It is ongoing. (Relationality 2: "Wrongs happen in relationships. Will you address the wrong?")
3. Coming to terms with the wrong, possibly through disagreement, is the way to maintain relationship. (Relationality 3: "Working through wrongs is part of good relationships.")

Because Callard does not see the relationship as the place of moral wrongdoing and so of anger, she underestimates Oded Na'amen's insightful reply that locates wrongdoing and working through wrong *in a relationship in process*:

> While anger focuses on a past violation of the norms of the relationship, expressed contrition on the part of the offending party shifts the background conditions of anger, signals to the wronged person that the offending party values the relationship, and can thus enable the continuation of the relationship and the fitting resolution of anger. *This suggests that anger is properly understood as fitting in the context of a crisis in a relationship—whether the relationship is a personal one or a general moral relationship between persons as such—though anger is not directly concerned with the relationship. It also suggests that the diminishing fittingness of anger is explained by a fitting process of repair, which is itself a process that one cannot normally carry through on one's own. The completion of the process is not the aim of anger, but it is in the context of this process that the occurrence, duration, and diminution of anger are made fitting. The relationship and the process of its repair are the background conditions of the reason for anger.*[29]

---

[29] Oded Na'amen, "The Fitting Resolution of Anger," *Philosophical Studies* 177: 8 (2020): 2417–2430, p. 2427, emphases mine.

I differ from Na'amen's insightful account only in that I do believe that anger is directly concerned with the relationship *in part* and that the process of repair follows along with the aim of anger, which is to maintain the moral relationship. To a large extent, this much is built into my view of wrongs.

As I view it, anger is the relation of protesting moral wrongs. It differs from protests that do not concern moral wrongs per se but things that it would be good to consider.[30] Many other things commonly called "anger" are better seen as frustration or irritability, even as negative anxiety expressed narcissistically. Anger is communicative within a moral relationship. As a protest, it puts forth something *moral* that should be considered in the eyes of the one(s) who wronged and before the eyes of any person who is basically moral. It makes a complaint and seeks moral repair – of the relationship primarily and, at the least, of the standing of the one who has been momentarily erased by the moral wrong. If the wrongdoer(s) will not own up to their wrong, the community that hears the protest can at least reinforce the standing of the one wronged. This community may be small in the instance – a partner, family, or friend-group. The public nature of angry protest affirms something that is morally considerable and thus *calls on* solidarity since it appeals to moral accountability. As a protest, anger is a call for moral community.

Also, note that this emphasis on anger as part of a moral relationship changes focus from Myesha Cherry's emphasis on "Lordean Rage" giving sustenance for long-haul activism against dominating systems.[31] The terms of her characterization of anger's benefits fall on the side of sustained *practical* action, with only one part of the relationship being emphasized, i.e., the self-recognition and self-determination of those who are dominated humanizing themselves through expressing anger. This is only part of the story, though, as *it is essential to moral relationships that the ones at whom the dominated are angry, be they perpetrators of a system or officials holding down a system, take anger as the beginning of a real relationship.* That relationship demands moral accountability. It is not clear that Cherry emphasizes opening a real relationship.

*

I profoundly disagree with Martha C. Nussbaum's critique of anger. In her major work on the topic, she sees anger as an emotion that is for the most part "childish

---

[30] For more on protest as witnessing before others to something that ought to be considered, see my "Reconsidering the Aesthetics of Protest."

[31] See her "Anger Can Build a Better World" and *The Case for Rage*.

and weak." These adjectives are oft repeated in Nussbaum's *Anger and Forgiveness*. They struck me most surprisingly in the context of an account of a couple with marital strife when Nussbaum argues that the woman who is begrudging should "get[...] on with her life," rather than hashing out complaints.[32] The instance struck me because one can readily imagine that the issue is communicative and that anger is epiphenomenal to that issue. Nussbaum's response suppresses the communicative problem, including the way it seems to involve psychological displacement that should be worked through for the good of the relationship.

Nussbaum's conclusions stem from what she presumes anger is. Locating her view in the *locus classicus* of anger's conceptualization in Aristotle's *Rhetoric*, she assumes that anger is a painful emotion showing upset at oneself or people about whom one cares being put down for no good reason (I have combined the first four conditions that Nussbaum isolates in a single sentence). It correspondingly involves a "desire for retribution."[33] The Aristotle reads, in Nussbaum's translation of it, that anger is "a desire accompanied by pain for an imagined retribution on account of an imagined slighting inflicted by people who have no legitimate reason to slight oneself or one's own."[34] Nussbaum calls anger's desire a "payback" wish.[35]

What makes anger immature and "weak" is that this payback wish flows, on Nussbaum's understanding, from "narcissistic vulnerability."[36] She elsewhere explains this as a fundamental challenge to childhood emotional development.[37] Faced with the loss of control over others – or the effects that others can have on us – and experiencing a painful and unjust demotion in the eyes of others, the angry person desires to get back at the perpetrator and to punish them. Retribution implies punishment in conventional English.[38] Presumably, this is an infantile way of reasserting "omnipotence."[39] It seeks to master the other's will.

One variant of payback involves demoting the perpetrator in kind. Nussbaum takes issue with this variant, which she calls "the road of status,"[40] because she accepts Aristotle's society's view of status as rank (e.g., hierarchical position or influential position) and inclusion in an in-group (e.g., Athenian citizens, men,

---

[32] Nussbaum, *Anger and Forgiveness*, 119.
[33] Ibid., 17.
[34] Aristotle, *Rhetoric*, 13778a31–33, quoted at *Anger and Forgiveness*, 17. For an alternate English translation, see Aristotle, *The Art of Rhetoric*, trans. Robin Waterfield (New York: Oxford University Press, 2018).
[35] Nussbaum, *Anger and Forgiveness*, 21ff.
[36] Ibid., 54.
[37] Nussbaum, *Upheavals of Thought*, chapter 2, section II especially.
[38] *Oxford American Dictionary*, "retribution."
[39] Nussbaum, *Upheavals of Thought*, chapter 4, section II.
[40] Nussbaum, *Anger and Forgiveness*, 28.

property-owners). But as I will have already suggested, things should change if we understand status – as Nussbaum elsewhere does in *Political Emotions*, *Frontiers of Justice*, and *Creating Capabilities*, for example, in terms of moral equality, much as, say, Honneth in *The Struggle for Recognition* or John Rawls in *A Theory of Justice* do.

But one can argue that expressing anger is vulnerable, trusting, and non-narcissistic. Anger expressed consistently with its moral core as a communicative act seeking moral repair is capable and grown up. Rage, irritability, passive aggressiveness, and active aggressiveness are different than anger. They remain locked up inside and treat others merely as objects. But *morally consistent anger remains in a moral relationship.* When someone becomes angry with me, they are being vulnerable and communicating in a highly intimate way, deep into their own personal world. Anger, then, whatever its protest, also calls for a renewal of relating. Relating implies the capacity to hold important differences between lives through respect, consideration, and accountability. In this way, morally consistent anger is a form of consideration demanding other possibilities within a relationship than the senselessness of wrongdoing. This allows us to view anger as a focused expression of positive anxiety shaking up the patterns of relationship involved in the wrong. As a moment of positive anxiety, anger belongs with wondering, challenging, and reconsidering the sense of things between us.

I disagree with Nussbaum's view of anger as much as I do in part because the disagreement bears on the possibility of a different kind of politics than one of interest-advancement, strategy, or identity-consolidation. Grown-up anger points to a politics in which disagreement is a relationship depending on the possibility of protest to open up, in moral accountability, what does and does not make sense between us. If people then learn to see disagreement and protest as grounded in wondering, they may develop a newfound understanding of the dynamics of isonomy in shared life between moral equals.[41] But in order to get to such a point, we need to see anger – the most contentious part of disagreement – differently than the philosophical tradition largely has taking its cue from Aristotle. What would politics born of honest moral relationships, not of interest-advancement, strategy, or identity-consolidation, be? It would be politics in which, at least, disagreement is a moral relationship, in which it is okay to be angry, and in which anger is moral and shows our social nature at its best: vulnerable, assertive of what is moral, communicative, and still believing in

---

[41] See my "Reconsidering the Aesthetics of Protest" and "How to Do Things Without Words."

another's moral capacity to recognize how relationships can be righted. To recall the last motet, such an understanding of politics even seems to me to be needed for healing past histories of domination.[42]

As I wrote, Nussbaum's initial analysis of anger is Aristotelian. Taking her cue from Aristotle's canonical definition of anger, she begins with five elements of anger.[43] It is interesting to note that none of these are strictly speaking emotional but instead include three relational elements, one narcissistic one, and one bodily state that may or may not be emotional:

1. The first she calls, from the Greek *oligōria*, "down-ranking." This is putting someone down in status and in this way humiliating them. Anger is said to respond to this.
2. The second is a down-ranking of oneself or people about whom one cares. Anger is said to reflect these relationships to self or to others.
3. The third is that something has been "wrongfully" or "inappropriately" done. Anger is said to arise over this inappropriate way of acting or relating.

Note that even this classical formulation of anger by Aristotle need not have a monadic logic as Callard construes anger. For Callard, anger is at a wrong that was done in the sense of a norm that was violated. But when anger is at something wrongfully done, the manner of relating can be at issue. The fixation is not on the perfectionistic norm that was violated but can be on the way of relating.

4. The fourth is that the perceived put-down or humiliation is accompanied by pain in the one angry. This is the bodily component of anger and presumably underscores it as an emotion.

Still, pain is not even strictly autonomic or reactive. It can be but need not be. It would therefore take two steps to link pain to emotion – first to link it to a "gut reaction," and second to link it to an emotion composed in part of such an autonomic reaction. But one can imagine coming to experience pain without having fight or flight reactions. Even with such reactions, one can imagine them processed in many emotional and non-emotional ways. Many kinds of people (e.g., athletes, monks, martial artists, soldiers, and even caretakers of children(!)) have trained themselves in such ascetics, levelheadedness, or calm in times for the sake of self and others.

---

[42] Cf. Murphy, *The Conceptual Foundations of Transitional Justice.*
[43] Nussbaum, *Anger and Forgiveness*, 17.

5. The fifth is a "desire for retribution." This is the "narcissistic" element in which we wish to make another go through what we (as wronged parties or parties to those wronged) went through, suffering a like humiliation.

Nussbaum links anger's narcissism to infantile helplessness's reactive desire for "domination and control" of others.[44] How does retribution do this? Presumably through subverting accountability into submission, as Callard does.[45] We might then be tempted to speak of a "narcissistic illusion" around anger, similar to a "transcendental illusion" around reason.[46] A "narcissistic illusion" might be *the tendency within reacting to being wronged to close down the interpersonal conditions of sense by subverting the autonomy of the other*, for instance, through forcing them to submit instead of holding them accountable.

Nussbaum criticizes and rejects the first and fifth of the Aristotelian elements of anger. She might also be read as criticizing and qualifying the fourth. If the pain one feels in anger is linked to the need to expunge injury through retribution – that is, if one is in pain because one has not gotten one's revenge[47] – then presumably such pain would be subject to Nussbaum's criticism of "magical thinking," which I discuss shortly.

Nussbaum rejects associating "down-ranking" with anger in two ways. On the one hand, she points out that much of what happens in moral wrongs isn't to be construed through relative status but in terms of suffering, injury, or trauma. "[I]sn't [viewing wrongs as down-rankings] a red herring, diverting us from the reality of the victim's pain and trauma ... ?"[48] The bully might have wanted to show you who's boss, but they also traumatized you by beating the shit out of you. On the other hand, Nussbaum argues that concerns about relative status misconstrue moral equality, especially when joined with the desire for retribution. "[D]own-ranking does not create equality."[49] To be focused on my rank rather than on my moral standing is already to have stepped outside of a moral point of view. Getting back at someone by down-ranking them only doubles down on such an extra-moral viewpoint.

Nussbaum's rejection of retribution in anger centers on a reading of the desire for retribution as infantile and narcissistic:

---

[44] Ibid., 29.
[45] Callard, *On Anger*, 18–20.
[46] Kant, *Critique of Pure Reason*, Section Division, Introduction, Section 1.
[47] See Callard, *On Anger*, 20 on how this might look.
[48] Nussbaum, *Anger and Forgiveness*, 28.
[49] Nussbaum, *Anger and Forgiveness*, 28–9.

The idea that payback makes sense, counterbalancing the injury, is ubiquitous and very likely evolutionary. Still, what else may make people cling to it? One factor surely is an unwillingness to grieve or to accept helplessness. Most of us are helpless with respect to many things, including the life and safety of those we love. It feels a lot better if we can form a payback project and get busy executing it ... than to accept loss and the real condition of helplessness in which life has left us.[50]

In other words, retribution is narcissistic, because it seeks to control one's helplessness by subjecting the out-of-control other who wronged one or those one loves to the pain, injury, or trauma that one or one's loved ones suffered. Presumably, this is narcissistic, because it refuses to accept the ways in which we are vulnerable and tries to deflect that vulnerability onto another who, by suffering, makes one feel powerful.[51] Nussbaum even goes so far as to suggest that this is "magical thinking" contradicting our basic striving as humans "to make sense to ourselves."[52] This acknowledgment of the vitality of making sense to ourselves, we have seen, attests to how important autonomy is for and in human striving. It also primes us to look for wonder without which we cannot search for sense authentically. I will return to these points.

Nussbaum also makes a practical argument against retribution. Seeking payback does "no good for the important elements of human flourishing that have been damaged" by the wrong.[53] What matters in a moral wrong, she implies, is that some injury has been done to one or to those one loves, and this injury is to be understood in terms of one's welfare, broadly understood (I imagine that she has the capabilities in mind).[54] To spend oneself on trying to bring about a similar injury in the wrongdoer is prudentially irrational. It does not work to heal the injury that one has suffered.

This last problem with retribution heralds Nussbaum's overall goal in her critique of anger. This is to rid us of seeing that anger makes sense except in a very narrow use – to motivate us to improve social welfare. She explicitly calls the very narrow use her "third road" of anger and names it "Transition Anger," stating that it is solidly "welfarist."[55] Only when anger motivates us to change the social conditions that led to or involve patterns of the wrong done to one or one's

---

[50] Ibid., 29.
[51] On the influence infantile helplessness has on leading to narcissistic behavior, see Nussbaum, *Upheavals of Thought*, chapter 4.
[52] Nussbaum, *Anger and Forgiveness*, 29.
[53] Ibid., 226.
[54] See her *Creating Capabilities* and *Women and Human Development*.
[55] Nussbaum, *Anger and Forgiveness*, 30.

loved ones, is it morally acceptable – and then only so long as it motivates us to improve society.[56]

> Transition-Anger does not focus on status; nor does it, even briefly, want the suffering of the offender as a type of payback for the injury. It never gets involved at all in that type of magical thinking. It focuses on social welfare from the start[, s]aying, 'Something should be done about this . . .'[57]

The acceptability of anger is *very narrow* here because the manner of one's motivation is not beneficial, she thinks, if it runs too hot. As she finds when studying Nelson Mandela's "strange generosity" that eschewed showing anger, "[a]nger [expressed to the one who wronged] does nothing to move matters forward. It just increases the other party's anxiety and self-defensiveness."[58] Note how Nussbaum views anxiety negatively here in passing. The only acceptable anger is kept inside in the face of wrongdoers and is channeled for social improvement. Nussbaum thinks that this is being practical. *We have to avoid more anxiety!*

*

Nussbaum's account and critique are partially Aristotelian in accepting a broadly Aristotelian ethics and partially Stoic in seeking to extirpate the passion of anger almost entirely.[59] The core problem in Nussbaum's hybrid Aristotelian and Stoic account of anger is its lacking the underlying logic of communicative relationship. To bypass that logic is to reproduce an alienated view of being human.[60] That logic, articulated by interpersonal relationships, personal attunement, and the moral accountability basic to moral relations, makes anger an important part of intimacy, trust, and what is social about us, namely that we can be vulnerable with each other and share what does and does not make sense to us on the basis of moral accountability. When Nussbaum does not emphasize these things about anger, her account becomes misleading. Nussbaum's belittling of anger as "weak" and "childish" preserves the illusion of anger as narcissistic.[61] Yet anger is really the opposite – an acknowledgment of vulnerability and a complaint against moral wrong that involves a plea for relationship. If anything, with Nussbaum's

---

[56] Ibid. "Transition-Anger, a Rational Emotion; Anger's Instrumental Roles," 35–40.
[57] Ibid., 36.
[58] Ibid., 230, in "Mandela's Strange Generosity," 226–32.
[59] See also Nussbaum's *The Therapy of Desire*, chapters 10 and 11.
[60] Marx, *Economic and Philosophical Manuscripts of 1844*, "Estranged Labor."
[61] Nussbaum, *Anger and Forgiveness*, 46.

critique of anger, Nussbaum's philosophy against narcissism has been carried into troubled waters.

Could it be that out of fear that the other's anger will be uncontrollably bad, difficult relating's been forgone? This would be ironic, since the critique of narcissism is central to Nussbaum's critique of anger.[62] In *Anger and Forgiveness*, Nussbaum underlines how important interpersonal and political trust are for society. She emphasizes that such trust depends on becoming comfortable with being vulnerable with each other, something which itself depends as much on social conditions as upon inherited practices and philosophical views.[63] Nussbaum should be on board with anger's communicative logic, especially given how important it is to repair moral wrongs.

The root of the problem is that Nussbaum and Aristotle begin in the wrong place, outside of moral and relational structure. Because morality is primary to how we must act as relational beings, conveying to others how you feel cannot license meanness, cruelty, or revenge. Let's not speak around the issue: *Aristotle's analysis of anger is intrinsically immoral.* It links the payback wish to anger. What would be moral comes from elsewhere, from justice.[64] We should then say that in Aristotle justice and anger are opposed. Nussbaum's analysis is accordingly morally ambivalent, even when it finds a narrow space for permissible anger. Her use of anger is ultimately only instrumental and presumes that nothing good for, true to, or beautiful in relationship comes of anger. The point is that since Aristotle and Nussbaum interpret anger almost entirely as a non-relational phenomenon, they miss what anger is about. In Nussbaum's case, this amounts to missing the way expressing anger in a manner morally consistent with anger's meaning is the opposite of narcissism. It is both mature and strong.

The beginning of anger signals an apparent wrong. Nussbaum actually agrees with this but misses how it discloses the relational reasoning implicit in anger.[65] This beginning can be emotional; it can be behavioral; it can involve forms of thought, or any combination of these three kinds of things. I might feel anger in my gut and begin to tremble, but I needn't feel anything at all. You might start pacing back and forth with furrowed brows, but you might not show any change in your behavior. They might start running the wrong done to them or their loved ones over and over in their mind. But they need not; they might space out.

---

[62] Ibid., 45.
[63] Ibid., 173.
[64] Cf. Aristotle's *Nicomachean Ethics,* book V, and Thompson, "What Is It to Wrong Someone?"
[65] Nussbaum, *Anger and Forgiveness,* 37.

They might not even think about the wrong, while meanwhile they walk around aimlessly or feel irritation spiking through their body like frenetic electricity. The form of the beginning is: "I was wronged," "you were wronged," or "they were wronged." What is implicit in this linguistic expression of a formal relationship is that the ones wronged were wronged by others who should have a considerate and accountable relationship in regard to those who were wronged. In this way, the beginning of anger reflects a moral relationship in the breach.

What of anger's life? The wrong is always a wrong of relationship, but it may not be that *the* relationship (as a whole) is wrong. It may be a wrong done in a relationship. What binds these cases together is that wrong always involves being inconsiderate of another – sometimes to the point that "being inconsiderate" is an inappropriate description of the failure to take another person and their life into account – for instance, when the failure is so severe or violent as to make the conventional English but conceptually precise "inconsiderate" sound trivializing. *The whole point of anger is to address the wrong of the relationship in a way that is morally consistent with relating.* The life of anger is relating, not closing off and deflecting the problems of the relationship into practical work. Turning Nussbaum's criticism of retribution's "getting busy" plotting revenge[66] against her idea of transition anger, one might argue that *transition anger's busyness in improving society could be a narcissistic deflection away from staying in relation.* In relationships, we're always vulnerable to another's will. Their will cannot be controlled if we're to still be in a relationship. Maybe it feels more in control to improve society instead. But that misses what the relationship is about. I don't relate to *you* by closing down what I'm experiencing about our interactions and throwing myself into a social justice group instead.

Anger attests to relationship and signals a real problem in it. This problem befell me, but it is *our* problem. You don't see it that way. Indeed, you wronged me. Even worse, perhaps the wrong you did in our relationship to each other reflected that "my bad is your good."[67] That's how bad a disagreement there is between us. Since, though, we are in relationship to each other – let us just say in the most basic way, as one human being to another, person to person[68] – I owe it to you, just as you owe it to me, to be accountable in the relationship,[69] and that means that I should tell you where I am. *By wronging me, you're missing me, and*

[66] Ibid., 29.
[67] Callard, *On Anger*, 19.
[68] Wallace, *The Moral Nexus*, and my "'Do you have a conscience?'"
[69] Darwall, *The Second Person Standpoint.*

so I should begin by helping you find me. The angry person should express to the wrongdoer that one feels that the wrong has been done.

As I've said, such an expression is a protest. It protests the wrong. But that can mean many things. It could mean that you weren't being considerate or, at the worst, that you failed to be moral at all. It could mean that the norms involved in a relationship are problematic and should be adjusted, reconsidered, or transformed. It could mean even that your understanding of the world is morally offensive and that we cannot share the world as things stand. But my protest still considers you as a person. It attests to the belief that you are capable of moral criticism and reflection. My protest attests to your capacity to relate differently. My anger even shares the world with you *in and through the anger,* even if the content of my protest is that I doubt that we can share the world.[70] Anger maintains relationship in situations of moral wrongdoing! It can certainly be painstaking, gut-wrenching, and all-consuming for the time, but the point is, the life of anger remains in the relating. One might even think of anger, formally, as a matter of moral integrity when faced with wrongdoing (using "integrity" in place of "consistency" to bring out how acting in a morally thoughtful manner is a virtue – that is, being morally angry attests consistently both to the wrong and to the moral relationship).

Morally consistent anger – which has no wish for payback but is about protesting a perceived wrong – is vital to moral relationships. Although it can be emotional and plausibly draws on evolutionary roots in our physiology,[71] anger understood consistently with its moral core is a moment in a moral relationship when one demands that a wrongdoer become accountable in and restore a relationship or that one's community support one's standing as a person deserving a life that makes sense. These are the two basic cases for the end of anger as opposed to its beginning or its life. *Either* the wrongdoer restores the relationship in some fitting way *or* one's community shores up one's standing as a person. The second possibility does not make up for the first, but it can address some of the wrong relationally, which is anger's point. When a community brings one wronged back into the world, so to speak, they make them know that they are relatable again – that there is a social space for them to make sense with others in the shared world. This is what happens in solidarity around anger.

---

[70] Compare my argument for disagreement holding people together in the shared world in *Involving Anthroponomy in the Anthropocene,* chapter 2.
[71] Prinz, *The Emotional Construction of Morals.*

Anger is "endless" when the wrongdoer doesn't become accountable – Callard is right about that, but not about what it means that anger is endless. Since anger is not an emotion and doesn't necessarily involve emotion, the endlessness of anger does not imply that I must hold a grudge or walk around poisoned by anger, as Nussbaum often suggests might happen.[72] Rather, anger's endlessness means that, in the face of an unaccountable wrongdoer, they are always to be *held in the space of my protest*. I will always hold open to them that they did wrong. This is tantamount to respecting their potential to be free, accountable beings, rather than disposable objects that I can simply write off. Bracket the amped-up emotions Callard and Nussbaum fixate on, and such an intentional and maintained openness to the other needing to be accountable can take many forms, even ones that are truly kind at the same time (i.e., wanting that the other, as a fellow person, live well). What is essential to anger is its logic when expressed consistently with its moral core, not the many ways that people fail to be consistent in their anger. Those matter, but they should not be blamed on anger. Rather, they should be blamed on poor facilitating environments and people not yet having come of age.

*

The basic moral relationship that people must have with each other if they are to be moral and of sound conscience is egalitarian. Nussbaum is also a moral egalitarian.[73] It is therefore surprising that she does not see how the subjection to which anger responds on the Aristotelian account should be interpreted *morally*. Being put down when one is a moral equal should call for anger. If Nussbaum were to acknowledge the breach of basic moral relationship to which anger fittingly responds, she might see that relationships of moral consideration are what anger is really about. If she saw that, then she might see that allowing anger to be associated with the narcissism of payback is incoherent, and that anger should be understood differently as part of a moral relationship with consideration being the central issue.

There are moments when Nussbaum comes close to such a realization. Her philosophy is, after all, concerned with affiliation, equal respect, sympathy, and even unconditional love.[74] At one point in her study of anger, she acknowledges that it is

---

[72] Nussbaum, *Anger and Forgiveness*, chapter 4, "Intimate Relationships: The Trap of Anger"; compare this to Na'aman, "The Fitting Resolution of Anger."

[73] See especially *Women and Human Development*, and in the vicinity of anger, *On Anger*, 28–9.

[74] See, respectively, *The Fragility of Goodness, Political Emotions, Frontiers of Justice*, and the focus of her admiration for Dr. King and for Mahler in *Anger and Forgiveness*.

a reasonable demand . . . that the wrongdoer acknowledge the truth: a wrong has been done. Being heard and being acknowledged is a reasonable wish on the part of the wronged party, and asking for truth and understanding is not the same thing as asking for payback.[75]

However, she then states that

often the *extraction* of acknowledgement shades over unpleasantly into payback and even humiliation, and this temptation should be avoided.[76]

Of course, she's right that such a temptation must be avoided. It is a temptation to subjection – to controlling someone to do something that they have instead to do freely for its sense to be authentic. But why should this worry rush in so quickly to close off thinking about how anger communicates a problem in the relationship that demands moral accountability and better relating? Elsewhere, Nussbaum thinks that a good way to be led by anger is to work through a conflict so that "relationships [are] preserved."[77] But it seems that her view is pessimistic about how well people can actually relate in the face of moral problems. That doesn't mean we shouldn't work to make a world where people *can* be angry.

This is one thing that the politics of wonder is about. In relationships, people *relate*. We relate to each other, and we relate to the world with each other. As relating actually occurs, things make more sense and the meaning of things is enriched and refined, or, as the case may be, made more sturdy and simplified of needless things. We come to be more understood and to understand others better. The world becomes more hospitable because it makes more sense. Moreover, the world becomes more open, just as people do. Avoiding people translates to inauthenticity as one loses faith in people being accountable in and through relationships and thereby loses confidence in one's autonomy within relationships. Subjecting people in any form becomes obviously wrong and inauthentic as one's living with the shared nature of sense-making comes undone. Especially when wrongs breach our relationships, the thing to focus on is not getting over anger, but on relating. The thing to do is to learn how to get angry in a relationship.

*

There is a politics of wonder inside the anger of relationships. To get to it, we should pause one last time on the threatening figure of narcissism in Nussbaum's critique of anger. Nussbaum thinks that

---

[75] Nussbaum, *Anger and Forgiveness*, 125.
[76] Ibid., emphasis hers.
[77] Ibid., 158.

people often grab onto anger and payback fantasies in order to exit from an intolerable condition of vulnerability and helplessness.[78]

This "narcissistic vulnerability"[79] repeats infantile reactivity, a homologous condition in infancy that is basic to emotional development as discussed in *Upheavals of Thought*.[80] Since infants get what they want by merely wishing it, they wish to control or dominate the world instead. Adults who are wronged likewise cannot wish away the person and the world that led to their injury, and so they feel that they must subject the person and control the world instead. Still, while wishing away the wills of others or trying to dominate them is narcissistic, we shouldn't accept the picture of vulnerability accompanying it.

We shouldn't accept that picture because it isn't truly *vulnerable*. The question is what it is to be vulnerable. In the context of the argument, vulnerability as Nussbaum understands it seems to be practical, focused on vulnerability to injury. But as I hope that I have shown, the vulnerability that enters into moral wrong is *relational*. It is a vulnerability we always have by virtue of being in relationship with others. In this way, it isn't simply negative. It is not simply vulnerability to another "injuring" us by subjecting us. It is vulnerability in relating. We relate only in so far as we are vulnerable with each other, letting down our guard and opening up. *This vulnerability is good for our flourishing.* It makes relationships possible and contributes through them to the possibility of our social flourishing. Such positive vulnerability, like positive anxiety, opens up sense-sharing between us and helps us, not leads us to contract and to be helpless. True vulnerability in relationships is both good and needed.

Nussbaum comes close to recognizing some such thing near the end of *Anger and Forgiveness* when she writes, "Intimate relationships . . . flourish only when parties are willing to be vulnerable with one another in major ways . . . Something similar is true in political communities."[81] But she doesn't compare the two senses of vulnerability that operate in her work, the one about being vulnerable to harm and disregard, and the other about being vulnerable with another in relating openly and letting down one's guard. Many of her works validate this second sense of vulnerability, however, ranging from what the basic capabilities must protect within socializing and sexual life,[82] to what works of literature explore,[83]

---

[78] Nussbaum, *Anger and Forgiveness*, 54.
[79] Ibid.
[80] Nussbaum, *Upheavals of Thought*, chapter 4.
[81] Nussbaum, *Anger and Forgiveness*, 173.
[82] Nussbaum, *Women and Human Development*.
[83] Nussbaum, *Love's Knowledge* and *Upheavals of Thought*.

to how relationships ought to work.[84] My point is that, beyond not disambiguating the two senses and inquiring into their difference or interconnection, Nussbaum does not see that, morally speaking, the second sense of vulnerability as a positive phenomenon is *primary*, for it opens up relating as such and makes the moral need for accountability be something other than defensiveness.

The narcissist has trouble relating to people and cannot abide the autonomous self-determination of people. So, too, with narcissistic moments in a life, such as those generating a payback wish. They lead those caught up in them to stop relating to the *object* (i.e., not the person!) of their control-fantasy and to seek to control that object, subjecting it to abuse.[85] What such an outline silhouettes is what should go on in a real relationship instead. A real relationship will consider the autonomous self-determination of others. It will subject one's fantasies of the other to critique so as not to leave the other an object. Even more, this critique will be led by the other's autonomous presence to which one will become attuned. Far from abuse being the modus operandi of interactions, relationships with others will flow from letting each other be how – and who – we are. We then have no need to have our guard up. The free play of our relating appears when, between morally accountable people, narcissism dissolves away and is outgrown. The free play of relating's openness is a positive kind of vulnerability with each other that makes much meaning and sense-making together possible.

Positive vulnerability helps posit relationships. Without openness to each other, no relationship can begin (again). In being open to each other and letting our guard down, we come to be present and to speak openly about our world and ourselves. This enriches the meaning of the world and clarifies the complexity of its sense by sharing the world in sharing of ourselves. The enrichment and complexity can take many forms, from an opening up of perspectives on things – and hence to multiple histories and cultures in relation to them – to the shading in of things so that they become more dimensional as they are shared. Moral accountability makes such vulnerability reasonable.

What is interesting about difficult relating is that it rests on the positive sense of vulnerability, yet involves the negative, conventional sense of being defenseless to wounding. "Vulnerability" includes the Latin root for "wound," *vulnus*.[86] Wrongs show us our negative vulnerability, the way we can be morally wounded.

---

[84] Nussbaum, *Sex and Social Justice*.
[85] Cf. Lundy Bancroft, *Why Does He Do That? Inside the Minds of Angry and Controlling Men* (New York: Berkley Books, 2002).
[86] "Vulnerability," *Oxford American Dictionary*.

But this should not occlude that even here the possibility of being morally wounded rests on the prior actuality of relating. *It is only because we are in relationship with each other that we can be morally wounded.* Yet to be in moral relationship with each other depends on being actual and honest people with each other. Only on such a basis can we even be accountable *to* each other. Positive vulnerability thus underlies the negative sense of vulnerability apparent in being morally wounded.

So, too, with disagreement. Disagreement can understandably involve being hurt when the disagreeableness of your world offends me, even leads me to want to drown you out or ignore you – both controlling reactions that would fit what Nussbaum calls "narcissism." But the possibility of getting hurt in disagreement rests on the prior actuality of positive vulnerability, whereby we can disagree only because we are in relationship first. Even more, only when we are honest and open people with each other can we truthfully be said to disagree.[87]

Anger, then, has an important place in being vulnerable. *In anger, I manage to remain open to another in the face of my being wronged by another.* The same applies *mutatis mutandis* to the frustrations of disagreement. Even more, since moral wrong is the worst disruption of sense between us, even worse than disagreement, anger is crucial to maintaining a world where we can make sense together, just as it is crucial for sustaining moral life as considerate and communicative. In the world where people do wrong to each other and where disagreement rocks the sense that the world can be shared well together, *being angry keeps open the possibility of making sense together,* strange as that sounds. In this, anger is like wonder. But is it actually wonderful?

*

The history of wonder involves many emotional associations. As we've heard, these tend to fall along a spectrum from delight and joyful surprise to awe, negative anxiety, terror, and even fear.[88] One emotion that is conspicuously lacking from talk about wonder, however, is the emotion commonly called "anger." That is striking, since anger as a moral relation that is sometimes

---

[87] Cf. Bernard Williams, *Truth and Truthfulness: An Essay in Genealogy* (Princeton: Princeton University Press, 2002).

[88] Vasalou, in *Wonder,* "DELIGHT," summarizes and reinterprets the groundbreaking history of Daston and Park's *Wonders and the Order of Nature, 1150–1750* as well as the conceptual genealogy linking Greek thought to post-Heideggerian thought in Rubenstein, *Strange Wonder.* One can add Fuller, *Wonder,* as providing a psychological history of wonder alongside the conceptual genealogy of Rubenstein, the history of thought of Vasalou, or the social and intellectual history of Daston and Park.

emotional opens up the possibilities in a relationship beyond where they currently make no sense and demands that the relationship, at least in part, be reconsidered. It is structurally homologous to wonder in this regard.

Consider what anger does with respect to moral wrong. Someone has wronged another, and that person has become angry. They protest the wrong to the wrongdoer and, if that fails to be heard, within their community. Their protest witnesses to what was ignored, neglected, or violated. It demands that the one who wronged consider the lives of others and their autonomy in living. It demands that the relationship between the one who wronged and the one who was wronged becomes stabilized so that they can share the sense of the world. The one who wronged thought it made enough sense to morally wrong others, and now this is being challenged by the anger of one wronged. That anger demands that other possibilities be considered; it protests that another world is possible than the one where wronging people "makes sense." "You must change your life"[89] – at least that part of your life where you thought you could do this! This protest isn't narcissistic control. It is a communicative demand for reconsideration. It calls the one who wronged to consider a different order of things and to reconsider their relation to others.

Insofar as the one who wronged hears the anger and is themselves moral, in so far as the one who wronged accepts the belief in their moral capability that is implicit in anger, they must reconsider their relationship to the one wronged and, in many cases, the things that they thought make sense in this world. If they thought that what they were doing was in some sense okay for them, now that is in question. On pain of inconsistency with their moral accountability, they must become lost while searching for the sense of things and of themselves in relationship with others anew. Another's anger, structurally homologous to wonder, has called them toward wondering.

The wondering of the one who wronged is, strictly speaking, anger's goal. Again, this protest isn't narcissistic. We cannot control others, even someone who appears immoral in the instance. We might have legitimate justification to coerce them but we can't make them change their minds of their own accord.[90] What can be summoned with some moral integrity, however, is the other as a moral being capable of reconsidering their life and how they relate to others reflectively. What can be summoned is another's capacity for wondering. This wondering need not be filled with "delight," "awe," or any of the other strangely

[89]   Rilke, "Archaischer Torso Apollos."
[90]   Marcello Oreste Fiocco, "Is There a Right to Respect?" *Utilitas* 24 (2012): 533–55.

exaggerated emotions historians of thought or psychology associate incorrectly with wonder as definitions of it. The conceptual form of wonder is what matters, that the one who wronged, still being a moral person, reconsider the possibilities of their life or of their relations, seeking to understand what makes sense in light of the protest of the one who was wronged. This is the core thing a moral person asks for in demanding accountability, despite what Nussbaum fears. To act morally, we mustn't wish to control others. But we can reasonably demand that we be accountable to each other. What anger does is to summon the other's reflection at the core of their accountability.

The goal of anger is for the other to become lost in reconsidering their world *with* others. Anger couples with wondering to lead people to reconsider the world and their lives in it together. Anger shows us one important way that it can take two to wonder about the basis of our life together.

*

A politics of wonder depends on sharing the sense of the world and what makes sense in our lives together. Insofar as the moment of politics involves confronting wrongs, too, politics depends on anger. Anger, in turn, calls for wondering. Moreover, the relational pairing disclosed in anger – anger from you with wondering in me as I try to reconsider my relationships – manifests a structure to disagreement between us. In disagreement, the claim that you demand I consider calls for my reconsideration of the way I act in the world and so of my understanding of the world that sanctions by action.[91] When things do not make sense between us in our relationship, we have to reconsider them as a matter of accountability to each other. We each make sense of our lives together, and to deny this in someone is to wrong them. It is to erase them epistemically and thereby to deny their autonomy.[92] Disagreement rests always on the possibility of anger being fitting, insofar as disagreement presents us with the demand to be accountable to each other and the possibility that we may fail to be so. Insofar as there is no politics without disagreement being possible, there is no politics purified of the possibility of anger. To seek to purify politics of anger is to misunderstand both anger and politics.

To share the world is to be open to wounding *and* to believe in each other's moral capacities. I see this everyday power of people as amazing, even virtuous.

---

[91] See my *Involving Anthroponomy in the Anthropocene*, chapter 2.
[92] Cf. Dotson, "Tracking Epistemic Violence, Tracking Practices of Silencing." I might call the injustice *epistemic deadening*.

Sharing the world may be the most common virtue, relatively incognito because of its ubiquity and basicness. Within this ordinary virtue, we find people being angry and working things out, rather than the fearful scenes the philosophers depict.[93] We find people being vulnerable in moments of profound disagreement.

Part of my argument with the philosophical accounts of anger I've discussed is that, despite their disagreements, they share a view of anger as the realm of immature or immoral relationships. They focus on extreme cases that burn themselves into our minds and neglect the widespread capability of ordinary people to get angry with each other and to work things out. I am leaving to the side for now a larger argument against a trend in my nation's culture to view anger as disrespectful and so to try to suppress it altogether in favor of upbeat interactions. Needless to say, I find such "positive" psychology immature and corrosive of moral responsibility. I find it negative – both distrustful of our capabilities and bad for our flourishing alone and together. One part of being vulnerable together is being lost together. We have seen how politics depends on being lost together. If sharing the world together is the task of politics, learning to be vulnerable together is part of that task, and being able to be angry with each other around apparent wrongs is involved. Can we see what we find when we communicate?

*

So here we are, sitting around the table, and I am mad at you. It isn't only that you have been harassing me with your political views. It's that you did not listen to me when I said I do not want you to send me letters at work or at home or to our extended family *and* my parents, harassing them in turn! To my mind, you have lost your moral bearing. In the name of politics, you have stopped considering people, stopped considering even your family. We are subjected to your need to control our ideology by drowning us out, bullying us, and refusing to listen to us and mind our limits, let alone wonder what we are thinking and why we think it. I am saying this on my own behalf and will let others speak for themselves: you wronged me. I am angry at you.

Our political views are another thing. There is a more basic politics at work here. We cannot share the world together when we are not morally accountable to each other. My anger and you sitting here become the political event that should matter to us, not anything else such as whom we vote for, to what rallies

---

[93] Cf. Judith N. Shklar, *Ordinary Vices* (Cambridge, MA: Harvard University Press, 1985).

we go, or what news channels we watch. Right here, not anything else. You and me. I am telling you that what you did was wrong. Will you hear me out?

I lost my sense of our family and of a relationship that I thought was sound. When thinking of our interactions, I felt a little more that the world had gone crazy and made little sense. I felt threatened and scared. Strange possibilities ran through my mind. I became anxious in a negative way. What you did was disorienting to me. The sense of things in our family and around the edges of the world frayed and even split apart as the harassment continued.

My anger is an expression of the way that I am lost. It also manifests my belief in the possibility of making sense of things between us again. I can imagine that being on the receiving end of my protest may strike you as my being vehement, and I have felt a lot of different things during the time that the wrong between us has unfolded. But I am capable of regulating how I feel so that we can communicate well. That much is demanded of me as a matter of respect for you.

I assume that you have reasons for the way you have been acting and that you have been offended, even you think wronged, by my silence. I can imagine that you think it is important to talk out how things are going in our country and that *you* are angry about the way things have ended up for you in this society. Maybe your talking things out and insisting on your viewpoint is a way of sharing your anger publicly within the family. Maybe what you wanted, in part, is an audience, and maybe what another part of you felt was that some of us in the family supported the very politics that you think has led to the unfair shake you've received when you acted in good faith for most of your life and still ended up on the shores of economic difficulty with your mind and capabilities underutilized and underappreciated. That makes *me* angry, too! You deserve better.

I don't fully understand how you could do what you did in relation to us, people in your family who've supported you. We've had many good laughs and good times. Maybe our past debating in good humor and our warmth, our support, and our reliability made it feel safe to vent around us or even *at* us. Maybe that same familiarity and warmth made it seem okay to blur the lines around us, to push more than we want, even to make us into enemies of a sort when we are not. Were things confusing on your end as well, and was your insistence to the point of harrying us just as much a call for stability and connection as it was a protest against wrongs you think have befallen you or those you support in your beliefs?

The reason I have been silent is that I have not been able to speak when my express wish for having my work and home boundaries respected was ignored. You have not treated me as a person but have up to now overridden my express request to sit down together. Up to now, you have bombed my work and home with mail. How can I speak when you have already ignored whether I am willing to talk? If I were to reply to you after you have ignored how I'm able to speak, I would merely be your object at your command. I would be subjecting myself in the name of speech. That, just as treating me as a thing to push around, is wrong. I can't do that to myself, and I can't do that to you.

I'm asking you to reconsider what you've done and how you related to me and to my nuclear family. My mother was struggling with cancer, my father was caring for her, and I was making a home. Into this, you introjected "politics," although I expressly said that I did not want to debate, and that in any event, I was not going to argue over email or in any other way than in person. I even told you that what you seemed to be assuming about my beliefs was false, that my beliefs might surprise you in some of their agreement with you. I both drew a limit and suggested that I wanted to relate to you face to face. I made an overture to move past hardened, simplified, and polarized positions. That you kept pressing the issue and bullied your way into our worlds, always ignoring the possibility of meeting face to face in a familiar way, that was what you did that was wrong. It wasn't your beliefs; it was your way of relating to me and to us that was wrong.

I'm asking you to reconsider your way of approaching things by reconsidering your way of relating to people when they are not simply available to hash out your emotional needs. How might your world work and appear differently if you related by giving others space to make sense of things *with you*?

That is for me the political question, not the policies and elected leaders and candidates for office whom you thought that we should debate. The political question begins with a moral one, about how we can share the world between us and then make sense together.

If there is anything fundamental about which we disagree in politics, it is this disagreement about the nature of the political. As far as I can tell, anything else about which we might disagree in polities and campaigns flows from or rests on the more fundamental disagreement about what we are doing when we are *being* political. I am committed to people working things out together, and I also have faith in it. The problems begin when people stop wondering with each other. This issue is moral and comes *before* debate. It's about a relationship between us that lasts *beyond* debate. As people together, we should feel free together.

This is what I wanted to say to you all along, but now all I have is a fantasy, imagining us sitting around the kitchen table and instead writing this imagined protest in a book. Have I betrayed my own word, that I would not discuss things with you except in person? But I have no idea where you are. For the third time in my life, I've had to cut someone out, and I am sorry.

My anger shows *me* how lost things between people are in my society. It makes me reconsider my life. I do not doubt the wrong and I do not doubt myself. Instead, I doubt that the society we tacitly maintain makes sense when it enables such senselessness within a family. I doubt this society for its lack of consideration and for its lack of wonder. Its harsh selfishness has closed down the space between us and left us *both* without a way to sort through the things that we need in order for our world to make sense.

But just as you cannot control my will, so I cannot control yours. The loss of our family breakdown is real. My anger, like some love, is unrequited. There is nothing I can do about that, and my anger can only go quiet. All I can do is mark it – and then leave it, setting myself free.

The wrong you did split apart the world I'd been given and made me confront possibilities I hadn't imagined. These possibilities weren't anger itself. They were my anger's lesson in wonder. This is the actual world I live in. It doesn't change that I love my family and that I love you. It changes how I love carefully.

"Croci (*Iridaceae*)," 2021

"With Wonder"

by
Misty Morrison

Prosperity Social Club, Cleveland, Ohio, June 2021

What were you doing with the series, "With Wonder"?
I have a hard time thinking about the series and how to explain it. I was trying to figure out what motherhood means. But I feel uncomfortable talking about it, because the idea of motherhood and art is a completely mundane idea, so mundane that the art world I know tends to dismiss it.

In the series, I was relating to this new life – or trying to – and how they relate to the world at a point where they are so alien that they cannot talk to you or even give you clear, non-verbal cues. I was thinking through wonder with Emet and with you as you wrote this book, through images – because that's how I think. Playing with objects is one of the ways Emet is figuring out the world; so, I was seeing the objects – or trying to – as I imagined he'd be seeing them.

Of course, I added my own layers of meaning. For instance, in *Duckies* (2020), I am seeing the bath toys in relation to our family, not simply Emet, and he might not see them that way – as the three of us and the three duckies in the image alongside the (unfinished) cup from the hospital where my post-partum uterine blood once was draining!

I think through what I see. I need to see things in order to make them real. That's especially true of relationships.

Through your seeing, what were you thinking about in relation to wonder?
I questioned . . . It shifts over the course of the year and a half that I painted. At first, I didn't know what wonder is. Whatever concept I had grew over time by talking together. At the beginning, I wasn't thinking of painting Emet. I was

thinking of what image would capture wonder. But then, because we were new parents and I was so new to Emet's world, I began thinking about what wonder is *when you don't think about it*. Wonder seemed then to me to be part of experience in the world, something you don't need to conceptualize first to experience it. I thought that if I watched Emet, he might give me a clue.

Now that Emet's almost 2 years old, and it's been a year since I've done a painting of him, it's only now that we're having moments when we can clearly see him wondering about the world. I think he was before, but part of it is just guesswork, and part of it is *my* experience of what he's experiencing. I think that's a lot of what was going on with the paintings: my imagining how *he* was experiencing the world was opening things up for how I could experience things. Openness is a big part of it, being receptive to *not* understanding what another person is experiencing. I think you have to get lost with a kid like that. "Being present" is an imperfect expression for it. With a kid, you have to let yourself get lost.

I feel like I learned a different *way of relating to wonder* from the work in this book and a different *way of wondering* from Emet.

Is there anything political that you relate to these images or the process of making them?
Let's start there – with the process of making them. I was making these images as you were writing this book during COVID-19, during the first year of being a parent, where I didn't have paid maternity leave; we didn't have support for childcare; childcare wasn't safe because of COVID; and I was painting at night after coming home from working at a job where COVID protocols were below state recommendations and yet flaunted.

If parents aren't supported with childcare in the child's first year of life when children are just sponges for the world and the bare minimum expectation is that we be present, then when *is* a child's experience of being open to the world supported? In this country, structurally, we don't support people being able to be open!

Even my own freedom to wonder about the world as a child and to not have restrictions put on my learning was in part *shaped by financial restrictions* for my family. I was homeschooled; my mom was a stay-at-home mom who could not pay for childcare, and we were also able to help around the house. So, I was able to wonder, but my parents were not able to be present for it. They had their own responsibilities to handle.

These images were made in the vacuum created by the absence of support for public goods.

*

Lomond neighborhood, Shaker Heights, Ohio, June 2022

When you were making "With Wonder," you were also reading about narcissism. Why did you do that, and what did it make you think about in relation to your visual art?
I had been reading about narcissism to help me understand my family system and also to understand how I relate to the rest of my life because of that system. With the birth of Emet, understanding my family became urgent because I didn't want to repeat bad patterns.

When I was working on "With Wonder," I was thinking a lot about how Emet relates to the world. As I was reading about narcissism in families, one of the things that came across is that children aren't free to be open to the world if their needs are being subsumed by someone else's. Through the work of painting, I was able to focus on the ways that Emet was being open to the world and to see what that looks like in healthy child development where his needs were being met.

That focus helped me to think about the direction of my visual art differently. The other thing that I've realized in reading and talking about narcissism, especially with you, is that I've used my visual art to navigate the world despite unhealthy familial patterns that shaped my environment. In my visual art, I began to think about what it would be to make understanding *what someone else sees* the focus of the art.

That in turn led me to think differently about how I relate to institutions and practices within the art world such as gallery representation, grant application, and general self-promotion. Despite what the prevailing attitude of working artists is, I had been taking a break from engaging with those things because the art that I wanted to make had an uneasy relationship to them. I wanted to do things that do not make sense within that world, such as making portraits to gift to their subjects rather than to be sold to them or to someone else. I did not want to focus on myself, how I am perceived, or why I should be given money. Making work that requires you to think from the perspective of another person or to attempt to relate to something outside of yourself is at odds with thinking about how to promote yourself.

Working on "With Wonder" led me to reverse engineer how I had been relating to the art world. Rather than thinking about how I could make my work fit that world, I realized that I should make the work that makes sense in my relationships and see where it takes me.

Thanks

The writing of this book took place on land in violation of an agreement made with the 1,100 chiefs and warriors signing the 1795 Treaty of Greenville. There is no way to be grateful for having inherited tyranny. But Native Americans enrich Northeast Ohio to this day, more than ten thousand strong from many older nations. I am grateful for the stewardship of the land their ancestors and Indigenous law have transmitted. What this book concerns has a role to play in undoing the narcissism of colonial society and leading settlers towards more caring relations with others.

To respond thoughtfully in deed is a way to insist on the reality of wonder in conditions of oppression.[1] I began this book from out of the first year of the Trump presidency and its subsequent treason, and I mainly completed it during the Omicron surge of the pandemic. My heart hurts thinking about everyone affected by the pandemic, and I am bitter about my nation's inability to try a president for treason of the highest order. But writing about wonder has helped me during these times.

Preparatory work for this book took form from academic papers[2] and more public essays.[3] I am grateful to all the venues and their editorial teams for giving me chances to think with others. In particular, this project emerged out of a community of scholars surrounding the Human Development and Capability Association (HDCA) annual meetings, especially the 2007, 2015, 2016, and 2019

---

[1] W. E. B. DuBois, *The Souls of Black Folk* (New York: Library of America, 2009), "The Afterthought."

[2] See my "From Humans to All of Life"; "The Politics of Wonder: The Capabilities Approach in a Time of Mass Extinction," in Mozaffar Qizilbash et al., eds., *The Cambridge Handbook of Capabilities* (New York: Cambridge University Press, 2020), chapter 12; "The Reasonableness of Wonder"; contributions to Urszula Lisowska, ed. "Discussing Wonder: A Seminar," *Studia Philosophica Wratislaviensia* 15:2 (2020): 7–74; my "Beneficial Relations between Species & the Moral Responsibility of Wondering," *Environmental Politics* 31:2 (2022): 320–27, and "The Other Species Capability & the Power of Wonder."

[3] "Reconsidering the Aesthetics of Protest"; "The Art of Protesting During Donald Trump's Presidency"; "Democracy as Relationship"; "Beyond Gestures in Socially Engaged Art"; "Fleabag, Let Things Get Lost!"

meetings at New School University, Georgetown University, Hitotsubashi University, and University College London. Thanks to Luke Craven, Breena Holland, Amy Linch, Urszula Lisowska, Martha Nussbaum, David Schlosberg, Rachel Wichert-Nussbaum (in memoriam), and Christine J. Winter. Thanks, too, to Jay Drydek for corresponding about domination and oppression following the 2020 virtual meeting hosted by Massey University.

After the New School University meeting, Martha Nussbaum encouraged my reading of the politics of wonder. I am grateful for her mentorship which began in 1995 at the University of Chicago during her first quarter there, even when she wasn't my advisor. Martha has consistently been open to frank criticism from her current and former students. It is such a wonderful quality.

Much imaginative work went into considering aspects of this project around an extended socially engaged art project in Cleveland that was interspersed with protest against the administration of Donald Trump. None of the project would have been possible without the generous financial support and university mission of the Beamer-Schneider Professorship in Ethics endowed by the Kent Smith Charitable Fund with heartfelt thanks to Phil Ranny (in memoriam) and William LaPlace as well as to the College of Arts and Sciences. I wish to thank John Levy Barnard and the College of Wooster and Steven Vogel and Denison University for the invitations to present early material in this project in 2017. Case Western Reserve University's Department of Philosophy also gave me space to speak publicly, and I remember Laura Hengehold's helpful comments. I wish to thank the Ethics Table (especially Bernie, Peter Whitehouse, Timothy Wutrich, Annie Pecastaings, Rachel Sternberg, Kevin Houser, Mae Elassel, J. P. Stephens, Evan Meszaros, David Beach, Stormy Sweitzer, and so many people whose names I am sorry not to remember at this very moment), the National Lawyers Guild, Tony Tenaglier and the Moral Inquiries (especially Patrice Yarnam, Em and Sylver Dragowsky, Dawn Ellis, Walter Nicholes – in memoriam – Cullen Brown, Ethan Moroh, Carlos Lewis-Miller, and many people whose names I cannot recall now that the website is down; thank you all for such a memorable, meaningful group), Elaine Hullihen, Sirjoon Elassal, and Amir Berbić.

Early feedback on the project that pushed me to develop more of my own position came from my college mentor, Susan Neiman – also a student of Nussbaum back then at Harvard. Susan's teaching on the problem of evil disrupted my life in the early 1990s and led me to focus on the conditions of senselessness in society, something that is behind this book's deeper interests.

An early stage of this project was presented at the University of Exeter in September 2019, following the HDCA meeting at University College London. I am grateful to the editors, publishers, hosts, and audiences of the venues listed in the last paragraphs, especially Jack Griffiths for organizing the Exeter workshop, Christopher Gill, and Anders Schinkel. I am grateful for Urszula Lisowska of University of Wroclaw for organizing the symposium on the politics of wonder for *Studia Philosophica Wratislaviensia* later that academic year.

Case Western Reserve University and its Department of Philosophy were supportive with a sabbatical leave in 2019–20. As sabbatical ended, I was fortunate to be able to start the Planetary Justice Virtual Community with Ben Mylius and then with many others. There, in addition to those previously named in other contexts, I thank Danielle Celermajer, Chelsea Fairbanks, Julia Gibson, Marion Hourdequin, Romy Opperman, Sebastian Östlund, Stefan Pedersen, and Charlotte Vyt. During the pandemic, this group demonstrated how academic work can be grounded in suppotive interpersonal relationships – even virtually and around the globe.

Charles Larmore corresponded helpfully at one point. Other memorable discussions include those with Sidra Shahid and Katherine Cassese, my co-editors for the American Philosophical Association's series *Into Philosophy*, Lynne Huffer who has developed a Sapphic ethics of wonder, and Kyle Powys Whyte.

For being in touch, I'm grateful to Anne-Christine Habbard. I will always be grateful for her example of being a scholar-activist while being a warm and real human being. She introduced me to the version of Kierkegaard that I relay in this book, albeit through my own interpretation.

The Baker Nord Center for the Humanities invited me to talk virtually about wonder in late 2020. Spring 2021's *Good Relationships* class at Case Western Reserve University gave me a chance to read Sadiya Hartman and Virginia Woolf again alongside several texts by Nussbaum. The Environmental Political Theory Virtual Community of the Western Political Science Association co-organized by Ross Mittiga and Gwen Ottinger workshopped the first part of this book in Summer 2021. My thanks again go to June Jones for her commentary.

I am deeply grateful to Daniel R. Scheinfeld, who reflected back and commented extensively on the first motet while he was dealing with the challenges of aging eyesight and working on a book of his own at 88 years of age. What a wonderful person and explorer Dan has been for the twenty years I've known him. His and Sandra's example of being welcoming and of being inspiring parents is one of those places I go in my mind to keep my sense of wonder open in this life.

I was lucky that Sidra Shahid and Rick Anthony Furtak accepted my invitation to review my manuscript in fall 2021. I want to thank Sidra for her moral focus, and Rick for his lucidity. He also recalled the Thoreau quote. Funds for Sidra's and Rick's work came from the Expanding Horizons Initiative of the College of Arts and Sciences at Case Western Reserve University and from the Baker Nord Center for the Humanities.

Lastly, I want to thank Colleen Coalter with her team at Bloomsbury, especially Suzie Nash, for their patience with this project. Thanks to Ben Harris, too, for copyediting, and to Merv Honeywood and Ben O'Hagen. Colleen was open to this project back in 2017, and it was good to talk with her at the American Society for Aesthetics meeting in New Orleans later that year. She supported my taking a more original direction than simply writing a secondary source. That made the project truer to the kind of dialogue true to Nussbaum's philosophy. She also reminded me of the value of a substantial introduction for a complex book.

Part of the process at Bloomsbury was final manuscript review, and there I was fortunate to meet, under anonymity, two generous and fair readers. Their comments were good. Had I two lives, I would have considered Hannah Arendt on the topic of wonder. I have always loved her dissertation and would want to think about love of the world from the starting point of wonder. I would also have read, or reread, many of the sources that were recommended by one reader with a strong grasp of the literature. But this book had its time. Misty and I were waiting on Ellery Abbie Ray Morrison, Emet's sister, to arrive!

*

For a friend around Cleveland, my gratitude goes to my buddy, Mattuck Meachum; for politics that burns with heat, my camaraderie goes to John Flores, and for being my emotional brother, my love goes to Stephen M. Rich. Lastly, for "beginner's mind," consciousness goes to Jeremy Levie and to Alex Shakar. But don't let me forget Rana Khoury and her family, and Emet's friend, "Sumi." And I am grateful for my elementary and high school choir teacher, Pat Clemens, thinking of us since my mom died.

This book wouldn't be possible without my family of origin, especially David Keymer, Esther Bendik (in memoriam), and Ruth Bendik. For a stretch of time, my mom, Esther, was an early childcare educator. Along with my dad, Dave, she created environments fostering sensation and creativity. Yet she herself struggled to find the kinds of supportive environments that would allow her to become autonomous in the disabling conditions of US society. I grew up with this contradiction, and in that mix, my dad first introduced me to the history of ideas (via Thomas More's *Utopia* and Jean-Jacques Rousseau's *Discourse on the Arts and Sciences*). The records on the turntables in the first half of this book came from him.[4] In addition to being a constant support, always showing up as a father, he introduced me to Nussbaum's work in the early 1990s before I knew that I would meet her. My dad's and my talks together have often been the stuff of life. I want to carry that on with Emet. This book could have been dedicated to Dave, too, except that he would want – with his whole, warm heart – that this book be for Emet.

Finally, my love goes to Misty Morrison for her series of paintings "With Wonder," and for her print that ends this book. Because Misty worked on the paintings during the first year of writing the book, what her painting taught me shaped how I wrote and what I saw in working out this study. This study would not be as real in the ways that I hope that it might be – where "real" means emotionally and interpersonally nuanced – if it were not for Misty's consistent attention to her relationships and to the complexity of people. I'm grateful also for her research into narcissism. Just as importantly, because we co-parent Emet, this book *literally* (!) could not have been written without Misty's parenting during the first half of the day or on those writing Fridays and crunch times during the pandemic. To come up from work to take walks with Emet after his nap and to give Misty time to re-energize left the writing in its place, making its purpose clear. It took a family to write this book.

*

There is a moment in Tarkovski's *Mirror* where the protagonist lets go of their weight in the figure of a bird. In late April 2022, Misty and I discussed some edits by the fire one spring evening, and then *this* is a more joyful version of that moment from *Mirror*.

Thanks, Emet, for your very self. And hello, Ellery.

- Shaker Heights, Ohio, USA / Land of Many Older Nations
  Summer 2022

---

[4]   In the book's second half, Windy & Carl came from Saleem Dhamee's radio shows at the University of Chicago in 1999 and Fela came from Steve Rich in 1992 and Neil Brenner in 1998.

Sources

Adorno, Theodor W. 1951. *Minima Moralia: Reflections on a Damaged Life.* Trans. E. F. N. Jephcott. Brooklyn: Verso, 2006.

Ahmed, Sarah. *Queer Phenomenology: Orientations, Objects, Others.* Durham, NC: Duke University Press, 2006.

Alighieri, Dante. 1320. *The Divine Comedy,* vol. I: *Inferno.* Trans. John D. Sinclair. New York: Oxford University Press, 1961.

Allen, Amy. "Rethinking Power." *Hypatia* 13:1 (1998): 21–40.

Allen, Danielle S. *Why Plato Wrote.* New York: Wiley-Blackwell, 2012.

Allison, Henry. *Kant's Transcendental Idealism.* New Haven: Yale University Press, 2004.

American Psychiatric Association. *DSM-5: Diagnostic and Statistical Manual of Mental Disorders.* 5th ed. Philadelphia: American Psychiatric Association, 2013.

Anscombe, G. E. M. 1957. *Intention.* 2nd ed. Cambridge, MA: Harvard University Press, 2000.

Aquinas, Thomas. *Summa Theologica.* Trans. the Fathers of the Dominican Province. New York: Benzinger Brothers, 1948.

Arendt, Hanna. 1963. *Eichmann in Jerusalem: A Report on the Banality of Evil.* New York: Penguin Classics, 2006.

Arendt, Hanna. *On Revolution.* New York: Penguin Classics, 1963.

Aristotle. c. 350 BCE. *The Art of Rhetoric.* Trans. Robin Waterfield. New York: Oxford University Press, 2018.

Aristotle. c. 350 BCE. *Nicomachean Ethics.* Trans. Christopher Rowe. New York: Oxford University Press, 2002.

Atwood, Margaret. 1972. *Surfacing.* New York: Simon & Shuster, 2012.

Bagg, Samuel. "Can Deliberation Neutralise Power?" *European Journal of Political Theory* 17:3 (2018): 257–79.

Bagg, Samuel. "Beyond the Search for the Subject: An Anti-Essentialist Ontology for Liberal Democracy." *European Journal of Political Theory,* published online (2018): 1–24.

Bancroft, Lundy. *Why Does He Do That? Inside the Minds of Angry and Controlling Men.* New York: Berkley Books, 2002.

Barthes, Roland. 1978. *The Neutral: Lecture Course at the Collège de France (1977-1978).* Trans. Rosalind Krauss and Denis Hollier. New York: Columbia University Press, 2007.

Basl, John. *The Death of the Ethic of Life.* New York: Oxford University Press, 2019.

Bass, Chloë. "An Artist Embarks on an Impossible Project for Tamir Rice." *Hyperallergic,* April 20th, 2015.

Bass, Chloë. *The Book of Everyday Instruction*. Brooklyn: The Operating System, 2018.

Bendik-Keymer, Jeremy. *Conscience and Humanity*. Dissertation submitted to the University of Chicago Department of Philosophy. Ann Arbor: UMI, 2002.

Bendik-Keymer, Jeremy. *The Ecological Life: Discovering Citizenship and a Sense of Humanity*. Lanham, MD: Rowman & Littlefield, 2006.

Bendik-Keymer, Jeremy. "Species Extinction and the Vice of Thoughtlessness: The Importance of Spiritual Exercises for Learning Virtue." In *Virtue Ethics and the Environment,* edited by Ron Sandler and Philip Cafaro, 61–83. New York: Springer, 2010.

Bendik-Keymer, Jeremy. "'Do you have a conscience?'" *International Journal of Ethical Leadership* 1:1 (2012): 52–80.

Bendik-Keymer, Jeremy. "The Sixth Mass Extinction Is Caused by Us." In Thompson and Bendik-Keymer, 263–80.

Bendik-Keymer, Jeremy. "The Moral and the Ethical: What Conscience Teaches Us about Morality." In *Morality: Reasoning on Different Approaches*, edited by Vasil Gluchmann, 11–23. Amsterdam: Rodopi, 2013.

Bendik-Keymer, Jeremy. "From Humans to All of Life: Nussbaum's Transformation of Dignity." In *Capability, Gender, Equality: Toward Fundamental Entitlements,* edited by Flavio Comim and Martha C. Nussbaum, 175–200. New York: Cambridge University Press, 2014.

Bendik-Keymer, Jeremy. "Reconsidering the Aesthetics of Protest." *Hyperallergic,* December 7th, 2016.

Bendik-Keymer, Jeremy. "The Art of Protesting During Donald Trump's Presidency." *The Conversation*, January 20th, 2017.

Bendik-Keymer, Jeremy. "Democracy as Relationship." *e-Flux Conversations*, April 30th, 2017.

Bendik-Keymer, Jeremy. "The Neoliberal Radicals." *e-Flux Conversations*, February 1st, 2017.

Bendik-Keymer, Jeremy "The Reasonableness of Wonder." *Journal of Human Development and Capabilities* 18:3 (2017): 337–55.

Bendik-Keymer, Jeremy. *Solar Calendar, and Other Ways of Marking Time*. Brooklyn, NY: Punctum Books, 2017.

Bendik-Keymer, Jeremy. "'This Conversation Never Happened.'" *Tikkun*, March 26th, 2018.

Bendik-Keymer, Jeremy. "How to Do Things Without Words: Silence as the Power of Accountability." *Public Seminar*, June 28th, 2018.

Bendik-Keymer, Jeremy. "Wonder, Capability Determination, and Epistemic Inclusion." Human Development and Capability Association Annual Meeting, 2018.

Bendik-Keymer, Jeremy. "Beyond Gestures in Socially Engaged Art: Community Processing and *A Color Removed*." *Public Seminar*, September 6th, 2018.

Bendik-Keymer, Jeremy. *The Wind ~ An Unruly Living*. Brooklyn, NY: Punctum Books, 2018.

Bendik-Keymer, Jeremy. "Fleabag, Let Things Get Lost!": "Wonder, Confusion, and Why Film Needs More of It". *Public Seminar*, September 19th, 2019.

Bendik-Keymer, Jeremy. *Involving Anthroponomy in the Anthropocene: On Decoloniality*. London: Routledge, 2020.

Bendik-Keymer, Jeremy. "Autonomous Conceptions of our Planetary Situation." *Studia Wratislaviensia* 15:2 (2020): 29–44.

Bendik-Keymer, Jeremy. "Wonder & Sense: A Commentary." *Studia Wratislaviensia* 15:2 (2020): 65–70.

Bendik-Keymer, Jeremy. "The Politics of Wonder: The Capabilities Approach in a Time of Mass Extinction." In *The Cambridge Handbook of Capabilities,* edited by Mozaffar Qizilbash et al., 227–44. New York: Cambridge University Press, 2020.

Bendik-Keymer, Jeremy. "Facing Mass Extinction, It Is Prudent to Decolonise Lands & Law: A Philosophical Essay on Respecting Jurisdiction." *Griffith Law Review* 29:4 (2020): 561–84.

Bendik-Keymer, Jeremy. "The Other Species Capability & the Power of Wonder." *Journal of Human Development and Capabilities* 22: 1 (2021): 154–79.

Bendik-Keymer, Jeremy. "Unacceptable Agency (Part I of *The Problem of an Unloving World*)." *Environmental Philosophy* 18:2 (2021): 319–44.

Bendik-Keymer, Jeremy. "Beneficial Relations between Species & the Moral Responsibility of Wondering." *Environmental Politics* 31:2 (2022): 320–37.

Bendik-Keymer, Jeremy, and Misty Morrison, "Trauma-feeding." *Cleveland Review of Books*, September 16th, 2019.

Berlant, Lauren. *Cruel Optimism*. Durham, NC: Duke University Press, 2011.

Berlin, Isaiah. "Two Concepts of Liberty." In *Four Essays in Liberty,* by Isaiah Berlin, 118–72. New York: Oxford University Press, 1990.

Biehl, João, and Torben Eskerod. *Vita: Life in a Zone of Social Abandonment*. Berkeley: University of California Press, 2013.

Bishop, Bishop. *Artificial Hells: Participatory Art and the Politics of Spectatorship*. Brooklyn: Verso, 2012.

Brandt, Jared, Brandon Dahm, and Derek McAllister. "A Perspectival Reading of *Acedia* in the Writings of Kierkegaard." *Religions* 11(2):80 (2020):1–22.

Brooks, Thom, and Martha C. Nussbaum, eds. *Rawls's* Political Liberalism. New York: Columbia University Press, 2015.

Buchanan, Larry, et al. "What Happened in Ferguson?" *The New York Times*, August 10th, 2015.

Callard, Agnes. "The Reason to be Angry Forever." In *The Moral Psychology of Anger,* edited by Myisha Cherry and Owen Flanagan, 123–37. Lanham, MD: Rowman & Littlefield, 2019.

Callard, Agnes. *On Anger*. Cambridge, MA: MIT Press, 2020.

Cavell, Stanley. 1958. *Must We Mean What We Say? A Book of Essays.* 2nd ed. New York: Cambridge University Press, 2008.

Cavell, Stanley. *Conditions Handsome and Unhandsome: The Constitution of Emersonian Perfectionism.* Chicago: The University of Chicago Press, 1990.

Chakrabarty, Dipesh. *The Climate of History in a Planetary Age.* Chicago: The University of Chicago Press, 2021.

Cherry, Myisha. "Anger Can Build a Better World." *The Atlantic,* August 25th, 2020.

Cherry, Myisha. *The Case for Rage: Why Anger Is Essential to Anti-Racist Struggle.* New York: Oxford University Press, 2021.

Chrétien, Jean-Louis. *La voix nue: Phénomenologie de la promesse.* Paris: Éditions de minuit, 1990.

Cobb, Jelani. "Ladies and gentleman, this is what you call uncharted territory." *Twitter,* @jelani 9, June 7th, 2020.

Cooley, Patrick. "Everything You Need to Know about the Michael Brelo Verdict." *The Cleveland Plain Dealer / Cleveland.com,* May 23rd, 2015.

Coulthard, Glenn. *Red Skins, White Masks: Rethinking the Colonial Politics of Recognition.* Minneapolis: University of Minnesota Press, 2014.

Critchley, Simon. "The Powerless Power of the Call of Conscience." Case Western Reserve University, April 12th, 2011.

Crowell, Steven. "Why Is Ethics First Philosophy? Levinas in Phenomenological Context." *European Journal of Philosophy* 22:3 (2012): 564–88.

Darwall, Stephen. *The Second Person Standpoint: Morality, Respect, and Accountability.* Cambridge, MA: Harvard University Press, 2006.

Daston, Lorraine, and Katharine Park. *Wonder and the Order of Nature, 1150–1750.* Cambridge, MA: MIT Press, 1998.

De Canonville, Christine Louis. *When Shame Begets Shame: How the Narcissist Hurts and Shames their Victims.* https://narcissisticbehavior.net/, 2018.

De Cruz, Helen. "Awe and Wonder in Scientific Practice: Implications for the Relationship Between Science and Religion." In *Issues in Science and Theology: Nature – And Beyond,* edited by M. Fuller et al., 155–68. New York: Springer, 2020.

Deerhunter. *Monomania.* London: 4AD, 2013.

Del Real, Jose A., Robert Samuels, and Tim Craig. "Black Lives Matters expands into movement embraced by the masses." *The Washington Post,* June 9th, 2020.

DeWylder, Jordan E. "An Argument for the Evolutionary Adaptiveness of Illusions." *Early Intervention in Psychiatry* 13 (2019): 720–1.

Dewey, John. 1938. *Experience and Education.* New York: Touchstone, 1997.

Diamond, Cora. *The Realistic Spirit: Wittgenstein, Philosophy, and the Mind.* Cambridge, MA: MIT Press, 1995.

Diamond, Cora. "The Importance of Being Human." *Royal Institute of Philosophy Supplement,* 28 (1991): 35–62.

Diop, Mati. *Atlantique.* Paris: Films du Bal, 2019.

Dostoevsky, Fyodor. 1879. *The Brothers Karamazov.* Trans. Richard Pevear and Larissa Volokhonsky. New York: Farrar, Straus & Giroux, 2002.

Dotson, Kristie. "Tracking Epistemic Violence, Tracking Practices of Silencing." *Hypatia* 6:2 (2011): 236–57.

Dotson, Kristie. "Making Sense: The Multistability of Oppression and the Importance of Intersectionality." In *Why Race and Gender Still Matter: An Intersectional Approach,* edited by Namita Goswami, Maeve M. O'Donovan, and Lisa Yount, 43–58. London: Pickering & Chatto, 2014.

Dryzek, John S., and Ale Y. Lo. "Reason and Rhetoric in Climate Communication." *Environmental Politics* 24:1 (2015): 1–16.

Duruflé, Maurice. 1960. *Quatre Motets sur des Thèmes Grégoriens.* Ensemble Vocal "Audite Nova" de Paris. Paris: Éditions Durand, 1986.

Edwards, Carolyn, Lella Gandini, and George Forman, eds. *The Hundred Languages of Children: The Reggio Emilia Approach to Early Childhood Education,* 3rd ed. Santa Barbara: Praeger Publishing, 2011.

Ellison, Ralph. 1952. *Invisible Man.* 2nd ed. New York: Vintage Books, 1995.

Emmerich, Roland, dir. *Godzilla.* Culver City, CA: Tri-Star Pictures, 1998.

Escobar, Arturo. *Pluriversal Politics: The Real and the Possible.* Durham, NC: Duke University Press, 2020.

Fingerhut, Joerg, and Jesse Prinz. "Wonder, Appreciation, and the Value of Art." *Progress in Brain Research* 237 (2018): 107–28.

Fiocco, Marcello Oreste. "Is There a Right to Respect?" *Utilitas* 24 (2012): 533–55.

Fisher, Philip. *Wonder, the Rainbow, and the Aesthetics of Rare Experiences.* Cambridge, MA: Harvard University Press, 2003.

Foot, Philippa. *Natural Goodness.* New York: Oxford University Press, 2000.

Foucault, Michel. 1979. "What Is Critique?" In *What Is Enlightenment? Eighteenth-Century Answers and Twentieth-Century Questions,* edited by James C. Schmidt, 382–98. Berkeley: University of California Press, 1996.

Foucault, Michel. *Abnormal: Lectures at the Collège de France, 1974-1975.* Trans. Graham Burchall. New York: Picador, 2004.

Front International. "Read More: First Edition of FRONT Generates over $31 Million in Economic Impact." *frontart.org,* December 17th, 2018.

Fuller, Robert C. *Wonder: From Emotion to Spirituality.* Chapel Hill, NC: The University of North Carolina Press, 2006.

Furtak, Rick Anthony. *Wisdom in Love: Kierkegaard the Ancient Quest for Emotional Integrity.* South Bend: University of Notre Dame Press, 2004.

Furtak, Rick Anthony. *Knowing Emotions: Truthfulness and Recognition in Affective Experience.* New York: Oxford University Press, 2018.

Freud, Sigmund. *Five Lectures in Psychoanalysis.* New York: Penguin Books, 1995.

Genel, Katia, and Jean-Philippe Deranty. *Recognition or Disagreement: A Critical Encounter on the Politics of Freedom, Equality, and Identity.* New York: Columbia University Press, 2017.

Glaveanu, Vlad P. *Wonder: The Extraordinary Power of an Ordinary Experience.* London: Bloomsbury, 2020.

Hartman, Saidiya. *Wayward Lives, Beautiful Experiments: Intimate Histories of Riotous Black Girls, Troublesome Women, and Queer Radicals.* New York: W.W. Norton & Co., 2019.

Haugeland, John. *Dasein Disclosed: John Haugeland's Heidegger,* edited by Joseph Rouse. Cambridge, MA: Harvard University Press, 2013.

Hawthorne, Susan. "Philosophers Fight Climate Change: Jeremy Bendik-Keymer." *Engaged Philosophy,* July 21st, 2021.

Hegel, G. W. F. 1807. *Phenomenology of Spirit.* Trans. A. V. Miller. New York: Oxford University Press, 1976.

Heidegger, Martin. 1929. "What Is Metaphysics?" In *Basic Writings,* edited by David Farell Krell, chapter 2. New York: Routledge, 2015.

Heidegger, Martin. 1927. *Being and Time.* Trans. Joan Stambaugh and Dennis Schmidt. Albany, NY: SUNY Press, 2010.

Heidegger, Martin. 1936. *Schelling's Treatise on the Essence of Human Freedom.* Trans. Joan Stambaugh. Athens, OH: Ohio University Press, 1985.

Hepburn, R. W. "The Inaugural Address: Wonder." *Proceedings of the Aristotelian Society, Supplementary Volumes* 54 (1980): 1–23.

Hitz, Zena. *Lost in Thought: The Hidden Pleasures of an Intellectual Life.* Princeton: Princeton University Press, 2020.

Honneth, Axel. *The Struggle for Recognition: The Moral Grammar of Social Conflicts.* Trans. Joel Anderson. Cambridge, MA: MIT Press, 1996.

Huffer, Lynne. *Mad for Foucault: Rethinking the Foundations of Queer Theory.* New York: Columbia University Press, 2009.

Huffer, Lynne. *Foucault's Strange Eros.* New York: Columbia University Press, 2020.

Hulsey, John. "Reconsidering the Aesthetics of Liberalism." *e-Flux Conversations,* January 18th, 2017.

Husserl, Edmund. 1939. *Cartesian Meditations: An Introduction to Phenomenology.* Trans. Dorion Cairns. Dordrecht: Kluwer Academic Publishers, 1987.

Inoue, Cristina Yumie Aoki, Thais Lemos Ribeiro, and Ítalo Sant' Anna Resende. "Worlding Global Sustainability Governance." In *Routledge Handbook of Global Sustainability Governance,* edited by Agni Kalfagianni, Doris Fuchs, and Anders Hayden, 59–72. New York: Routledge, 2020.

Irigaray, Luce. *Sharing the World.* New York: Continuum, 2008.

Jackall, Robert. *Moral Mazes: The World of Corporate Managers.* 2nd ed. New York: Oxford University Press, 2009.

Kant, Immanuel. 1781. *Critique of Pure Reason.* Trans. Norman Kemp-Smith. New York: St. Martin's Press, 1929.

Kant, Immanuel. 1784. "An Answer to the Question: What Is Enlightenment?" In *What Is Enlightenment? Eighteenth-Century Answers and Twentieth-Century Questions,* edited by James C. Schmidt, 58–64. Berkeley: University of California Press, 1996.

Kant, Immanuel. 1788. *Critique of Practical Reason.* Trans. Mary Gregor. New York: Cambridge University Press, 2017.

Kant, Immanuel. 1790. *Critique of Judgment.* Trans. J. H. Bernard. New York: Hafner Press, 1951.

Kant, Immanuel. 1793. *Religion within the Limits of Reason Alone.* Trans. Theodore M. Greene and Hoyt H. Hudson. New York: HarperOne, 2008.

Karatani, Kōjin. *Isonomia and the Origins of Philosophy.* Trans. Joseph A. Murphy. Durham, NC: Duke University Press, 2017.

Kierkegaard, Søren. 1843. *Either/Or, Part II.* Trans. Howard V. Hong and Edna H. Hong. Princeton: Princeton University Press, 1987.

Kierkegaard, Søren. 1844. *Eighteen Upbuilding Discourses.* Trans. Howard V. Hong and Edna H. Hong. Princeton: Princeton University Press, 1990.

Kierkegaard, Søren. 1844. *The Concept of Anxiety: A Simple Psychologically Orienting Deliberation on the Dogmatic Issue of Hereditary Sin.* Trans. Reidar Thomte. Princeton: Princeton University Press, 1980.

Kierkegaard, Søren. 1846. *Concluding Unscientific Postscript to* Philosophical Fragments. Trans. Howard V. Hong and Edna H. Hong. Princeton: Princeton University Press, 1992.

Kierkegaard, Søren. 1849. *The Sickness unto Death: A Christian Psychological Exposition for Upbuilding and Awakening.* Trans. Howard V. Hong and Edna H. Hong. Princeton: Princeton University Press, 1980.

Kieślowski, Krzysztof. *La double vie de Véronique.* Paris: Sidéral Films, 1991.

Kieślowski, Krzysztof. *Trois couleurs: bleu, blanc, rouge.* Paris: MK2 Productions, 1994.

Kitcher, Philip. *The Ethical Project.* Cambridge, MA: Harvard University Press, 2011.

Kitcher, Philip. *Moral Progress.* New York: Oxford University Press, 2021.

Korsgaard, Christine M. *The Sources of Normativity.* New York: Cambridge University Press, 1996.

Korsgaard, Christine M. *Fellow Creatures: Our Obligations to Other Animals.* New York: Oxford University Press, 2018.

Kuti, Fela Anikulapo & Africa 70. *International Thief Thief (I.T.T.).* New York: PolyGram, 1980.

La Caze, Maguerite. *Wonder and Generosity: Their Role in Ethics and Politics.* Albany, NY: SUNY Press, 2013.

Larmore, Charles. *The Morals of Modernity.* New York: Cambridge University Press, 1996.

Larmore, Charles. *The Practices of the Self.* Trans. Sharon Bowman, Chicago: The University of Chicago Press, 2010.

Larmore, Charles. *What Is Political Philosophy?* Princeton: Princeton University Press, 2020.

Lisowska, Urszula, ed. "Discussing Wonder: A Seminar" *Studia Wratislaviensia* 15:2 (2020): 7–74.

Lisowska, Urszula. "Wonder and Politics in the Anthropocene: Beyond Curiosity and Reverance," MS, 2022.

Lloyd, Genevieve. *Reclaiming Wonder: After the Sublime.* Edinburgh: University of Edinburgh Press, 2018.

Luhmann, Niklas. *Love as Passion: The Codification of Intimacy* Trans. Jeremy Gaines. Cambridge, MA: Harvard University Press, 1987.

Malecki, W. P. "Against Wonder." *Studia Wratislaviensia* 15:2 (2020): 45–58.

Manne, Kate. *Down Girl: The Logic of Misogyny.* New York: Oxford University Press, 2018.

Marion, Jean-Luc. *Reduction and Givenness: Investigations of Husserl, Heidegger, and Phenomenology.* Trans. Thomas A. Carlson. Evanston, IL: Northwestern University Press, 1998.

Marion, Jean-Luc. *Being Given: Toward a Phenomenology of Givenness.* Trans. Jeffery Kosky. Palo Alto: Stanford University Press, 2002.

Marion, Jean-Luc. *In Excess: Studies of Saturated Phenomena.* Trans. Robyn Horner and Vincent Berraud. New York: Fordham University Press, 2004.

Marion, Jean-Luc. *The Erotic Phenomenon.* Trans. Stephen E. Lewis. Chicago: The University of Chicago Press, 2006.

Marx, Karl. 1932. *Economic and Philosophical Manuscripts of 1844.* Trans. Martin Milligan. Mineola, NY: Dover Publications, 2007.

McCammon, Christopher. "Domination." *Stanford Encyclopedia of Philosophy,* 2018.

McCarthy, Tom. "Tamir Rice: video shows boy, 12, shot 'seconds' after police confronted child." *The Guardian,* November 26th, 2014.

McDowell, John. *Mind and World.* Cambridge, MA: Harvard University Press, 1994.

McKittrick, Katherine, ed. *Sylvia Wynter: On Being Human as Praxis.* Durham, NC: Duke University Press, 2015.

McQueen, Steve. *Small Axe.* London: BBC, 2020.

Meagher, Thomas. "Ethics of Freedom, Politics for Decolonization: Thoughts on Devin Shaw's *Philosophy of Antifascism.*" *Blog of the APA,* August 17th, 2021.

Merleau-Ponty, Maurice. 1964. *The Visible and the Invisible.* Trans. Alphonso Lingis. Evanston, IL: Northwestern University Press, 1969.

Mill, John Stuart. 1859. *On Liberty.* Indianapolis: Hackett Publishing.

Mitchell, Roscoe. *Nonaah.* Chicago: Nessa Records, 1977.

Morrison, Misty, "An Interview about *Oblivion,*" https://soundcloud.com/mistymorrison/an-interview-about-my-upcoming-show-oblivion-and-the-process-behind-it, 2021.

Murphy, Colleen. *The Conceptual Foundations of Transitional Justice.* New York: Cambridge University Press, 2017

Na'aman, Oded. "Reasons of Love: A Case against Universalism about Practical Reason." *Proceedings of the Aristotelian Society* 115:3 (2015), 315–22.

Na'aman, Oded. "The Fitting Resolution of Anger." *Philosophical Studies,* 177: 8 (2020): 2417–2430.

Nancy, Jean-Luc. *The Experience of Freedom.* Trans. Bridget McDonald. Palo Alto: Stanford University Press, 1994.

Nancy, Jean-Luc. *The Birth to Presence*. Trans. Brian Holmes et al. Palo Alto: Stanford University Press, 1994.

Neiman, Susan. *The Unity of Reason: Rereading Kant*. New York: Oxford University Press, 1994.

Neiman, Susan. *Moral Clarity: A Guide for Grown-Up Idealists*. Rev. ed. Princeton: Princeton University Press, 2009.

Neiman, Susan. "Learning from the Germans: Tarantino, Spielberg, and American Crimes." Case Western Reserve University, April 11th, 2013.

Neiman, Susan. *Evil in Modern Thought: An Alternative History of Philosophy*. Rev. ed. Princeton: Princeton University Press, 2015.

Neiman, Susan. *Why Grow Up? Subversive Thoughts for an Infantile Age*. New York: Farrar, Straus & Giroux, 2015.

Neiman, Susan. *Learning from the Germans: Race and the Memory of Evil*. New York: Farrar, Straus & Giroux, 2019.

Nichols, Rob. *The World of Freedom: Heidegger, Foucault, and the Politics of Historical Ontology*. Palo Alto: Stanford University Press, 2014.

Niemeyer, Simon. "Intersubjective Reasoning in Political Deliberation: A Theory and Method for Assessing Deliberative Transformation in Small and Large Scale." *Centre for Deliberative Democracy and Global Governance* 4 (2019): 1–36.

Nussbaum, Martha Craven. *Aristotle's* De Motu Animalium. Princeton: Princeton University Press, 1985.

Nussbaum, Martha C. 1986. *The Fragility of Goodness: Luck and Ethics in Greek Tragedy and Philosophy*. 2nd ed. New York: Cambridge University Press, 2001.

Nussbaum, Martha C. *Love's Knowledge: Essays in Philosophy and Literature*. New York: Oxford University Press, 1990.

Nussbaum, Martha C. *The Therapy of Desire: Theory and Practice in Hellenistic Ethics*. Princeton: Princeton University Press, 1994.

Nussbaum, Martha C. *Poetic Justice: The Literary Imagination and Public Life*. Boston, MA: Beacon Press, 1995.

Nussbaum, Martha C. *Cultivating Humanity: A Classical Defense of Reform in Liberal Education*. Cambridge, MA: Harvard University Press, 1997.

Nussbaum, Martha C. *Sex and Social Justice*. New York: Oxford University Press, 1999.

Nussbaum, Martha C. *Women and Human Development: The Capabilities Approach*. New York: Cambridge University Press, 2000.

Nussbaum, Martha C. *Upheavals of Thought: The Intelligence of the Emotions*. New York: Cambridge University Press, 2001.

Nussbaum, Martha C. *Hiding from Humanity: Disgust and Shame in the Law*. Princeton: Princeton University Press, 2004.

Nussbaum, Martha C. *Frontiers of Justice: Disability, Nationality, Species Membership*. Cambridge, MA: The Belknap Press, 2006.

Nussbaum, Martha C. *The Clash Within: Democracy, Religious Violence, and India's Future*. Cambridge, MA: The Belknap Press, 2007.

Nussbaum, Martha C. *Liberty of Conscience: In Defense of America's Tradition of Religious Equality*. New York: Basic Books, 2008.

Nussbaum, Martha C. *From Disgust to Humanity: Sexual Orientation and Constitutional Law*. New York: Oxford University Press, 2010.

Nussbaum, Martha C. *Creating Capabilities: The Human Development Approach*. Cambridge, MA: The Belknap Press, 2011.

Nussbaum, Martha C. *The New Religious Intolerance: Overcoming the Politics of Fear in an Anxious Age*. Cambridge, MA: The Belknap Press, 2012.

Nussbaum, Martha C. *Political Emotions: Why Love Matters for Justice*. Cambridge, MA: Harvard University Press, 2013.

Nussbaum, Martha C. *Anger and Forgiveness: Resentment, Generosity, Justice*. New York: Oxford University Press, 2016.

Nussbaum, Martha C. "Human Capabilities and Animal Lives: Conflict, Wonder, Law." *Journal of Human Development and Capabilities* 18:3 (2017): 317–21.

Nussbaum, Martha C. *The Monarchy of Fear: A Philosopher Looks at Our Political Crisis*. New York: Simon & Shuster, 2018.

Nussbaum, Martha C. *The Cosmopolitan Tradition: A Noble but Flawed Ideal*. Cambridge, MA: The Belknap Press, 2019.

Nussbaum, Martha C. "Crucified by the War Machine: Britten's *War Requiem* and the Hope of Postwar Resurrection." In *Cannons and Codes: Law, Literature, and America's Wars,* edited by Alison L. LaCroix, Jonathan S. Masur, and Martha C. Nussbaum, chapter 7. New York: Oxford University Press, 2021.

Nussbaum, Martha C. *Citadels of Pride: Sexual Assault, Accountability, and Reconciliation,* New York: W.W. Norton & Co., 2021.

Nussbaum, Martha C. *Justice for Animals: Our Collective Responsibility*, New York: Simon & Schuster, 2022.

Ober, Josiah. "The original meaning of 'democracy': capacity to do things, not majority rule." Princeton/Stanford Working Papers in Classics, version 1.0, September 2007.

Opperman, Romy. "Haunting and Hosting." *New School University Gender and Sexuality Studies Institute*, November 10th, 2020.

Oxford American Dictionary. Apple Inc., 2005–20.

Oxley, Julinna. "Feminist Perspectives on Power, Domination, and Exploitation." In *Philosophy: Feminism*, edited by Carol Hay, chapter 4. New York: MacMillan Reference USA, 2017.

Parker, Emily Anne. *Elemental Difference and the Climate of the Body*. New York: Oxford University Press, 2021.

Partzsch, Lena. "'Power with' and 'Power to' in Environmental Politics and the Transition to Sustainability." *Environmental Politics* 26:2 (2017): 193–211.

Pasternak, Shiri. *Grounded Authority: The Algonquins of Barriere Lake Against the State*. Minneapolis: University of Minnesota Press, 2017.

Pedersen, Jan B. *Balanced Wonder: Experiential Sources of Imagination, Virtue, and Human Flourishing*. Lanham, MD: Lexington Books, 2019.

Pène du Bois, William. *Bear Party*. New York: Viking Press, 1951.

Pettit, Philip. *Republicanism: A Theory of Freedom and Government*. New York: Oxford University Press, 1998.

Petit, Philip. *On the People's Terms: A Republican Theory and Model of Democracy*, Cambridge: Cambridge University Press, 2012.

Pico della Mirandola, Giovanni. *Oration on the Dignity of Man, A New Translation and Commentary*. Trans. Francesco Borghesi, Michael Papio, and Massimo Riva. New York: Cambridge University Press, 2012.

Piketty, Thomas. *Capital in the Twenty-First Century*. Trans. Arthur Goldhammer, Cambridge, MA: The Belknap Press, 2014.

Pilkington, Ed. "After 15 days of stunning antiracist protests ... what happens next?" *The Guardian*, June 10th, 2020.

Prinz, Jesse. *Gut Reactions: A Perceptual Theory of Emotion*. New York: Oxford University Press, 2004.

Prinz, Jesse. *The Emotional Construction of Morals*. New York: Oxford University Press, 2007.

Rakowitz, Michael. "A Color Removed." Case Western Reserve University, April 7th, 2015.

Ramsay, Lynne. *The Swimmer*. London: BBC Films, 2012.

Rancière, Jacques. 1974. *Althusser's Lesson*. Trans. Emiliano Battista. New York: Continuum, 2011.

Rancière, Jacques. 1987. *The Ignorant Schoolmaster: Five Lessons in Intellectual Emancipation*. Trans. Kristin Ross. Palo Alto: Stanford University Press, 1991.

Rancière, Jacques. 1995. *Disagreement: Politics and Philosophy*. Trans. Julie Rose. Minneapolis: University of Minnesota Press, 2004.

Rawls, John. 1971. *A Theory of Justice*. 2nd ed. Cambridge, MA: The Belknap Press, 1999.

Rawls, John. 1996. *Political Liberalism*. 2nd ed. New York: Columbia University Press, 2005.

Reich, Steve. *Music for 18 Musicians*. New York: ECM, 1977.

Ridley, Matt. *The Origins of Virtue: Human Instincts and the Evolution of Cooperation*. New York: Penguin Books, 1998.

Rilke, Rainer Maria. 1908. "Archaischer Torso Apollos." Widely reprinted.

Rilke, Rainer Maria. 1923. "Duino Elegies." In *Duino Elegies & The Sonnets to Orpheus: A Bilingual Edition*. Trans. Stephen Mitchell. New York: Vintage, 2009.

Rimbaud, Arthur. 1870. "Sensation." Widely reprinted.

Rimbaud, Arthur. 1870. "Roman." Widely reprinted.

Rousseau, Jean-Jacques. 1762. *Émile, or On Education*. Trans. Alan Bloom. New York: Basic Books, 1979.

Rousseau, Jean-Jacques. 1778. *The Reveries of the Solitary Walker*. Trans. Charles Butterworth. Indianapolis: Hackett Publishing, 1992.

Rubenstein, Mary Jane. *Strange Wonder: The Closure of Metaphysics and the Opening of Awe*. New York: Columbia University Press, 2011.

Sartre, Jean-Paul. 1943. *Being and Nothingness: A Phenomenological Essay on Ontology.* Trans. Hazel E. Barnes. New York: Washington Square Press, 1984.

Schelling, F. W. J. 1800. *System of Transcendental Idealism.* Trans. Peter Heath. Charlottesville: University of Virginia Press, 1993.

Scheinfeld, Daniel R., Karen M. Haigh, and Sandra J. P. Scheinfeld. *We Are All Explorers: Learning and Teaching with Reggio Principles in Urban Settings.* New York: Teachers College Press, 2008.

Schinkel, Anders. "The Educational Importance of Deep Wonder." *Journal of Philosophy of Education* 51:2 (2017): 538–53.

Schinkel, Anders. *Wonder and Education: On the Educational Importance of Contemplative Wonder.* New York: Bloomsbury, 2020.

Schürmann, Reiner. *Heidegger on Being and Acting: From Principles to Anarchy.* Trans. Marie Gros, Bloomington: Indiana University Press, 1987.

Scott-Heron, Gil. "The Revolution Will Not Be Televised." *Small Talk at 125th and Lenox.* New York: Flying Dutchman Records/RCA, 1970.

Shahid, Sidra. "Genealogies of Philosophy: Lynne Huffer (part I)." *Blog of the APA,* March 5th, 2021.

Shahid, Sidra. "Genealogies of Philosophy: Lynee Huffer (part II)." *Blog of the APA,* April 2nd, 2021.

Shahid, Sidra. "Understanding Academic Precarity with Iris Marion Young: Who's Responsible?" *Blog of the APA*, December 31st, 2021.

Shahid, Sidra Shahid, and Jeremy Bendik-Keymer. "A Little Place to Oppose Insecurity in the World." *Blog of the APA*, June 25th, 2021.

Sholette, Gregory, Chloë Bass, and Social Practice Queens, eds. *Art as Social Action: An Introduction to the Principles and Practices of Teaching Social Practice Art.* New York: Allworth, 2018.

Shklar, Judith N. *Ordinary Vices.* Cambridge, MA: Harvard University Press, 1985.

Sierra (sop.), Nadine, and Rachel Willis-Sørensen (sop.). "Duettino-Sull'aria." In Wolfgang Amadeus Mozart, 1786, *La Nozze de Figaro.* WQXR Radio, November 30th, 2017.

SPACES Gallery. "SPACES Is 40 and Fabulous: 2018 Annual Report." SPACES Gallery, 2018.

Steinhauer, Jillian. "An Artist Honors Tamir Rice, One Orange Object at a Time." *The New York Times,* July 29th, 2018.

Sumpter, Sam. "Conditions of Empowerment." *Philosophy and Activism*, August 10th, 2021.

Suzuki, Shunryu. *Zen Mind, Beginner's Mind: Informal Talks on Zen Meditation and Practice.* Boston, MA: Shambhala Publications, 2011.

Táíwò, Olúfémi. "Who Gets to Feel Secure?" *Aeon,* October 30th, 2020.

Tarkovsky, Andrei. *Mirror.* Moscow: Mosfilms, 1975.

Taylor, Paul C. *Black Is Beautiful: A Philosophy of Black Aesthetics.* Malden, MA: Wiley-Blackwell, 2016.

Thompson, Allen, and Jeremy Bendik-Keymer, eds. *Ethical Adaptation to Climate Change: Human Virtues of the Future.* Cambridge, MA: MIT Press, 2012.

Thompson, Michael. "What Is It to Wrong Someone? A Puzzle about Justice." In *Reason and Value: Themes from the Moral Philosophy of Joseph Raz,* edited by R. Jay Wallace, Philip Pettit, Samuel Scheffler, and Michael Smith, 333–84. Oxford: Clarendon Press, 2004.

Thompson, Michael. *Life and Action: Elementary Structures of Practice and Practical Thought.* Cambridge, MA: Harvard University Press, 2008.

Van Jaarsveld, Jessica. *Towards an Environmental Ethic: Revising Nussbaum's Capability Approach.* Dissertation submitted to the Department of Philosophy, University of Johannesberg, 2002.

Vasalou, Sophia. *Wonder: A Grammar.* Albany, NY: SUNY Press, 2016.

Wailers, The. "Small Axe." On *Burnin'.* London: Island Music/Tuff Gong, 1973.

Wallace, R. Jay. *The Moral Nexus.* Princeton: Princeton University Press, 2019.

White, E. B. *Charlotte's Web.* Illus. Garth Williams. New York: Harper & Brothers, 1952.

Whyte, Kyle Powys. "Indigenous Climate Change Studies: Indigenizing Futures, Decolonizing the Anthropocene." *English Language Notes* 55: 1–2 (2017): 153–62.

Whyte, Kyle Powys. "Settler Colonialism, Ecology, & Environmental Injustice." *Environment & Society* 9 (2018): 129–44.

Williams, Bernard. *Moral Luck: Philosophical Papers, 1973–1980.* New York: Cambridge University Press, 1981.

Williams, Bernard. *Making Sense of Humanity, and Other Philosophical Papers, 1982–1993.* New York: Cambridge University Press, 1995.

Williams, Bernard. *Truth and Truthfulness: An Essay in Genealogy.* Princeton: Princeton University Press, 2002.

Wilson, Nick. *The Space that Separates: A Realist Theory of Art.* New York: Routledge, 2019.

Windy & Carl. "Balance (Trembling)." On *Consciousness.* Chicago: Kranky Records, 2001.

Winnicott, D. H. *Holding and Interpretation: Fragment of an Analysis.* New York: Grove Press, 1986.

Wittgenstein, Ludwig. 1953. *Philosophical Investigations.* 4th ed. Trans. G. E. M. Anscombe, P. M. S. Hacker, and Joachim Schulte. Malden, MA: Wiley-Blackwell, 2009.

Wittgenstein, Ludwig. 1969. *On Certainty* Trans. G. E. M. Anscombe. New York: Harper Perennial Modern Thought, 1972.

Wolterstorff, Nicholas. *Art Rethought: The Social Practices of Art.* New York: Oxford University Press, 2015.

Woolf, Virginia. 1927. *To the Lighthouse.* New York: Vintage Books, 2005.

Yumusak, Ege. "The Organizer's Anti-Utopian Imaginations." *Philosophy & Activism,* June 8th, 2021.

Young, Iris Marion. "Asymmetrical Reciprocity: On Moral Respect, Wonder, and Enlarged Thought." In *Intersecting Voices: Dilemmas of Gender, Political Philosophy, and Policy*, edited by Iris Marion Young, 205–28. Princeton: Princeton University Press, 1997.

Zeldin, Theodore. *An Intimate History of Humanity.* New York: HarperCollins, 1994.

Index

An index is a way of pointing toward something so as to reveal it. "Index" is related to "indicate" from the Latin meaning "toward" "making something known" (or possibly "saying" it).[1] Since this book depends on striving to get lost in revealing the sense and meaning of things, I spirited the index into provoking interpretation and reflection. Instead of providing a comprehensive grasp of the book's entire weave, I pulled on four important threads different from the "little words" of the motets and let these threads unravel the book as possibilities for reading. Along the length of each, I methodically moved through the book and marked what was revealed of the discussion. This method showed that, for instance, working through "anxiety" preoccupies the first half of the book, only to lessen in the second half. Interestingly, "morality" works inversely, becoming frequent as the book concludes. Or, more particularly, you could see that R. Jay Wallace's The Moral Nexus ended up being an important book for this one and that "governing together" ended up being a much-discussed aspect of "politics." The result of making the book known in the manner I chose is a cluster of thematic patterns, each one a different take on the book:

[1] "Index," Oxford American Dictionary (Apple Inc. 2005–2020).

In *The Moral Inquiries,* 153, 164
And the human good, 8, 17, 19, 38, 42,
    47, 52, 60, 64, 70, 74, 78, 91,
    93, 97
  As a basic human need, 8, 33, 86, 95,
    106, 125–6, 130, 137, 160
  In striving, 43–4, 47, 49–51, 61, 81,
    112
And life between us, 32, 72, 121–2,
    125–6, 139, 146, 158, 181, 195
And love, 11, 17–18, 72, 98–9, 101, 119,
    128, 199
And meditation, 43, 45, 68, 73
And the mind's excitement, 15, 21, 23,
    47, 72
And the motet form, 1, 6–7, 9, 34, 43,
    45–6, 72
And "original joy", 33, 94–5, 104, 108,
    135, 160
As subversive or revolutionary, 11, 27,
    158, 163, 170
Born to, 5, 71, 83, 84, 86–7, 95–6, 109,
    119, 161
  "Into the shores of light," 83, 94
  Supported by environments, 7, 63,
    70, 84, 86–7, 98–9, 102–3,
    107–8, 202
    At the Chicago Commons
    "Reggio Emilia" family
    centers, , 142–8, 159
Continuum view of, 48–9, 60–2, 64, 67–8,
    73–4, 75–6, 93, 105–6, 120
Definition of, 12–13, 15, 21, 60, 94,
    105
  And phenomenology of, 19, 43, 67
    77–8
Drained by domination, 4–6, 15, 86,
    125, 161
Filling in a world, 50, 62–4, 69, 71, 73,
    75, 76, 77–8, 94, 141, 145
Freedom in and with, 7, 45, 50, 122,
    125, 126, 129–30, 133, 136,
    140, 143, 160
Getting lost in, 9, 15, 38, 42, 44, 50–1,
    68–9, 75, 119–20
  Together, 25, 116, 122, 132,
    157–8
In the drive to understand, 9, 19, 32, 42,
    48, 64

Behind consciousness, 21, 23, 42,
    50, 64, 70, 73, 95, 105
Within imagination, 13, 42, 43–4
  Or Aristotelian *phantasia,* 41–2,
    44, 54
In good relationships, 8–11, 17, 23–4,
    29, 34, 36, 112, 127, 129–30,
    190, 204
  Against narcissism, 9, 17, 22, 26, 43,
    70–1, 121, 126, 156, 203
  And "subtle interplay," 8–9, 11,
    102–3, 129, 133
  That are personal, 33, 87, 100–2,
    106, 109–11, 133
  With anger or conflict in them,
    29–31, 122–3, 134, 136, 139,
    157, 168, 170, 181, 190,
    193–5, 199
In Glaveneanu's work, 8, 9, 21, 49, 62,
    64, 67, 68
In Llloyd's work, 9, 43, 48, 49, 58, 60, 62,
    63, 64, 70, 105
In Morrison's series, 7–8, 201–4
In protest, 7, 30–3, 170, 181
In Rimbaud's poetry, 20–3, 89–90,
    113–14
In Schinkel's work, 43, 44, 49, 57, 59, 60,
    61, 62, 63, 71, 73, 74, 93, 128,
    141, 145
Not an emotion, 9, 21, 45, 59, 96–7,
    193–4
Not Humean, 9, 21, 45
Nussbaum's implicit understanding of,
    15–17, 29, 33, 64, 72–3, 91,
    93–4, 104–5, 123–4, 133,
    156
  And Nussbaum's core idea, 17–19,
    121, 131
  In music, 28, 127–8, 138, 159
Opening up politics, 7, 23, 25–7, 32, 36,
    121, 198
  And needed in it, 27, 30, 121
Over the child as a wonder, 87, 89–90,
    107–11, 201–2
Over sense and meaning, 43–4,
    50, 55–6, 59, 63, 71, 74,
    86, 84, 195
"Over" vs. "about", 106–7
Post-Kantian, 9, 21, 42, 45

JEREMY BENDIK-KEYMER works as Professor of Philosophy in the Department of Philosophy of Case Western Reserve University and as Senior Research Fellow for the Earth System Governance Project, Universiteit Utrecht. A graduate of public schools in New Hartford, New York (on Haudenosaunee land), Yale College and of the University of Chicago, his previous monographs include *The Ecological Life: Discovering Citizenship and a Sense of Humanity*; *Solar Calendar, and Other Ways of Marking Time*; *The Wind ~ An Unruly Living*; and *Involving Anthroponomy in the Anthropocene: On Decoloniality*. He is currently thinking about a book on planetary justice.

MISTY MORRISON is a visual artist from Ohio, trained in figurative painting at Lyme Academy College of Fine Arts and in printmaking, with a specialization in lithography, from Ohio University. Her work mixes visual art with installation, dramatizing and exploring the complex roots of family systems. Recent solo shows include *If You See Something* at Majestic Gallery, *Oblivion* at the Pittsburgh Center for the Arts, and *The Family System I ("I ain't got no home in this world anymore")* at Unsmoke Systems. Her lithographs and prints are in the Ohio University permanent collection, and her portraits are in several private collections.

Made in the USA
Columbia, SC
23 July 2024

39017033R00130